YANNI IN WORDS

YANNI

IN WORDS

with David Rensin

miramax books

HYPERION

NEW YORK

ISBN 1-4013-5194-8

First Edition
10 9 8 7 6 5 4 3 2 1

Text design: Stanley S. Drate/Folio Graphics Co. Inc.

for Sotiri and Felitsa

My father once said,
"If the whole world wants to go left and you feel
like going right, go right. You don't have to
follow. You don't have to make a big deal about
which way you're going. Just go. It's very easy."

CONTENTS

• • •

I believe music represents humanity's soul. Confucius, in his travels throughout China, used to say that he was able to see the mood of each province by listening to its local music. He knew if the people were happy, content, angry, getting ready for war. When I compose I blend a rainbow of styles and ethnicities and witness the souls of many cultures come together obviously and easily. The result is more color, beauty, and strength. A seamless mesh. Unity.

I do it all the time. I feel it, and it's not at all awkward or unusual. In fact, it is completely natural.

When I see how our musical souls come together in art, I ask myself, "Why can't we do the same?"

The answer is that we can. We must. I know the world is in turmoil, but I believe that we are on a one-way street, and that to survive we have no choice but to become a global community. I believe that what I see in the music means that the human race has the chance to find common ground. You can say I'm a dreamer, as John Lennon once sang; I'm supposed to be a dreamer. I'm supposed to see how the world *can* be. I'm an artist. I am about instinct, not logic or history.

If our souls can come together in music, they can come together anywhere, and as a race we can achieve harmony and peace.

• • •

YANNI IN WORDS

PRELUDE

When I was thirteen, I took a long walk with my father through the summer-parched foothills above Kalamata, the small port on Greece's Gulf of Messinia where I was born. We did this often, and as we strolled he would talk to me about life, about simplicity, about appreciating nature. He liked to say that the best things in life are available to everyone because they're inside us: truth, imagination, creativity, love, kindness, compassion.

We hiked for a while in silence, then stopped to watch the sun set into the blue-green waters that stretch from the southern end of the Peloponnese peninsula to the Mediterranean.

"What do you think?" my father asked.

"It looks . . . nice," I said.

"Yes, it's beautiful," he agreed. "But does it make you feel *happy*?"

"I . . . I don't know," I said.

My father smiled patiently. "If looking at that makes you feel happy, then you'll be a very happy man, because there are lots of sunsets to come in your life," he explained. "But if it takes buying a house or a car . . ."

Thirty years later, walking again through those familiar hills, we paused in our usual spot as the light began to fade. This time I watched the sunset through more seasoned eyes and thought about the question my father had asked me so long ago.

I had never spent wildly on material things, but my father's point—as ancient as the Greek philosophers themselves—was still valid: The less you want, the richer you are. The more you need in order to be happy, the more miserable you'll be. I'd heard him say this in one way or another for years but had pushed it to the back of my mind as I chased the dream of having my music heard by more and more people. When the dream came true, I spent too little time enjoying the rewards and too much time reaching for bigger dreams. Now, I'd come home to find my health and the boy from Kalamata I seemed to have lost along the way, and I could no longer shut out the truth of my father's wisdom. I've failed myself, I thought, as the sun slipped into the sea.

Most people would insist I had no reason then not to be thrilled with my life. I was forty-three, music had been my career for more than twenty years, and my journey from having nothing to everything was an odyssey that made both my family and me proud. After all, I had often asked myself, what are the chances that a poor kid from Kalamata who doesn't read music but taught himself to play piano at eight, who doesn't dance, doesn't sing, doesn't write lyrics, doesn't conform to any particular musical style, and doesn't want to play the show business "game"— what are the chances that this kid will *ever* succeed, much less become known worldwide? It's laughable. It's against all the odds. But it can happen. And it did.

Along the way I tasted much: I became a Greek national swimming champion at fourteen, moved to America at eighteen to earn a B.A. in Psychology at the University of Minnesota in Minneapolis, and played in an assortment of wild midwestern rock bands. I scored some movies, wrote music for television commercials, even worked as a dishwasher and an employment counselor. But mostly I just wanted to bring the songs I heard in my head to life.

In college I played piano whenever I could. After graduation and in between rock 'n' roll gigs I confined myself for months to a makeshift studio I had built in the basement of my sister's house in Brooklyn Park, Minnesota, and recorded my first solo album. It went nowhere. Five years and too much rock 'n' roll later, I made another album and finally got a record deal. I moved to Los Angeles, where I once again became a monk and lived in my home studio—when I wasn't on the road.

As my records began to sell I came to the attention of actress Linda Evans, who called to say how much she loved listening to my albums. We spoke often on the phone, met, and began a miraculous nine-year relationship. Linda was a mentor as well as a lover; being with her gave me insight into myself and into show business, and she gave me the support I needed to grow in my career. Driven by my relentless ambition to be heard despite limited radio and television exposure (neither medium could figure out how to classify my music—I just didn't fit in), I invested everything, including most of my money, into creating new opportunities.

My biggest professional and personal risk was to return to Greece to film and record three concerts with a band and full symphony orchestra at the ancient Acropolis in Athens. The reward was overwhelming: global exposure, millions of new fans, and finally a grudging respect from the media and music business.

With that momentum I planned a world tour and played at the Toji Temple in Kyoto, the Taj Mahal in India, and the Forbidden City in China. The logistics were hell, but I was driven.

I drove myself off the edge. My father could see it coming. "Get a life," he said. My closest friends echoed him. "Travel for pleasure. Go to a barbecue. Burn some hot dogs. Drink a beer. Hang out with your friends. Do nothing." They were right, only I didn't know how to do nothing. I could risk $20 million on a tour, fight in the Supreme Court of India to be the first musician to play at that country's most sacred monument, and charm Chinese dignitaries. I could lock myself in a studio for days, not eat, and hardly sleep. But I didn't know how to just go out for dinner and see a movie. I'd dealt with many cultures and experienced some of the most spectacular places on the planet, but I couldn't just relax and have fun.

Linda and I grew apart and broke up just after New Year's Day, 1998. The end was melancholy and unresolved, but we parted amicably and stayed friends while I kept touring, appearing in five different cities a week. I got up at 5 A.M. for television shows and interviews, put on makeup, and posed for pictures. I worried about selling more albums and more tickets. I tried to take responsibility for the hundreds of people that I dragged across the continents, living in an endless series of hotel rooms.

By summer 1998, I couldn't go on. I was at the height of my career, but I'd lost what I'd once believed was an infinite ocean of optimism. Everything seemed flat, dark, without meaning.

My father taught me that one of the most important abilities in life is to be able to take the pain and persevere, and for years this lesson had served me well. But even my toughness couldn't help with my deeper problem: I had fought the battles, taken the risks, and somehow won—and I didn't know what to do with the rewards.

So I quit. After speeding at 160 miles per hour, nonstop, for more than six years, everything screeched to a halt overnight. After my last concert on July 5, 1998, what I had thought of as my life for so long was gone. I woke up the next day with nowhere to go and nothing to do. But I was neither at peace nor happy. I was wired and tired and frustrated and angry and beaten. I didn't want to talk to anyone, even my closest friends. I was a warrior without a war, a man who not only no longer knew himself but also had forgotten the person he was when the journey began.

Although I would emerge stronger and more determined than ever, with a greater understanding of myself and a more balanced view of life, at the time all I could do was lie in bed and stare at my hands. I realized without a shred of emotion that I didn't care if I ever touched a piano again.

1

ALLOWING

People always ask what drew me to music. The truthful answer is that it was a way to get attention in my family. I remember being three years old and listening to my mother sing; I loved it. I also noticed how adoringly my father looked at her when she sang. Even at that tender age I made a mental note of his reaction.

When I was five my uncles and aunts came by for dinner a couple of times a week. Afterward someone would pick up a guitar or play the piano, and there would be dancing and singing. The music was traditional Greek. My mom would harmonize sweetly with my uncle Yianni, and everyone always complimented and encouraged each other. I got goose bumps listening and I wanted to be part of it.

Later, music became a great way to reach girls. On beautiful summer nights my brother, a couple of friends, and I would go to the lighthouse by the breakwater, where all the ships came in, and sit on the benches and play guitar and sing. Sometimes we'd serenade our sweethearts right under their bedroom windows. One time, a girl's father threw a bucket of water on my head after I woke him up with my lovesick warbling. I wonder if he realizes that he was probably responsible for my writing only instrumental music?

A love of music ran in the family. When my father was a boy he longed to play the violin but there were none available, so he found an old, untuned piano in the church and got permission from the priest to play it when the church wasn't being used. My mother dreamed of being an actress and singer. She had the opportunity to study theater in Athens as a girl, but my grandfather forbade it as inappropriate and her passion was silenced. Those early experiences didn't stop my parents from encouraging my older brother, Yorgo, my younger sister, Anda, and me to play music, and they showed tremendous interest when we did. (They supported almost *anything* we did.) Whether I played the piano or picked at the guitar, my mother paid attention. My dad would come home from work late and still ask to listen to whatever song we'd been working on in the afternoon.

My father earned only $200 a month, and we had no money to spare, yet he bought a piano for the house. It cost more than a year's salary, so he paid it off monthly. To give you an idea of what a luxury it was, we had no television, we didn't own a car, and my father rode a bicycle to work. He had only two suits and both had holes in the pants. "You're crazy," one of my aunts chided him, "buying a piano when you don't even have proper clothes to wear!"

But my parents were wise. They knew that if we had the piano around while we were still young we'd discover it and some magic might happen. The alternative was waiting years until they could afford the instrument—if they were lucky—only to have us just walk right past it as if it were another piece of furniture.

Mind you, they never forced us into music; they gave us the opportunity and let us make the choice. And there was also a limit. Although my parents held music in high esteem and be- lieved that knowing how to play refined a person and that it could be a friend for life, they encouraged music *only* as a hobby, not as a profession. We could love it but we weren't to depend on it. This wasn't a surprise. Too many Greek musicians ended up poor, playing for a handful of drachmas at the local bar. My par- ents did not want that life for their kids. On the other hand, they weren't pushy, saying, "You must have a career, and you must make money, and you must, must, must." Mom and Dad were all for personal power, resilience, and, especially, individuality.

Without much thought I accepted my parents' gentle guid- ance. I had no clue that I'd become a musician, not even in my wildest dreams, until one day when I would realize that I never really had a choice.

Music was like a time bomb inside of me waiting to explode.

My family's story is also born of explosions, but real ones.

My father, Sotiri, was born in Mani, in 1923. Mani is a re- gion in the southernmost end of the middle peninsula of the Peloponnese. This is one of the most beautiful places in Europe: spectacular ocean views of clean blue water and rocky shores, breathtaking mountains, low humidity, no bugs; in other words, a dream neighborhood. Mani was also the only Greek territory untouched by the Ottoman Turks, who destroyed Byzantium— as Greece was called then—and occupied the country for 400 years, until the early 1800s. The Ottoman Turks wanted Mani because it was the last outpost of resistance. Its people not only were well-trained tough-asses who'd become skilled over the cen- turies at thwarting occupation forces, but they also provided refuge to fighters from enslaved regions who fled to Mani and lived to fight another day. They'd hide in the Taygetus Mountains that run along the peninsula's spine to the sea and attack the Turks with hit-and-run guerrilla tactics. While Mani is rugged and gorgeous, with wide coastal plateaus that drop precipitously to the water, the terrain is harsh and dry, and lacks much in the way of natural resources. In the end it just wasn't worth the trouble to try to crush the people of Mani. The Ottoman Turks tried several times, and with each attempt they were defeated; the last battle was like a Greek version of the Native Americans massacring Custer.

The Turks eventually left Mani alone and focused their barbarism on the rest of the country. Big mistake. In 1821, the men of Mani—big, strong, boisterous, spirited, independent, with an in-your-face attitude toward life—attacked the Ottoman occupation forces in nearby Kalamata, and the revolution began. Eight years later, the Ottoman Empire that had outlawed our schools and churches and tried to pretty much eradicate our culture—it's a miracle we even speak Greek today—was driven north. It was the beginning of the end of Turkish domination.

Everyone says that my father's father, also named Yianni, was a special man, soft-spoken and wise. He was a teacher and a huge influence on my father, who still talks about him in the same reverent tones I reserve for my own dad. Grandpa Yianni was blue-eyed and blond. In fact, our name, Chryssomallis, means "golden hair."

My mother says Grandpa Yianni was one of the sweetest people who ever walked on the earth. He died from colon cancer when I was five, and although I barely knew him, I have a hazy memory of his taking us to a little city garden called Kiparion. He'd peel an orange for the kids and let us play. My mother told me that once he had to punish me for some infraction. "Put out your hand," he'd said. Then he tapped me a couple of times on the open palm with a little stick. I got mad, so he let me hit his hand in return, with my little palm. When my mom asked him why he let me do this, he said, "Let him get the anger out; it's okay. You don't want to break the spirit."

My mother has treated me that way ever since. As a result, when I'm mad, or if I've been hurt, I let the person know very clearly, very succinctly, sometimes loudly. These days I rarely get angry, but when I do I don't hold on to anger or emotions and come back later. My father also took special care never to discipline his kids in a way that would leave us scarred, or to push us to conform to a society determined to treat us like sheep. He knew better.

Tolerance and consideration of the spirit are the main characteristics of my family. A great example is how we handle religion. My mother is a devout Christian. She can focus intently while praying, and we all think God listens to her when she prays. I've literally watched life change around her. She gets her way.

My father doesn't go to church. He used to just drive my mom there and wait outside for the service to finish. It's a matter of respect, he says. "Because I don't believe what the people inside believe, it would be wrong for me to go in and pretend I do." My father taught us to never try to shake anyone's faith no matter what a person believed in. He always set an example of tolerance, acceptance, and respect.

Around the age of thirteen I began asking questions about religion. I didn't really know if anyone was listening to my prayers, but I wasn't afraid that a thunderbolt would strike me because I doubted. I couldn't imagine a God who would be so vengeful as to hurt a kid like myself who was stupid enough not to believe in him.

Growing up in a home where no one took shots at one another over differences as fundamental and powerful as religion was a great lesson by example. Today I'm not part of any organized religion. My connection to the Creator is very personal, and I'm suspicious of anyone who tries to save my soul. I believe that when the time is right we all find our Creator.

As a rule I also avoid the establishment. I don't follow schools of thought. I'm open enough to study any religion, to go to temples, churches, and mosques, and to listen to ideas. There's beauty in every path. Buddhists believe that there are as many paths to Enlightenment as you care to take. I'm not Buddhist, but I like that concept.

For all his gentility, my father's childhood was at times surprisingly harsh. He told us of people dying in the streets, bloated from malnutrition. He and my mother were teenagers during World War II and the German occupation; they shared with me the fear they felt when German boots clomped through the streets. Would the storm troopers stop at their houses? Would they even wake up the next morning?

My dad helped Allied soldiers escape the Germans by ferrying them offshore to waiting sea vessels. Once, using only a flashlight, he flagged down a destroyer off the coast in the middle of the night, not knowing if it was German or English, but obviously hoping for the latter. Incredibly, he got it to stop. He took his little boat to the ship, found it was English, came back, put four English soldiers in his boat, and took them out to the destroyer. On the way, one soldier asked my father if he wanted to come along; they were headed for Egypt. My dad thought about it but realized that if he went, his family would think he'd drowned. He couldn't do that to his parents.

After World War II, there was civil war in Greece. My dad was a sergeant major with the government forces. He doesn't like to talk about this time, and never brings it up, but recently, because I was older and pushed a bit, he did. I heard gruesome stories of living in the mountains, of being shot at, of people cutting throats in the villages, of mutilation.

"The human beasts were out," he said.

My father's brother, Yorgo, was killed during the civil war when he braved enemy gunfire to retrieve a wounded comrade. The man was prone and screaming. Yorgo couldn't stand it anymore, so he carried him in over his shoulder. As he slipped the injured man into the trenches, Yorgo caught a bullet in the head. Yorgo was a true patriot. His death was ironic. He had his army release papers in his pocket. He could have gone home, but he stayed around a few more days because he didn't think it was the right thing to leave with a big battle coming. Thanks to him, the wounded soldier lived a long time.

When Yorgo died my dad freaked. He had to pick up the body. Afterward he burned every article of my uncle's clothing, as well as anything else that reminded him of his brother. Only one picture of Yorgo remains. That tragedy changed my father's life. Ever since, he has hated war and has done everything he could to keep us from becoming indoctrinated and seduced by a violent way of thinking.

But the most incredible part of my father's story is his attitude. As he says, "You know, it's really amazing that we ended up being the people we are despite these experiences." To this day he is soft-spoken and gentle. No matter what happened, he just wouldn't be bitter.

My mother's name, Felitsa, is short for Triandafelitsa, which means "rose." She comes from Kalamata. The town, known worldwide for its succulent black olives, is just north and over the mountains from Mani, and about forty miles from Sparta. As a kid, I could also go to the ancient Olympic stadium and run and play. There, I could touch the old monuments and temples and feel my heritage.

As in Mani, Kalamata's air and water are wonderfully clean. The climate is similar to Southern California's—as low as forty degrees, usually sixty to eighty-five—but we often get a cooling breeze off the bay, and we're protected by the mountains behind us from the northern winds during the winter. We *do* have a winter in the sense that there's snow on the mountains, but it has only fallen in town once in the last seventy-five years.

Unlike Southern California, Kalamata is still underdeveloped; the population is maybe sixty thousand, and it doubles in the summer. Ten years from now, I don't know if that will still be true. I don't think I want to know, either.

My parents met in Kalamata. They had seen each other from a distance and asked mutual friends to introduce them. To get to know each other in those days they'd take a walk, with family members and friends—not quite official chaperones—trailing behind them. I have a wonderful picture of them strolling together when they were young and in love.

I can understand why Sotiri and Felitsa were attracted to each other. My mom is warm, beautiful, affectionate, full of life, and always has a smile on her face. She has a sweet voice. She's a great cook and is completely devoted to my father and the kids. She never treated one child differently than another. She just loves to give. When I was a teenager, we'd come home with our friends and she'd fix us all dinner, giving each of us what we wanted. Later, when the group dragged back in after midnight, we'd find her sleeping on the couch. My mom wasn't worried or checking up; she just didn't want to miss us, or the chance to cook a late dinner of eggs, sliced tomatoes, and fried potatoes. She's a nightbird (which also happens to be her nickname for me) who loves to hang out and socialize at any hour. If we stay up until six in the morning, she'll be right there with the best of us. Mom is joyful and can make friends with anybody. She loves to sing and dance and party. She loves to laugh. She loves life.

Once I complained to her about growing old, and she said, "It's only by living that you grow old." I understood immediately. Growing old is better than the alternative. Can you imagine how hard it was for me to find a girlfriend when I had a mother like that?

My father is an introvert, which is why he takes long walks alone. He has no patience for a busy mouth, particularly if it just likes the sound of its own voice. My father doesn't offer unsolicited advice, or say, "This is how I feel about life. This is what I think." He'll never be in your face. He'll never start talking to you and trap you there, and he assumes you won't do the same thing to him. If he doesn't like the conversation, he'll just get up and wander off—even from the dinner table, after the meal. No insult to you. One of Linda Evans's girlfriends affectionately called him "The Shadow." However, my father can easily stick around, tell off-color jokes, and get a good laugh out of just about any situation. He just doesn't like to waste your time or his.

My father worked at the National Bank of Greece in Kalamata most of his life. He began at the bottom and eventually became the manager. He taught himself five languages—English, Italian, French, Spanish, and Portuguese—in addition to Greek. As a result, he handled the bank's overseas correspondence, and because he was so sharp they wanted to send him to run branches in Chicago or New York or London. But that meant he would have had to leave his family. He wouldn't.

Sotiri is also much more than a banker. On his own he studied philosophy, psychology, and medicine. When I took psychology at the University of Minnesota in the mid-seventies, he would often say, "Well, of course you know this a lot better than I since you're studying psychology now . . . ," then he'd tell me something brilliant. I would ask, "How do you know about that?" He'd respond, "Well, a few years ago I read an article in the *Journal of the American Medical Association* and . . ." He always surprises me.

I believe my passionate desire to succeed and the single-mindedness needed to do what it takes to achieve my goals comes from both my parents. My mother is tolerant but made of steel. She is sweet and will sometimes say what she thinks you'd like to hear—then do what she wants to anyway. My dad does not play that game at all. For instance, in Greece it is much more important to celebrate your "name day" than your birthday. On his name day my father skips out of the house and takes a long walk because he doesn't want to have to answer the phone calls wishing him *Hronia Polla,* or Happy Name Day.

As with most kids, I'm a combination of my parents. Like my mother, I enjoy staying up late. When I was two and three years old I wouldn't sleep unless she sang for me—hence the "Nightbird" nickname. Sometimes she was so tired she'd start to pass out, only to hear me wail from the crib. "You tortured me a lot," she told me.

From my mother I also inherited my ability to walk on-stage. I've always been something of an exhibitionist. Our home was right next door to an outdoor movie theater. It wasn't a drive-in; there were chairs instead of cars, and one big speaker. If you sat at the top of the staircase outside our house you could see the movie. When I was five my uncles taught me a very popular song, and one night, during a break in the film, the theater played the tune. I heard it and sang along—loudly. My mom says that everyone at the theater turned around and looked at me—and that I liked it.

Yet like my father I'm also a recluse and a monk, the deep

thinker who can't be social for long periods; then I can be as boisterous and obnoxious as the next guy.

Now that I'm older the quieter part dominates.

I was born on November 14, 1954, the middle child. In English my name means John, in honor of St. John the Baptist. My name day, when all the Yiannis celebrate, is January 7.

In Greek tradition, the firstborn child takes the father's father's name. But my older brother was named Yorgo, to honor our uncle, leaving Grandpa Yianni's name to me. (In proper Greek, if you were to talk *about* me, you'd refer to me as Yiannis; all male Greek names have the "s" at the end. Speaking *to* me, you'd call me Yanni. What few people know is that until I first went out as a solo artist I spelled my name "Yianni." Dropping the first "i" wasn't even my idea. Someone suggested, "Maybe if the 'i' is missing, you could still pronounce it 'Yanni,' and it would have fewer letters and look better.")

In Greek there are many words to describe the different kinds of love. My parents raised their kids with *agape*—meaning "unconditional love." Simply put, no matter how we acted, if we did something "wrong," our parents never withdrew their love or threatened to. That's crucial.

Whenever I got into trouble, instead of raising his voice or his hand, my father got very quiet. He would take me into another room to talk calmly. The worse my transgression, the calmer he got. There was no punishment. I don't remember him ever saying, "Because you did this, from now on you're not going to . . ." or, "You stay in your room." My father's approach was much more difficult to deal with than anger. Sometimes I hated those serious talks, but he and my mother insisted on treating us with respect and kindness, and we all learned to hold ourselves to that standard. I loved them both so deeply that I couldn't bear to hurt or disappoint them.

The embarrassing childhood misadventure that I most regret certainly merited my father's anger. I was maybe thirteen, too energetic to sit still, and looking for trouble. One night three friends and I were outside a movie theater when we saw a couple of motorcycles. They looked pretty tempting so we decided it would be fun to ride them for a mile or two. We weren't thieves; we didn't want to keep them or destroy them. We just wanted some kicks.

After daring one another to actually do it, we finally agreed that two of us would take one, and two of us the other. I didn't drive, but held on behind. My friend and I rode "our" bike for a couple of miles, winding through the back streets until we got close to my house. We stopped a quarter mile away, left the bike, and walked to our homes.

I didn't know if my other two buddies had made it back safely, but I found out soon enough. Two hours later my doorbell rang. Fearing the worst, I tiptoed into the front room and peeked through the curtains while I tried to keep from hyperventilating. Maybe it was my friends. No such luck. Outside I saw flashing lights and the police. My knees buckled; my palms got wet. But I had to let them in. The police took me to the station. My friends on the other bike had hit a pothole, spilled, and injured themselves. They made it home and explained their bumps and bruises by saying that they'd been hit by a car that had driven off. One boy's father called the police, who knew a couple of motorcycles were missing. They inspected the kids' wounds—mostly scratches, not something you'd get from being struck by a car—and confronted them. During their confession someone mentioned my name.

My parents were out and when they got home, they learned

from my siblings that I was at the police station. My father came to pick me up. I could hardly face him. When we got to the house he led me into the bedroom and very quietly said, "After all I've put into you, it really hurts me to see my son bring himself to such a low level. It's painful and it makes me wonder if the way I've been raising you is the right way. I don't know what else to tell you. You know right from wrong. I can't believe you did this."

For a few days he walked around the house, visibly hurt. After that I never dared to do something so stupid again. My father didn't have to rant or yell or threaten or withhold. He didn't have to punish me because I punished myself. It was embarrassing, even agonizing, for me to see the man I respected the most look so miserable.

I got a lesson in compassion, too, because the motorcycle owners gave us a break and did not press charges. We were from a small town; everyone knew everyone. The owners felt sorry for us and didn't want to ruin our lives over a stupid prank.

To tell you the truth, I've never heard my parents lash out at or openly bad-mouth anyone. Sure, they get upset sometimes, but they release that stuff quickly. Two minutes, and then it's gone. My mom lives with love. She will find any excuse to explain why someone acts strangely, or badly, and she always allows for their redemption. Same with my dad. He doesn't dwell on the negative. He is optimistic and trusts the future. Whenever I had problems, or struggled with a situation, he'd say, "You're smart enough and strong enough to take care of it, so fix it. You will survive and move on, and it won't happen again because you'll learn from experience. Keep your eyes open. See what happens. Analyze. Be truthful with yourself."

Linda Evans once told me that this parental love—she called it "allowing"—goes to the core of my being, that I have a trust in life that carries me everywhere. If that's true—and I think it is—then I am one of the lucky ones. My trust is not stupidity or foolishness; I see the same stinkers and slimeballs everyone else sees. The music business certainly has its share. I have been nicked, but I haven't been cut badly. People have lied to me, stolen from me, taken advantage of me, but I've never gone back to get even—even if I've wanted to. I just got smarter and learned to see it coming. I thanked them for the lesson and moved on.

My parents invested a lot of time in their kids. My dad would say, "I didn't ask you if I could bring you into the world, therefore you owe me nothing and I owe you everything." One of his most important gifts to the family was an appreciation of nature and of doing things outdoors. In the winter he would come home tired from the bank, but instead of taking the traditional afternoon nap we would walk, maybe three miles a day. He'd introduce us to the flowers and the trees and tell us a story about an animal; we'd discuss the weather, the clouds. What are thunderstorms, where do they come from, how do they work? If there was any way to feed us outside instead of on a table indoors, my parents would do that. Sometimes they would rent a rowboat, take us out on the bay, and eat there.

When my brother, sister, and I were very young my father decided he wanted to teach us how to withstand the cold. He didn't just send us outside without jackets on a winter day and tell us to be brave. As always, he was more creative. He took us to the beach in January.

We all watched as he walked into the water and began splashing around, saying, "Wow. This is fantastic. Great." Even in southern Greece, the ocean is cold enough at that time of year to make your head hurt. We didn't know that, of course. Dad just seemed to be having the time of his life, which made us want to come in too, just as he had anticipated.

"I don't know," he said, when we asked for permission to join him. "It's very cold, but I suppose you can try if you want to." We didn't think twice and plunged right in; we were highly competitive and probably dared one another. Boy, was it cold. But we got used to it quickly and soon we were having too much fun to get out.

The real lesson here is one that my father taught us over and over in every way possible: The most important battle is the one to conquer yourself. You've got to overcome pain and discomfort and control your urges. Learn how to rein in your desires. This wasn't about sexuality or morality; his advice was purely practical.

He told us not to overeat, to learn about vitamins and exercise. Your body hurts because you're working out? That's okay. It's a good thing. Trust me; you'll be very happy later in life because you won't have the same health problems as your friends.

My father led compassionately and by example. He was very clever. He never said, "You *must* do what I do, otherwise you're nothing." He let us find our own ways, and as I get older, I benefit from his lessons each and every day.

My childhood was idyllic. With the beach right outside our door you could say that I grew up in a big sandbox. I walked to school and never worried about encountering guns or knives. I didn't have to lock my bike so no one would steal it. I could stay out past midnight without fear of being abducted or molested or robbed or killed. I never felt threatened or worried, and that was a great thing.

Though our family life was simple, I wasn't aware that we were poor. Maybe we didn't have many possessions, but we never went hungry, were cold, or lacked love. Yes, my soccer ball was homemade—a tin can wrapped in cloth and tied up with string—but I could kick it in an open field, by a gorgeous ocean, with my friends.

My parents wanted us to appreciate our good fortune. Kalamata had an orphanage, and some of the locals thought the kids there were worthless. Not my mother. Some weekends she would invite one or two of them to come eat with us. And sometimes she would send me to eat at the orphanage. I still remember the long tables and the bad food.

The piano in the house was not my first instrument. Perhaps *you* can imagine me hefting an accordion, but I never could. I played it only long enough to get an idea of how music was constructed, then I quit taking lessons. One reason for my haste was that when my brother played the piano all the girls looked at him. When I played the accordion, everybody left the room. I got the message.

My brother was a virtuoso, a big talent who'd mastered Mozart, Chopin, and Liszt. My parents offered me piano lessons, too, but I refused. For some reason I wouldn't let myself be taught. Instead I picked at the piano keys and found my own way by copying from memory what my brother played. Other times, when I heard a movie soundtrack wafting up from the theater next door—say, some Ennio Moricone, from a spaghetti western—I would try to play it on the piano even though I didn't know what key it was in. I also spent a lot of time listening to music on a battered old shortwave radio in my room.

Whatever I tried to play, if I didn't like the way the original melody went, I had no problem going in a completely different direction to suit my taste. I let my emotions take me. When something inside pushed to get out, I just let it come.

But I couldn't do everything by memory. I realized I had to be able to write down what I heard. I couldn't write music and had no tape recorder, so I developed my own shorthand notation—a combination of numbers, a few symbols, and Greek words—as a memory post. I began by taking a piece of paper to the movies, where I'd sit in the dark scribbling the chord progressions in my private code. Soon I could chart them as well as the key, the time signature, the main melody, and more. Today it has developed into a very quick and accurate system.

Within a year or two I realized that I could also instantly recognize notes just by hearing them. This ability is called "absolute" or "perfect" pitch. I don't believe I was born with perfect pitch, but by the time I was eight or nine I had it because I'd worked so hard for it.

Some might regard what I have as a gift. I take issue with the idea of "gifts," not because I have any problem with exceptional talent, but because the concept of a gift means that some people have it while others do not—and it's just their tough luck. This implies that my accomplishments have little to do with spending sixteen hours a day in a room, for twenty years, working obsessively, and that my "talent" is a result of God looking down at his children and saying, "Hey, let this independent, dark-haired kid from Kalamata have the ability to write music."

I say no. Absolutely not. That's so untrue. And it's so misleading, especially to young people.

I'm not talking about eye or hair color, being tall or short, or having a certain bone structure. That's all part of your genetic inheritance. I mean gift in the sense of it being a winning lottery ticket, something given to you that you have very little to do with—and no matter how hard those who don't have the gift work at it, they won't get it. Again, no. All you need is passion. If you have a passion for something, you'll create the talent. Just love it. And then bust your ass. You'll become great at it. Passion is the fuel.

I will agree, however, that we are born with potential, some of which is realized, some of which, for whatever reasons and life circumstances, will never be discovered. If Mozart's father had not been a music teacher, and if Mozart had been born in the middle of nowhere with no musical instruments at his disposal, I don't think Mozart would be Mozart.

Music quickly touched my soul and consumed me. Suddenly anything related to music got my attention. From copying what I heard on the radio and in the movies to developing my system of notation, I put in a lot of work.

At first I struggled with musical notes; eventually they just spoke to me. I think of notes as words, like Do-Re-Mi-Fa-So-La-Ti-Do. For example, a song might go: Do-Me-So-Fa-Me-So-Fa-Me-So-Do. At the piano, I don't only hear the pitches, but my mind knows the words and my fingers just do it.

Ironically, I don't listen to much instrumental music at home because the "words" force me to pay attention; music is like an audiobook telling me a story. The story affects me emotionally and I respond in kind. I don't need to hear lyrics that say, "I just woke up, you're not here because you left me yesterday. I haven't slept all night. I miss you." I know from the music that the composer is in pain, or happy, or romantically involved. If you listen to Mozart, Beethoven, Stravinsky, Chopin, or Tchaikovsky, you know everything they're "talking" about. Their souls, their existence, can be studied without reading a single word about them; just listen to their body of work. With a painter, look at her paintings; you'll know her soul. These artists put everything that they're about into their art. That's what I do. Everything I'm about is in my music.

Though I loved music I was not at the piano every chance I had. Mostly I was outside doing something athletic. Early on I developed a passion for soccer and played it in the sand, quickly developing my lungs, heart, and endurance. I also boxed. I had good balance, heavy shoulders, solid thighs. I put the gloves on and a couple of friends who were heavily into the sport trained me. We whacked each other around just for fun. A single punch can feel like a giant headache, but when you're in the middle of a fight you don't really feel it that much. If you take a fist in the face, you notice it most when you smell your own blood.

The training came in handy. I'm not especially proud of this story, but when I was sixteen I fought with a player on Kalamata's local pro soccer team. I caught him pushing around a friend of mine. I was already five foot eight and very strong. I hated that kind of injustice and couldn't help myself.

It happened at the soccer field, where the team practiced and our high school class took gym. I saw my friend being slapped around. I asked the guy to stop. He didn't, and swung at me instead. I ducked, hit him twice, and he went down. That was the end of it. He wasn't a boxer. I was.

The fight gave me a reputation. I was already known as an occasional hothead, and this confirmed it. Just beat up somebody really big and nobody ever fools with you. It's not what I wanted, but it came in handy. Although my brother, Yorgo, is very athletic and today runs marathons, I also saved him from beatings a couple of times. He was a "pretty boy" and all the girls went after him, and vice versa. This resulted in a few stolen girlfriends. The jilted boyfriends would band together and wait for Yorgo after class. My friend Armenis—not a great fighter, but strong as a bull—stood with my brother and me. You didn't want to mess with both of us at the same time. (I ran into Armenis recently and even after all the years we reminisced about our battles.)

Now, who would ever imagine me, the gentle musician in white, as a fighter?

My brother was into war and toy soldiers. I loved electronics. I built a rudimentary arc light, like the kind used to illuminate projectors in old movie theaters, by using the carbon from a couple of D-cell batteries.

The fun part is putting something metal through the arc; it's so hot that even metal will instantly melt and drip. Some got on the table in my bedroom and burned a hole in the Formica top. It's not easy to do that to Formica; it's even more difficult to explain it to your mom.

I also loved to blow up stuff. I used gunpowder, which I could just buy at the store, and fuses. I would make little bombs out of playing cards and fishing line. I don't want to describe how to do it, but it sure made a lot of noise when it exploded. I'm lucky I still have my fingers. Of course, nobody knew what my friends and I were up to until my mom found the boxes of gunpowder I'd hidden in the basement. "You could have blown up the whole house!" she said.

I shared a bedroom with my brother. It had a cool terrazzo floor, covered with a shaggy white carpet—a *flocatta*—between the beds. My father put a world map on the wall on my side, a clever trick to make me aware of the planet. Even better would have been a poster of Farrah Fawcett; but no. At the foot of the bed stood the little table I'd burned, otherwise used for studying.

Most of all I loved my Phillips shortwave radio, which was made of dark brown plastic, with a light cream cloth-covered speaker. I remember lying awake nights, after lights out, with the radio next to my ear, twisting the dial through the crackle and hum, searching for channels, overjoyed at discovering the world: I could pick up stations from Algeria, Egypt, Italy, Germany, the Middle East, and Greece. I'd listen to whatever I could, from rock 'n' roll to jazz to Middle Eastern songs. The experience opened my mind to different music and time signatures. I realized that one culture could find beauty in places another culture didn't understand, but that given a chance, that beauty could be shared through melody. I began to appreciate those differences—and similarities—and my affinity for both grew as I spent more time exploring the world beyond myself.

I was also ready to explore a world much closer at hand.

The idea of sex itself was not a mystery to me. My father was very liberal. He had no problem with mild "bad language." Mom was a little more uptight, but although she giggled and turned red in the face, she didn't reprimand my dad for talking that way. In Europe, sexuality is much more accepted than in America, which, frankly, was a big shock to me when I came to the United States, because in my experience Americans—at least on holiday abroad—had always seemed so uninhibited.

My first kiss was from a girl I liked in school, but that's as far as it went. I had my first full sexual experience in a local bordello, right next door to my school, of all places. I was thirteen and a half. It was perfectly legal by the way—if you were over eighteen—but no one looked too closely.

Why did I do it? Well, some reasons are obvious, but an unspoken one was that my brother, a year older, already looked like a male model. I never thought I was ugly, but the girls never went for me the way they went for him. Still, none had gone *all the way* with him, so it was very important for me to go there before he did.

An older friend took me in on a Saturday afternoon. The waiting room was tiny, dingy, and dimly lit, and reeked of cigarette smoke and alcohol. I waited for twenty or twenty-five minutes, and then the *Chacha*—the madam—came out of a door on the left, her office, and led me through a door on the right.

A bleached blonde with big breasts waited. She looked really old to me, though she was probably in her mid-thirties. But what did I know? I had no television; I had no *Playboys* under my bed, no Internet. I knew which parts fit where, but that was about all. Otherwise I was as nervous—no, scared—as I could possibly be.

The woman was really nice. She sat on the dirty, crumpled sheets, motioned me over to the bed, and helped me out of my clothes. I was so naïve I asked if I should take my socks off. Then she washed me in a little basin of water and put my penis in her mouth. Holy shit! I didn't know someone could do that. I wish I had had a camera then, not to record the act, but to take a picture of my face. I'm sure it revealed exactly what I was thinking: *You can do that? Is that legal? Do Mom and Dad do this?*

I was so nervous that it took me a few minutes to get aroused, but she took it easy with me, and said, "Come on. Relax. Feel good," and everything worked as it was supposed to. It seems funny now, but afterward I remember thinking, You had sex, now you're a man.

When I left we had some beers and celebrated the loss of my virginity and having beaten my brother at something important. He made the trip himself two weeks later because he couldn't stand the thought of his younger brother having one up on him.

Now that I was a man, there was only one "problem." I liked sex. A lot. But I didn't have enough money—the drachma equivalent of about ten dollars—to keep going back. I'd had to save for a long time just to show up in the first place. That left me in a quandary. No fourteen-year-old girl at my school was having sex. And although I may have looked mature for my age, the older girls, eighteen or nineteen, were not going to have sex with a fourteen-year-old boy. A brothel was my only option, and I couldn't afford it.

So my friends and I sometimes went from bordello to bordello just to check out the girls. There was no rule that you had to get laid. You could browse just like in any store. We'd go in, buy a drink, and pretend we wanted to buy some company. A girl would come out and say hello. I'd examine her closely and shake my head. The next one would come and I'd do the same; and the next one, too. Eventually, I'd say, "Well, we were just thinking about it. Thank you," and leave.

Of course, the madams probably knew we couldn't afford the girls. As long as we bought drinks they made some money, and they knew that one day we'd grow up and spend a little more.

I think now that maybe it was unfortunate to have started so young with sex because it only added to the frustrations I had begun to experience in other parts of my life.

2

LEARNING

With the bay virtually outside the town's front door, everyone in Kalamata swam. I was in the water all the time. I loved breaking through the waves, fooling around with my friends, and seeing who could swim the fastest. I also made bets with my friends about who could swim farthest underwater. I could make it out to a boat anchored 50 meters (about 150 feet) offshore and come up on the other side without taking a breath, and always won. The loser had to buy sodas afterward.

Our high school, which began in the eighth grade, had a swim team. Unfortunately, we had no pool and no real coach who could tell us how to train or win. We were just kids fooling around, although I got some pointers from my uncle Yianni, a water polo player and regional swimming champion.

Near the end of each term students from the different area high schools gathered at the beach for races. Our "pool" was the ocean between two wooden barges that floated on great metal drums, inside the breakwater. The barges were set approximately

50 meters apart—one Olympic pool length, though the distance varied with each small swell that passed—and were connected by ropes, to make lanes.

I entered my first official meet when I was a freshman, and came in first. The prize was a trip to Athens for the national championships. Because we didn't have a coach, a gym teacher from another high school went along as chaperon, with instructions to keep order and bring us back alive. Naturally, we expected to get our asses kicked because the city kids had heated Olympic pools and trainers and took their swimming seriously.

My mother packed my little brown suitcase and, with my brother and maybe twenty other students, I settled in for a twelve-hour train ride to the capital. I'll never forget the journey: It was June, and hot. We had no air-conditioning. The train stank of coal smoke, and soon my short-sleeved shirt and khaki shorts did, too. The hard wooden seats hurt my ass, and we stopped at every little town along the way.

But no matter. This was all an adventure. I stared out the window as we rolled along through the countryside, thinking, Can I do this? Maybe I can.

"You know," I said to some kids near me, after reading the race qualifying times in the newspaper, "this doesn't seem very fast. I think *I* can go this fast."

I had no idea if that was true. I'd been timed, but when your lane is the rope line between two barges that might be 49 meters apart one second and 52 the next, there was no such thing as accuracy. I just knew I usually came in first.

The chaperon overheard me. I can't recall his exact response, but it was more or less, "Stop the boasting, kid. You're just going on a little vacation. Don't think you can beat anyone up there. You ain't got a chance."

His words upset me, but he was probably right. The guy

just wanted to protect us all from having unreasonable expectations and from coming home terribly disappointed. But he didn't know me. At almost fourteen, I was much stronger than most kids my age. I'd been playing beach soccer almost every day since I was six. I lifted weights and boxed. I had tremendous lung capacity.

Maybe I could do it. I'd certainly try.

We arrived in Athens after sunset. An official told us the schedule. The 50-meter freestyle heats were in two days. No problem. I'd have a chance to rest and maybe see some of the city. I hadn't been in Athens since I was eight years old; compared to Kalamata it was huge, intimidating, and promising. I feel the same way now when I go to New York. Everybody pushing, energetic, going places. Horns blare. The air smells like a city.

Our accommodations were hardly better than our seats on the train: an old army barracks with what seemed like endless rows of cots. Trying to relax and sleep that first night was almost impossible with kids throwing pillows, making noise, roughhousing, going nuts.

The next morning I had a big breakfast, including lots of milk, bread, butter, marmalade, and everything you're not supposed to eat before swimming. But I had a day to kill. Before exploring the city, I went to the pool with the team to watch a few events. When we walked in, someone told our coach that there had been a mistake: The 50-meter freestyle heats had just started and I was in heat number three. Not only did I barely have time to run downstairs and get into my suit, I wouldn't be able to warm up. I'd counted on that because I'd never actually been in a pool or unsalted water.

I was in a heat with seven other swimmers. The current

under-fourteen, 50-meter freestyle Greek champions had already won their earlier races and no one really expected any of the kids in my heat to qualify. But despite the badly timed heavy meal, I felt strong. I looked at the other racers and realized that my shoulders were bigger and I was more fit. I may not have trained under ideal conditions or every day, even in winter, but I knew that the 50-meter freestyle was a power event. It's all about speed. It's straight ahead, one pool length. There's no endurance involved. It all just comes down to how strong you are.

I took three or four good deep breaths, the starting gun fired, and we dove in. My plan was to breathe as little as possible while I was swimming and to use the pain of my lungs about to explode as an incentive to touch the opposite pool wall before everyone else. My muscles would get less oxygen, which is like depriving an engine of fuel; however, it takes about eighteen seconds for a breath to distribute its benefits to the body, and the distance was short enough not to make that a major issue if I could get enough air at the outset.

After I hit the water I never looked up. I didn't know if I was ahead or behind. I just swam straight and fast until I touched the wall, thrust my head out of the pool, and gulped air. The first thing I noticed was my brother standing to the right of the official timer on my lane. He stared at his watch, then shook it. I looked into the pool and saw everyone else still swimming, a good 5 or 6 meters to go—an enormous distance in this race. My brother ran up to me and said, "I don't know if this is right, but Jesus, this is fast. This is really fast!" And then I heard "A new national record!" on the loudspeaker. I clocked 28.6 seconds, and I was stunned. The second-place swimmer was at least 5 seconds behind me.

I got out of the pool and everybody screamed. My team-mates lifted me into the air. The chaperon who had rebuked me the day before was now all hugs and smiles. I didn't bother to say, "I told you." We both instantly accepted what had happened and forgot about the past. That's what I love about athletic events. The results are not a matter of opinion. They are what they are.

Swimming in freshwater is indeed different from swimming in the ocean. The ocean is more buoyant, and the salt water creates much more resistance. Your arms don't move as fast. You can't push or pull as hard, though with every pull you cover more distance. Think of bicycle gears. Ocean water is like a higher gear. You work harder, and go farther. Freshwater is like a lower gear. You can pedal faster and more easily, but you cover less ground.

After my win—and a celebration—I was surprised by a feeling I'd never had before: self-doubt. I tried to rest that afternoon, before the evening finals, but I couldn't. It wasn't just the dormitory noise. I was nervous. Rather than feeling elated, I was racked with questions: How could *I* have won? Maybe it was a mistake. Or a freak accident! I didn't know if I could do it again, and this time I would be swimming against the champions.

Beyond those doubts lay an even more uncomfortable realization: Before the race I'd been of one mind, focused on winning, no questions asked. Now I had a mind divided. I tried to bury my anxiety by napping, but sleep wouldn't come.

By evening, the media had already begun to make a big deal out of me—bigger than I was. As the dark horse, I was the story of the day. The race even took on social and political overtones. Decentralization movements were afoot to try to get the Greek government to spend money outside Athens for education and a variety of activities. Suddenly I was the poster boy: Look, this kid came out of nowhere and doesn't even have a coach. Imagine what he could do with training . . .

Moments before the final race, one of the two Greek champions walked by and tried to intimidate me. "I've never lost," he said confidently. "No one can pass me. No one." He was at least a foot taller than me. "This is a real race," he added, as we stepped up on our platforms. I was in lane four. He and the other Greek champion flanked me. I stood there, waiting, shaking, scared. The only good news was that it seemed that some of my competition was just as nervous. Instead of concentrating on the race ahead, they were looking over at me, with expressions that asked, "Who is this guy? Who's teaching him? Why is he here?" I guess I'd have felt that way too if some kid out of nowhere had just that morning beaten my record by a long shot. Suddenly I felt better. My confidence returned.

The official announced the race. We took our marks, got set, and . . . false start. Someone moved before the gun and we all ended up in the water. The starter gun was fired a second time, to let the swimmers know the situation. Warning flags were dropped in the water about 8 to 10 meters out in case someone didn't hear the gun. We got out of the pool and took our places again, the tension even greater.

Another false start.

A third false start would mean disqualification for anyone who ended up in the water.

The official held up the starting pistol: "On your marks, get set . . ."

I saw the swimmer in lane five move just before the gun went off. I assumed once again that the race would stop, and the swimmer would be disqualified, so I struggled to hold myself back and stand up. But there was no second shot, and no warning flags. The officials didn't want to disqualify a Greek champion, so they let it go—and everyone hit the water but me.

You make that big a mistake and you don't recover, but I didn't stop to think. I just dove in and swam as if my life depended on it. If I breathed at all, I don't remember.

Here's what I do remember: I won—and my time was identical to that morning's. Now I really owned the record.

The media fussed over me. The newspapers and radio kept asking, "Who is this Chryssomallis kid from Kalamata, and how is this possible?" The mayor of Kalamata gave me the "Best Athlete of the Year" award, a handmade silver cup. And the town hired a team swimming coach who knew all the latest training techniques.

People swim a lot faster today, but I think my win was miraculous. My definition of "miraculous" is that there was no way an untrained kid could reasonably expect to enter his first official event and beat swimmers who had dedicated their young lives to the sport. Yet in both races I looked around and thought, There's no way any of you are going to get ahead of me. The miracle was in my innocence, and I've learned that in innocence there is strength. When you're naïve, you don't question. Years later, this applied to my music when I was learning how to set up the best conditions under which to create it. The more I questioned and the more I doubted, the more I destroyed my songs. A naïve person believes things are possible that others, who think they know better, don't—or can't. I'm not saying that the innocent *always* triumph, but maybe knowing better isn't always better. Sometimes the knowledge you've been given in school or by an elder—"This is just the way it is"—keeps you from accomplishing because it traps you in a box in your mind and limits your freedom to discover.

Openness has always been the key for me. I won the swimming meet in part because I believed that anything was possible, or at least because I didn't put together everyone else's "facts" and believe that winning was *impossible.*

I became serious about swimming and trained twice a day, from six to eight in the morning, and from six to eight in the evening. From five to six in the afternoon, I lifted weights. I was in bed by nine thirty. On Sunday I trained just two hours, plus I lifted weights. I even worked out on my birthday because I knew that if I missed practice sessions it would take me days to get back to peak shape. Swimming is a particularly difficult, demanding, and physically brutal event. My pulse rate sometimes reached nearly 180 beats per minute. Watch a swimmer's chest after he's done interval training and you can actually see his heart beating against his skin. If my body could have spoken it would have screamed, "You're killing me!"

I refused to give in. I acknowledged my pain but I would not let it destroy me or change my course. Then I went back for more. Endurance is mind over matter, mind over muscle. I have tremendous respect for athletes; when I watch the Olympics I know the kind of agony these competitors have been through.

For the next few years I won almost every race I entered, from the 50-meter freestyle to the 100-, 200-, and 400-meter distances. I did it in the under-fourteen and over-fourteen age categories. I collected a lot of gold medals and cups—my parents still have them in the house—and continued to do well right through high school. But I didn't do as well as I wanted to. The best swimmers are tall and slim; my muscled, five-foot-nine frame began to show its limitations. I was more built than sleek. I had natural ability, but that wasn't quite enough anymore.

As a junior, I remember walking around Athens one day by

myself, in the rain, crying, bummed out at having not lived up to my high hopes in an international swim meet. I'd been very sick the week before and the illness had drained me—but knowing that didn't seem to help. After having been so positive for so long, I doubted my competitive future, and I decided to quit. The coaches and my friends tried to talk me out of it. "You're still a kid. Come on, how could you give this up?"

"You have a great talent!"

"You can go to the Olympics."

Maybe. But at that level of competition there is absolutely no room for doubt. Either you're 1 million percent convinced that this is the only thing you want to do, or you get out. You can't *just kinda* do it. You won't succeed. It's a waste of time. Also, swimming had once been fun; it was hard work but also a social event. Now most of the fun had disappeared and I knew I no longer had the passion to continue.

My mom says I always hated injustice. If I knew I had done something wrong, I accepted the consequences. I put my head down and didn't say a word. But if I did not agree that I'd done anything wrong, she could never punish me because I would object loudly. Once, but only once, I grabbed the dining room table and turned it upside down.

Sometimes my desire for fairness and justice caused problems at school. In the eighth grade I was in gym class playing basketball when the rest of the school was called to an assembly outside. We didn't have to go, so my coach asked me to get him something from the dressing rooms. I took off, past all the kids, and ran into the composition teacher. He didn't like me. "The principal's talking," he snapped. "You're being disrespectful." I tried to tell him I was on an errand for the coach but he wouldn't let me finish. "I said you're being disrespectful," he barked. "You've *always* been disrespectful. I know your kind." I stood there, speechless. "Go back to your class," he ordered.

"I can't go back," I protested. "The coach . . ."

That's when he grabbed me and started shaking me. "Listen here," he yelled. "You'll do whatever I tell you to do."

The Greek school system was strict and unforgiving, and many of the teachers had the bad habit of getting physical. Sometimes they'd even hit. I didn't like it, so without much thought, I grabbed his arms and pushed them away, forcing him to let me go. For my trouble, I was suspended for a few days.

This teacher's attitude was part of the reason I hated school. I resented being treated like a little kid. I didn't like to be pushed around, hit, or handled in an uptight military manner. It was always "Move this way, turn this way, look up, look down, sit to the left, sit to the right." Even worse, it was also "Think this way, not that way. You're wrong, we're right."

A couple of years later in religion class somebody made a noise or giggled and the teacher got mad. He asked who did it and no one would confess. Then for some reason the instructor decided I knew and should tell him.

"I have no idea," I said.

"If you don't tell me," he threatened, "I'm going to kick you out of the class."

"I don't know," I repeated.

"Tell me," he insisted.

"Look," I said, "I don't know. And even if I did know, I wouldn't tell you. And you're not going to kick me out of class for nothing."

I shouldn't have let my frustration get the better of me.

He marched to my desk, grabbed my arm, and tried to pull me out of my chair. I weighed a lot more then than I weigh now, and my biceps were twice their current size. (I could do 137 push-ups nonstop.) Unfortunately for the teacher, I sort of lost it and reacted instinctively by backhanding him on the chest. Not the face, the chest. And only once. But I must have hit him harder than I realized because he fell backward on a desk and went down in a heap with some students. It all seemed to happen in slow motion and I remember thinking, Now I've done it. I've just hit a teacher, it's over. I'm never going to finish high school. They'll kick me out forever. My future is screwed.

Even though I saw my whole sorry life flash before me, I still had the presence of mind to leave the classroom immediately, on my own, and go to the principal's office. He was at his desk. He saw me, smiled, and said, "What's up?" The principal liked me; he thought I was a good kid, which is why I went to him in the first place.

"I just did something really bad," I said. "I'm really sorry, but I just lost it." After I explained, I added that I was just exhausted from getting up at 5 A.M. every day and training so hard for the swim team. Most teachers understood and cut me some slack. More important, I also said, "My father doesn't hit me. I don't get dragged around like that in my family. I don't expect anyone here to grab me, either. It was just instinct. My arm did what it wanted to do."

From the look on the principal's face I could see he was trying to figure out whether or not to believe me, so I said, "I know you can't give me a break, so I'm going home now."

I was totally embarrassed to tell my parents. My father, who never condoned violence, always said, "You gotta be cool." (Of course you don't actually say "cool" in Greek, but that's what he meant.) You don't use your fists, you don't yell, you don't jump up and down. Strength is in your mind and heart. We went through all that. But I still had a little bit of a cowboy attitude.

My dad believed my story, and so did my mother, which surprised me because most of the time she went the other way and stood up for the teachers whenever I complained. It wasn't that she didn't support me, but my mother wants to do the right thing and the good thing, to be socially and politically correct, to get along. Part of me is that way, too—but only part.

Because word traveled fast around school and I became a hero for decking the teacher, the principal made me stay home for a week. It could have been much worse. In those days, if you didn't have excellent behavior on your high school release papers, the government wouldn't give you a passport to study abroad. My parents' dream was for all their children to go to college in America. I didn't want to mess that up. Luckily the principal protected me. I promised myself to take a deep breath before losing my temper again.

As for the teacher, they let him go a couple of months later.

If only discipline were my biggest complaint about the Greek school system. But it wasn't. I loved my country and admired its culture and heritage, but I objected to the way children were educated. Those core beliefs about teaching remain with me today.

Once, an instructor stood me up in front of the entire class because my brother and I had to take a few hours off from school for a music recital. He was upset that I had to leave for something "as ridiculous as playing music."

"You just can't do so many things," he said. "If you go to school, do music, take languages, play sports—all at the same time—you'll be no good at any." And this was the wisdom of a man teaching life's truths to impressionable young minds? No wonder I disliked the—you guessed it—composition teacher whose arms I had pushed away when he grabbed me.

In high school we spent an enormous amount of class time translating ancient Greek into modern Greek. We focused on the works of Plato, Socrates, and so on. We had ten lines to translate every other day. That would have been fine had the teacher also made some attempt to help us understand what the texts were about. What had these sage men advocated? Why do we still read them today? What had they disagreed about? Did they get along? We spent 99 percent of our time translating and 1 percent discussing. To say this made me angry is an understatement. I asked the teacher why the ancients wrote down their philosophy in the first place if not to communicate their ideas and encourage debate. No answer.

Most of my early educational experiences were similar, and to this day I regret the time wasted by school at an age when my mind could have absorbed so much. Of course, I didn't expect my teachers to be Aristotle or Plato or Socrates, but I also didn't expect them to be just disciplinarians who frustrated me and made me hate school. Maybe it wasn't their fault; rather than being structured to encourage individuality and creative thinking, the system was set up simply to test my ability to remember on Wednesday what I was taught on Monday. But there's a difference between a teacher who loves his students and wants to stimulate their minds through exploration, and one who stresses memorization. Maybe learning is best when it isn't a grind but opens your mind instead.

Great teachers usually have wise teachers themselves. Again, think of Socrates, who taught Plato, who taught Aristotle, who was personal tutor to Alexander the Great—who in turn conquered most of the known world in his time. I don't think that's a coincidence. The teachers I responded to were those who encouraged thinking outside the box. That's how my dad treated me at home. There I had respect and positive reinforcement to the nth degree. He taught self-reliance, freedom of thought, and that it's okay to be different. "If the whole world wants to go left and you feel like going right, go right," he would say. "You don't have to follow. And you don't have to make a big deal about which way you're going. Just go. It's very easy."

At school, I couldn't go anywhere. I had to fit in, find my place, stay there, not ask too many questions, make no waves, be a slave—a microcosm of what society wants from most people.

It was hard to reconcile my father's approach to life with one that told me to get in line and sell out like everyone else standing there with me. I've always thought that if you can bring good to those around you, be productive and not a drain on society, avoid hurting people or feeding off of them, then you should be allowed to live the way that you want to live. Find a way to contribute: Take out the garbage, build, cook, paint a house. There is always a way.

The older I got, the more I wanted to rebel. Sunday nights were the worst time of the week for me because Monday I had to go back to school. When my mother reads this page she will be surprised and think, But you were such a good student, what do you mean? Well, remember how I spoke of being trained to take pain? No matter how depressed I got on Sunday nights, I didn't complain.

A few times I discussed these feelings with my father. Even though he also disagreed with the system, he knew I had to go to school and do well simply to achieve my goal of going to America. He tried to help me get along. "Just ignore it," he'd say. "It's fine. They don't understand." He worked to nurture my individuality, but he also knew I had to deal with the situation. "You're right, they're wrong, but you still have to show respect. Don't take it personally. Don't shortchange yourself. Look beyond now; focus on your future."

I confess I contributed to the problem. From as early as I can remember, starting with the piano, I didn't particularly like to be taught. This is my personality, I know. I've always been more teachable when I teach myself. I don't want problems solved for me. I want the fishing rod, not the fish. My whole family's like that. Sometimes when we have a discussion over dinner I say, "You know, no one in this family listens to anyone."

I've learned the hard way. I've made mistakes, spent hours tinkering, experimenting, obsessing. But I'm glad I made discoveries on my own. To write my music, I must face the unknown. I call it "the black." Most people are frightened by the unknown. I find it exciting because of the abundance of possibilities. I'm comfortable there. The unfamiliar is very familiar to me. I don't have a "you can't do this" voice in my head. Freedom is beautiful.

It's not that I don't value teaching. I do, especially when it comes from instructors who understand that their job is to teach students how to function without them, how to confidently face the unknown without a backup. That takes more than just memorizing a bunch of facts. You need a mind open to possibility, conditioned to love the creative spirit we all have inside ourselves.

Look at Dick Fosbury, the 1968 Olympic high-jump champion. Instead of leaping like everyone else, he went over headfirst and backward. They called it the "Fosbury Flop." At first people laughed, but Fosbury broke the world record. Now everybody jumps headfirst and backward.

When I began to play piano seriously, I looked at the keyboard and my fingers and thought, What would I like my hands to do? Okay, I'd like to be able to press this note and that note. I tried, and if it didn't work I experimented until it did. Did I need a teacher to show me how? Teachers can make it easier as long as they don't imply that there's only one right way to do something and cut off access to original thoughts.

Original thinkers have always fascinated me.

Take the idea that the universe is made up of small "building blocks," or atoms. The name is derived from the Greek word *atomos,* which means "indestructible particle." The concept is commonly attributed to Democritus, an ancient Greek philosopher who lived from 470 to 380 B.C. Democritus was first to use the word "atom," but he built on the ideas of his teacher, Leucippus. Democritus's student, Epicurus, went further and enquired into the movement of atoms. Some say the original thought behind the atom came even earlier, with Anaxagoras and others, and it's difficult to know exactly, but the point is not who actually came up with what, *but that they came up with anything at all.* How in they heck did they think of this stuff? What made someone arrive at the picture of an atom in his head? I always wanted the kind of mind that could give birth to a thought that no one else had had.

Today, largely because of the creative process I employ to make my music—which I will describe in more detail later on—I realize I do have that kind of mind. *And so does everyone else on this planet.* It's just a matter of how that mind is nurtured, encouraged, and trained. It begins when we're young, with our parents, and continues in school, where the key is not to teach in a way that breaks the spirit—or ignores it—so that the student never explores or takes a chance. Supporting creativity and eliminating the fear of facing the black is the path that works for me and allows the mental quantum leap. If I were raising children, my primary focus would be to expose them to a wide spectrum of subjects. I wouldn't push; I would find a way to let the new experiences attract and entice the children. That way they would follow of their own accord. And once they did, I'd let them soar.

Unfortunately, my vision of how things work best was not the standard when I went to school. And even now, there are so many students and so few teachers. Classrooms are crowded; all kids don't learn at the same speed. It's next to impossible to give individual attention and cater to everyone's needs. Some kids are visually oriented, some aurally, some tactilely, and sometimes those who are not equipped to pick up information in the standard fashion, or who are slower, are considered dumb, if not by their peers or the teachers, then by themselves. They become traumatized and think they're not good enough. They drop out, and it's over.

Self-judgment is the destroyer.

It doesn't have to be.

The famous psychiatrist Alfred Adler performed a test many years ago in which he went to different schools and found kids at the bottom of the class, took them away for a year, and taught them while highly emphasizing and reinforcing self-esteem. When he returned them to their schools they went to the top 10 percent of their classes. Adler believed in relationships established on the basis of equality. He supported creativity, improvisation, invention. He understood the uniqueness of each person and adapted his methods to the individual.

We all have special needs. If they're met early, our brains will rise to the occasion.

I have a suspicion that if you check into the lives of some gifted children, you'll find something in their homes and families or somewhere along the educational line that inspired their brains to hang on to a lot of those billions of neurons that most of us drop along the way. They were probably stimulated in every way possible without worries about what they'd be when they grew up, without love being withdrawn for making mistakes. It may seem like they lack direction because sometimes they go in all directions at once, but it's not so. The engaged mind stays sharp and retains tremendous capacity. Those kids learn how to solve their own problems, gain confidence from doing it, and are not afraid to face the black.

When I was still in high school I met a man named Bill MacDonald. He was the Dean of the College of Liberal Arts at the University of Minnesota. He, other professors, and their students would come to Greece in the summers to excavate archaeological sites near my town and study the culture. They wanted to discover the origin of the Greeks. Eventually MacDonald wrote a book about it.

I got to know Bill because of my father, who got involved with these people through a good deed he had performed a few years earlier for a young American couple named William and Esther Loy. They came into his bank when they were in Kalamata making maps for the future excavation.

The story is so characteristic of my dad.

The Loys asked a bank official if a check from the University of Minnesota had arrived. The answer was, "It's not here yet." The problem was a post office strike, which went on for forty days, and they desperately needed money.

My dad was assistant manager then. One day he realized he'd seen the Loys come in again and again, always leaving frustrated. He assumed they must be in trouble, so he took them aside and heard their story. They couldn't pay the rent or buy food. To help, my dad did something anyone else would have considered foolish—he gave them money out of his own pocket. He said, "I'm sure your check will come, and when it does, just give the check to me."

What? The Loys freaked. Can you imagine: In a foreign country, some local banker just gives you money without collateral? The Loys could have walked out and never returned. A smart person would never have given them a loan. But my dad is great at reading people. He knew they weren't lying. He has always told me, "Intelligence is a wonderful thing, and you must be intelligent. But intelligence without discernment, judgment, without being a good judge of character and a good judge of a situation, is useless. You will always shoot yourself in the foot. Intelligence is not enough."

Maybe a week later, when the strike ended, the check came and the Loys repaid my father. Then they became friends. My father brought them to the house. My mother cooked and baked. We all went swimming and hiking. The next summer, they visited again.

As the excavations approached, the university needed someone to handle the business end in Greece, to buy land and get permissions from the government's antiquities department. The college turned to my dad. He got land clearances and helicopters, and built them the expedition house. My dad made money from these dealings, but the biggest benefit was that his openness cleared the way for his kids to go to college in the United States at the University of Minnesota.

My father would sometimes take me to the dig, where I met the professors—including Bill MacDonald. Bill was my hero, an inspiration. He was the first adult much more important to me than any teacher or authority figure, except for my father. Where others treated me as a child, ignoring or deflecting my inquisitiveness because my mind was housed in a kid's body, he considered my questions seriously and engaged me in dialogues.

Bill had humility; my regular teachers were absolutists. Bill was one of the first people to be sympathetic toward my young views about my education. It's a sign of my bond with him that I felt free enough to discuss them in the first place. My opinions weren't fully formed then; I was just a kid with a sense that something was very wrong. But when I complained to him about how we were taught, instead of brushing me off or patronizing me, he said, "You're right; it's wrong." I felt a great sense of relief.

Bill was always ready to talk. Once I asked him, "How do we know that a historical event really happened? How do you know that a certain battle took place with this many Persians and that many Greeks?"

His answer: "That's just it: We don't know. We cross-reference one primary source with another. If more than one account from different cultures in existence at the time say the same thing about the same event we tend to believe it."

Maybe this is no big deal to American students, but no teacher I'd ever known had been so open. Bill didn't even like the grading system, believing instead that students should either pass or fail. Grades, he said, misrepresented knowledge and intelligence—and often confused them. I wondered then why I couldn't have more teachers like him. He was there at the right time, saying the right things to spark my imagination. He showed me I wasn't crazy, that there *were* different approaches to learning. Before he died a few years ago, I would call him whenever I had a serious question about early civilizations, archaeology, or history, and we would have long talks. At one point, after I had become famous, he said that if I ever found myself in a position to be able to affect society and do something about revamping the educational system, that I should do so.

I went to my last two years of high school in Athens on a swimming scholarship as part of the Greek national team. Although my brother was also in school there, I lived in an apartment by myself. Before I left for the city I asked my father for an allowance, and he agreed. In fact, he gave me a family checkbook.

"What can I take out a week?" I asked.

"Whatever you need," he said.

"No, I mean *how much?*" I wanted him to say, "Fifty or a hundred dollars a week." Something specific. But he refused.

"Whatever you need," he repeated. "But of course if you spend too much there won't be any left for the rest of us to live on."

"Why," I asked him many years later, "would you trust a sixteen-year-old with that kind of responsibility?"

"Because I raised you," he said. "I know what I put into you. You understood responsibility."

To this day we joke about that moment, but he was right. Once again he had treated me like an adult, and it had worked.

Around the time I quit swimming I had also, not so coincidentally, fallen in love with psychology. My father had passed on to me his love of exploring why we are the way we are. There is no single answer, of course, but I loved thinking about it so much that my athletics suffered. But that was okay with me, and I made the difficult choice to go in a completely new direction. I read and absorbed every text I could find. I was well into Freud, Adler, and Jung by the time I turned seventeen. That's young, perhaps, but not if you grew up with my father. He always talked to me about the human condition. He was interested in what made people tick and tried to explain it nonjudgmentally.

Years later, in college, I studied dream analysis. I think dreaming is one way our brain educates itself. To process our mishmash of experiences during the day, it runs various scenarios at night, based on the information we've absorbed from the world. This includes situations we're afraid of or think might happen, and outcomes that make us happy, sad, or indifferent. Dreams just connect the dots—without judgment—and through them we get to experience a possible future and react fully. Then if it ever really happens, we'll be more prepared because we've already been there. If anything, dreams are self-protective, educational survival mechanisms.

For example, my sister used to see my father dying in her dreams. She thought it meant something was going to happen. But I think she just loves my dad so much and is so connected to him that she's probably going to be devastated when he dies. Those dreams are her way of preparing for the future by letting her become accustomed to her feelings now, a desensitization that also works when you're awake. When I see people cry, I say, "Please: Cry. Go for it." It hurts you? Good. Please cry. Let's think about it again tomorrow. The next day it won't hurt as much. Pretty soon you can handle your feelings. Suppressing anything only makes it worse.

All our brains go into overdrive at night. Mine focuses on music. If I work on a song at the end of the day and have unresolved problems, I know when I wake up the next morning I'll have the answers. My brain does that for me because music is the last thing I think about at night—intentionally. No TV or books.

I brush my teeth and go to sleep. The next morning I wake up smarter about the song.

Attending college in America isn't cheap, especially for a foreign student. To make it possible for us to go, my father did what many would consider unthinkable: He sold our house, moved into a rental, and used the money to buy plane tickets and help all three children get started in school. That took enormous balls. My father was in his fifties, approaching retirement. His salary would soon stop. But Mom and Dad had discussed it and agreed that nothing was more important than us going to America.

It wasn't only the educational opportunities. From 1967 to 1974, Greece was ruled by a U.S.-backed military junta. The government tried to change history by rewriting the schoolbooks. Boys, me included, had to get a crew cut. They also changed the language in an effort to make it more "proper." The police and army had ultimate and absolute power. There was no freedom of the press. There was no political dissent allowed. We were told not to say anything against any government official because we could be arrested and thrown into jail with the other political prisoners. We also heard stories of people "disappearing."

After the junta was overthrown, Greece was not such a bad place if you could focus on the country's history and its hopes for the future instead of on its day-to-day struggles with bureaucracy and corruption. Today, Greece has worked through a rite of passage, has come a long way, and is looking at a brighter future.

Nonetheless, as my father recently and bluntly told me, had I not come to America there would be no Yanni. He's adamant about that. He believes I've reached whatever levels of creativity I have because I was stimulated by changing cultures, by moving to a land with greater challenges and more of everything. And, of course, because of who I am. Maybe he's right.

My brother went first, to the University of Minnesota, where he studied chemical engineering. (He earned a Ph.D.) His freshman year he stayed with one of the professors, which helped financially.

A few days before I left, I visited my aunt Xanthe and I told her that I would not come back until I did something right, until I had made something of myself. I understood my parents' sacrifice and I believed in my heart there was no chance I'd allow myself to fail.

The day before my flight to America I walked with my father to the little pier on the bay where I used to swim. I looked out over the water and found the horizon, but hard as I tried I couldn't see the horizon inside my head. I had no idea what the future would hold. "I would give anything to be in this spot ten years from now," I told my dad, "to know what is actually about to happen to me."

Was I scared? Maybe a little, though danger always feels to me more like excitement, like pins and needles. When I throw everything in the air, up for grabs, that's when great things happen for me. I don't live in fear, but if I don't have a *little* fear about what I'm about to do, then I know I'm just repeating myself, not stretching. I look for the little bit of doubt; I need to ask myself the question: Can I do this?

However, at that moment, I had a stomach full of butterflies and I wanted desperately to see through the curtain of time.

My father wanted to make the unknown okay. "What you're about to do is extremely difficult," he said, "so if it doesn't work, come home and don't feel bad about it." Then he opened the door a crack more and said, "Most kids wouldn't succeed at this. You don't really speak the language. It's a change in cultures; you don't know what to expect and you don't know what you'll find. We think it's best that you go and try, but if it doesn't work, no one is going to blame you. You can go to the university here."

He gave me permission to fail without ever implying that he expected I would. With that, he took the pressure off. Dad is a clever man. He understood the source of my stress. My mom, too. I heard her voice in my head, saying, "If your own mind does not beat you up, a thousand people can't do it, either." In other words, she knew I had self-control and focus and that I would do my best.

I forgot about that moment until years later when I returned to Greece after a long absence. I walked with my father to the bay and stood on the pier in the same spot where we'd talked so long ago. I remembered our good-byes and my wish to know the future. That's when the circle finally closed. Suddenly, I felt like an eighteen-year-old again. I had tears in my eyes.

3

CHANGING

When I came to America I wanted to be free and open to change. I wanted to try new foods, a new culture, and new ideas. I understood that to do so I had to cut the cord to Greece. You have to give up some of the old so that you can make room for the new. You need not to be full of yourself in order to move on. I had no intention of getting stuck in the past, and I couldn't have chosen a better way to do it than to leave the cocoon, get on an airplane, and wind up in Minnesota.

I didn't even call myself Yanni. I was John. John Chryssomallis, the name on my passport and enrollment forms.

I had this "keep moving" attitude even as a kid. My instinct was to taste it all, because the more I stimulated my mind, the better off I was. Now that I'm older, I *know* that I can never sit still. That's the beauty of life. It never stops. We change constantly, both physically and in our perceptions. That's not to say that other instincts don't pull in the opposite direction. No matter how old you are, at times you will find a place and say, "Hey, this works for me. This is good. Why don't I stay here?" But even if you could, even if nothing bad ever happened, even if it was Heaven, I suspect you'd be bored out of your mind. Eventually you'd want to change—so you might as well not resist when it happens naturally.

I wouldn't mind having a younger body if I could keep my mind the way it is today. Many mornings I wake up and look at myself in the mirror—and it's kind of a bummer. "Hey guy, what happened to you?" I'm not happy about getting hurt more easily and taking longer to heal, but as my mother has said, what's the alternative? These changes are part of what keeps me interested and excited. Life won't let me keep coming at it from the same angle.

I said good-bye to my parents at the Kalamata airport and took a puddle jumper to Athens, where I boarded a TWA flight to New York. I arrived in America on November 8, 1972, a week before my eighteenth birthday. I had to change terminals at JFK for my flight to Minneapolis. The airport bus charged a quarter, but I didn't have any American money, so I just got on and walked to the back while the driver yelled at me to pay him—I think: I barely spoke English and he talked too fast. Fortunately, a nice woman said, "It's okay," and paid for me. Then, being a Good Samaritan, she gave me a handful of coins and said, "This is a quarter. This is a nickel. This is a dime."

My brother met me at the end of the jetway in Minneapolis. We'd been virtually inseparable all our lives and it was great to see him after a year apart. We hugged, then picked up my bag, which was much larger than the old brown suitcase I'd taken to Athens for the swimming championships. But as soon as we exited the terminal I wanted to turn around, reboard, and fly home. The wind howled and it must have been ten below zero. My skin had never experienced anything remotely as cold. My lungs hurt so bad I could hardly breathe. My ears were on fire and felt like any second they'd crack off my head and fall into the snow. Yorgo had said it would be cold, so I wore a coat, figuring, How cold could it be?

Let's just say it wasn't the right coat for Minnesota in the winter.

I'd also never touched snow before. Ignoring the chill for just a moment, I picked up a handful of the slushy white powder, squeezed it into a lump, and threw it. Eventually I learned to love the snow, but had I realized then that the ground would still be frozen and covered six months later, I might *actually* have gone home.

Yorgo drove us to Territorial Hall, our dormitory at the university. We'd be roommates on the second floor. I lugged my bag up the stairs and we walked down a long corridor. Suddenly, I smelled something burning; it was pungent, acrid, and everywhere.

"Yorgo," I said. "What's that smell?"

"Marijuana," he said. "Pot."

"*That's* what it smells like?" I had never been exposed to it. "But it's so strong."

He laughed. "Oh, that's because everyone's smoking right now in their rooms."

The whole place? This is going to be great, I thought, and not because I wanted to get high. Compared to Greece, everything was wide open here and the possibilities seemed endless.

The first thing I did was grow a beard and stop cutting my hair. Soon I looked like a cross between Cat Stevens and Che Guevara. Since coming to America, I've shaved my mustache only once, and I didn't like it. There's nothing funnier–looking than a guy who has a mustache one minute and not the next. It takes him a year to get used to his face again.

Back home, I'd had to take some examinations, wait for grades, and deal with endless emigration red tape before I could leave the country, so I wasn't able to start college in September. That meant I had to kill time until the next quarter began in January, 1973. I didn't mind because I had to work on learning English. After only a year in Minnesota, my brother spoke quite well. I hardly spoke English at all, despite a few years of study at high school. Most kids in Greece had to take English, but mostly we joked our way through class, and I didn't absorb much.

My brother, who is extremely intelligent and has great problem-solving abilities, made my challenge clear. "Look," he said. "From now on you just don't speak Greek anymore. If there's something you don't understand, I'll explain it in Greek. But don't talk to me in Greek." Very clever. He knew the difference between English lessons back home and speaking English in America. Nobody slows down.

I struggled, but I kept up.

I also needed a job. The next day I found one as a part-time dishwasher at the university Campus Club, where my brother worked and the professors ate. I'd never had a job before. My father had figured we'd work for most of our lives anyway, so he didn't push us as teenagers. I earned $1.29 an hour, five hours a night, to grab plates, with cigarette butts stubbed out in the un-eaten food, off the conveyor belt and scrape and scrub them bright and clean. I'd never washed a plate in my life, either; my mom was the best dishwasher in the world. I even hated touching food with my fingers. In Greece, I'd only eat chicken with a fork and knife, even the drumstick; it was too greasy and oily.

Because we lived in the dorm, the cost of meals was covered, though you can imagine how they compared to my mother's cooking, which had spoiled me forever. Once a week we went across the street to the Red Barn, where I stared at the pictures of the hamburgers and French fries and struggled to decide whether I could afford the large fries for fifty-nine cents or had to stick with the small ones for thirty-nine cents. If I could afford an extra cheeseburger it was the highlight of the week—that is, once I got used to American hamburgers. They always came with onion, ketchup, and pickle. I almost threw up after my first fast-food experience.

But I soon got used to it all. The job became like a big party. The kitchen crew played practical jokes on one another, we threw towels around, and once in a while I'd make a big mistake and break a bunch of plates. Not on purpose, of course, but if you know anything about the culture, you have to wonder if dishwashing, of all things, is really the right job for a *Greek*.

When I wasn't working I'd hang out in our little two-beds-and-not-much-else dorm room and study English or read, which amounted to the same thing. Otherwise, I had little to do: We didn't own a television, and I had no car. In some ways it was just like being back home—except that outside it was freezing cold, I didn't know my way around, and I had no friends. One thing remained the same, though: My brother, who'd lost none of his magic touch with women, was usually off with a girlfriend.

After reading for hours straight I had to take a break or go crazy. One "escape" was to start smoking. At first I had only one or two cigarettes a day, and it seemed like no big deal, but that's how you get hooked. It took me years and a lot of pain to quit.

Sometimes I would wander into the communal room. An old television set hung from the ceiling and everyone watched shows like *Sanford and Son*, with Redd Foxx. I couldn't understand what anyone said and I thought, I'm never going to learn English. I asked my brother, "What language are they speaking?"

"You'll get used to it," he said. "It's slang."

When I saw Johnny Carson for the first time, I thought, What is that? A guy standing in front of a drape, telling jokes. I didn't think it was that funny.

My brother told me Carson *was* funny, but I'd have to know more English and listen more closely. I took his advice, paid attention to Carson's speech patterns, and learned to tune my ears. Fortunately, he spoke clearly, with simple words. Yorgo was right. Johnny was very funny.

Most of the time I preferred to relax by playing a brown, beaten-up, out-of-tune upright piano in the first-floor student lounge. Late at night I'd go downstairs, sit in the near-empty room, and make up melodies on the spot. No particular song. No words. Even then I wasn't a big fan of three-and-a-half-minute formula tunes. Most of them didn't seem that creative, and besides, I couldn't connect with the "I love you, baby" and "Since you left me" lyrics. My idols were Beethoven, Mozart, Stravinsky, Tchaikovsky, Bach—and the world music I'd heard on my short-wave radio at night.

Playing piano was a way for me to shift focus and pass the time. I wasn't that good, but I still found it easy to surrender to whatever emotion I felt and express it musically. It was a way out of feeling lost and a way into myself. To my surprise, I really took to it. The kid who had never thought of becoming a musician suddenly had a tremendous urge to play for hours. The melodies just poured out. I remember wondering what was going on, but it should have been obvious: Music was simply a part of me.

My mother recently reminded me that until I took up swimming, I had played music all the time. Often, I would gather everyone in the living room, which doubled as our music room. My brother played the piano; a friend of ours, Christos, played the drums; Stathis played the guitar; I played the guitar and the accordion; my mom and my sister sang. I'd tell everybody what to do. "You were conducting us even then," my mom said.

Soon I brought a cheap cassette tape deck with me into the student lounge, to put on the piano and record some ideas. Later, I'd play back my tapes before I went to sleep. It was purely for pleasure because I enjoyed the mood the music created. Today I understand that music follows a natural emotional flow from its creator. That's the advantage of writing your own song: You write it precisely the way you like it. I enjoy the improvisation. I don't agonize over it.

I'd only been playing in the lounge for a few weeks when I noticed that people began to fill the couches and chairs around me. Particularly women; they'd walk in and stay. Now *that* was music to my ears. I realized, Wow, this works great for me! Lonely coeds, or girls tired of studying, would sit and listen and, when I finished, would come over and say, "That was beautiful."

Oh yeah? Wait 'til you hear this.

To be honest, I didn't have a problem meeting girls. I wasn't as classically handsome as my brother, but in Minnesota we were more on par. So many of the local women were blonde, and they just *loved* dark men. I enjoyed the benefits of being the Greek guy.

Girls wanted to cuddle me, take care of me, feed me. My halting English was suddenly adorable, and they wanted to show me the ways of America. "Okay," I said. "Show me. Show me!"

Could life be more pleasant and beautiful? Perhaps not, but it could get more complicated.

On my second day at work I had noticed one of the Campus Club waitresses, and she noticed me. Her name was Janice. She was, atypically, a brunette. We spoke during our break and one thing led to another. We ended up in my room, between the sheets. Remember, it was the seventies and it was very normal to meet someone and have sex—no AIDS, no big deal. Afterward we said an affectionate, "Nice to meet you. See you at work. Bye."

The next day, Janice had the shift off and I noticed another waitress, a blonde. Cute as a button. I thought, Wow. I want to meet her! I did, and we ended up in my room that night. Sweet. Great. No problem. Nice meeting you.

The fourth day, it all blew up in my face when both girls worked the *same shift.* I walked in, punched my time card, saw them, stopped to think about what I'd done, and nearly had a heart attack.

Then I found out they were roommates!

Both were casual about the whole affair. Janice said, "I don't mind sharing," which, frankly, blew my mind. Of course, I didn't mind either, but it didn't really work out. I preferred Janice's friend, and I ended up going with her for a while.

From then on I made sure the girls I went out with didn't work where I worked.

Making love was one thing; making good friends was another. Those first few months in America I had plenty of the former, none of the latter. As lucky as I was to have female company, I was also lonely. I hadn't been in Minnesota long enough to get close to anyone, but understanding that didn't make me feel any better. I was depressed.

It all hit me at once on New Year's Eve, 1972. My brother was off with a girlfriend. I couldn't call home because it was too expensive. (I used my cheap tape deck to record letters to my parents.) The girls I'd met and sometimes slept with were scattered throughout Minnesota and the Midwest, home for Christmas. I had no money, no car, no anything. I wished I were in Kalamata with friends, a couple of gifts, and my mom's cooking. I'd never been alone for the holidays before and I missed my family. I'd have slept off the emotional turmoil if I could have, but I had a serious case of cabin fever.

Without thinking, I wandered out of the dorm and across the campus toward the Mississippi River and the West Bank Bridge, which led into town. I wore a green army jacket and blue jeans, and my hair looked pretty much as it does now. I was halfway across the bridge when I figured out how cold it really was—and that I was dressed like an idiot. Not even a scarf or a hat. Mistake of my life. My head almost froze off.

The bridge comes out onto Franklin Avenue; that was Nowhere Land to me because I'd never been in town. The neighborhood was dark, looked unsafe, and seemed as empty as I felt. Then I saw a neon sign, and underneath it a door into a bar. I opened it and walked inside. I just wanted to get warm.

I stepped into a dark foyer. To my right was a window that looked into a small, empty bar, closed for the night. In the shadows I noticed a guy on a stool. He saw me and said, "Shhh," and cocked his head toward another guy in the bar, trying to break into the cash register with a screwdriver. No one could see them because the main room was beyond a swinging door at the far end of the entryway. I was too cold to have enough sense to ask myself, What the hell am I doing here? and walk straight out. Instead, I pushed through the far door into a room full of Native Americans. I sat in the back, shared a few drinks with the locals, said nothing about what I had witnessed, and got along fine. An hour into 1973, I walked out. The guys trying to jimmy the register were long gone.

This time I crossed the bridge on the inside, under the covered walkway used by normal folks who were not dumb-asses like me. I stopped in the middle and looked out over the frozen river, under a starless January sky, and decided once again that I could take whatever pain would come my way. I knew what I was doing in America: trying to become somebody. The loneliness and disorientation were part of the price I had to pay. I wouldn't have the luxury of being able to wallow in my gloom, anyway. The semester started in a few days and I had to think about what lay ahead, not what had just happened. I picked up the pace and hurried back to Territorial Hall and whatever the future held in store.

The first quarter I took three classes: calculus—in Greek high school we had a lot of math and physics; French—I already spoke quite a lot; and Psychology 101. My psych course had a 400-page textbook. Every fifth word was unfamiliar. I'd never been so frustrated, but as they say, what doesn't kill you makes you stronger. I studied with the book, a notebook, and a Greek/English dictionary. I'd read a word: "Preface." Pre-face? What the hell is pre-face? I'd write it down, look in the dictionary, then put the Greek word next to it. This happened so often that it probably took three hours to get through the first page. Plus, almost every word or sentence had a few possible translations. But I'm a worker. I'd sit for eight, ten, twelve hours—whatever it took—

[64]

and at the end of each day, I'd cover up Greek words, look at the English side, and try to recall the Greek. Then I'd do it the opposite way. I also threw the book up against the wall more than a few times, but I had faith the work would get easier.

Reading that textbook is how I finally learned English. The inadvertent beauty of my method is that I ended up going through it about ten times. I not only got a perfect score on my final, I aced all my finals and made the dean's list. That really encouraged me.

Another benefit of getting A's was financial support. Foreign students pay three times as much as local students. I knew my father's money would last maybe a year, but after that I'd be on my own. Great grades meant a full scholarship. All I had to decide was whether I'd rather wash dishes for money or read books. The answer was a no-brainer.

As an honor student I had also earned the right to take more classes than I needed, without my advisor's signature. Fifteen credits was the general maximum, but some quarters I took twenty-one, or twenty-four. Once, I took twenty-seven credits. My life became single-minded study, but I saved an enormous amount of money and graduated early. I took just about every psychology class offered at the university even though I didn't need them for my degree. I also signed up for computer classes—with state-of-the-art IBM punch card computers—without actually registering, and learned programming for free. But that's what I was there for: to learn.

My first summer in America I went to Northfield, Minnesota, where I had two jobs: coaching some high school swimmers whose families knew that I was a Greek swimming champion, and lifeguarding at the municipal pool.

The next semester a psychology professor decided I was a hard worker with good ideas and he hired me to work with lab rats. Though I was an undergraduate student, I got two rooms in the psychology department and they paid me. I wonder if my professor would recognize the John Chryssomallis he knew then as Yanni today?

The rats were black and weighed maybe a pound each. I fed and cared for them and conducted experiments. We know that rat hearing is pretty close to human hearing and we were trying to prove that there's a gain-control mechanism in the human ear that interprets sound.

I trained the rats to perform sound discrimination tasks. I created a box and a Plexiglas tube with a nose press in it, and two slots on either side. Imagine the rat's head going inside the tube—they're very inquisitive and usually stick their noses in anything—and pushing the nose press. Its ears would pop up on either side of the tube and two bursts of white noise would oc-cur. If the two sounds were equal in volume, the rat had to press the left bar to respond correctly. If one sound was louder than the other, the rat had to press the right bar. For the correct answer the rat was rewarded with a bit of sweet milk. The trick was how to get the rat to keep its ears in one spot while the sounds hap-pened. If you could come up with a way to keep the head steady, you could study them.

I designed the box, the nose press, the whole experiment. And it worked. I could train a rat to learn that task in one af-ternoon.

Here's the weird thing: A journalist once asked me—jok-ingly?—if this is when I learned I could psychologically manip-ulate millions of people with sound. I suppose he wanted to figure out how a guy who plays instrumental music that some critics think is fit only for elevators, coffee shops, and putting callers on hold, managed to sell so many albums and fill so many concert halls. Of course, I don't believe he thought that I actually brainwash people, but it's true that you can intentionally manipulate sound to cause emotional reactions. It's done in the movies all the time. A low frequency tends to be scary, probably because it's reminiscent, at a primal level, of a large animal or an earthquake. In other words, it intones impending death. A hissing sound recalls snakes. I'm sure this is all programmed into our genes.

I also know it's possible to have a tremendously profound experience while listening to music. Music at the right moment is the facilitator, the catalyst to get your body—and, I believe, soul—to vibrate at a certain frequency, to transport you to a different perspective.

When I compose I'm not trying to produce a specific reaction in any listener, but if my listeners connect with what I'm feeling at the time (every artist's sincere hope)—or if it sparks an emotion of their own—that's good enough for me. If my music can change someone's mood for the better even a little bit, that's amazing. What's wrong with taking a bad frame of mind and making it good?

It goes deeper. In 1993 scientists reported on the "Mozart Effect." They claimed that listening to certain of his works had a positive effect on spatial reasoning. Other international research has suggested that some musical compositions can reduce the number of seizures in people with epilepsy. Then, my music was added to the list—particularly "Acroyali/Standing in Motion"—because, according to the *Journal of the Royal Society of Medicine*, "it was similar to Mozart's K448 in tempo, structure, melodic and harmonic consonance and predictability."

Whether a person is spiritual or not, we all seek to get away from the stress, anger, and anxiety of everyday life. Some people drink, do drugs, or do worse to escape, and they hurt themselves in the process. Some people listen to music, mine included, and feel better. As I come to experience life on different levels, I can use music to express what those levels feel like to me. I believe the listener can be transported to this understanding as well, just by listening to the music. Based on the letters I get, and the stories I've been told by fans, apparently I've done this for many people. If, like me, you're interested in how you're doing on the planet, then that kind of feedback is pretty nice to get.

In the summer of 1974, between my sophomore and junior years of college, I went back to Greece for a brief visit. When I returned to Minneapolis for the new school year my brother and I moved out of Territorial Hall and into a one-bedroom apartment in the slums. I like to say that the kitchen floor was self-cleaning because it lay at an angle; anything you dropped rolled into one corner. My brother got the bedroom; I put a mattress on the floor in the pantry and still had space for a small table and chair. The living room was for company. We stayed there for a year, surviving on bologna sandwiches and peanut butter. I thought it was a beautiful life.

Between my studies, music, fun, and new friends, I fell more and more in love with being in America. I cherished both the freedom and the anonymity. A beautiful thing about changing cultures is the ability to reinvent yourself. In Greece, I was Yanni the swimming champion; in America, I was John the nobody. In Greece I was the weird kid who didn't smoke, had problems with school, and disliked the teachers. In America I was the kid with an insatiable appetite for learning, who wanted good teachers and to expand my mind. And just because I'd started off as a dishwasher didn't mean I had to stay a dishwasher forever. Americans take that malleability for granted; people from some other countries don't. Had I stayed in Greece I would have faced people who resisted my changes and hoped to keep me in a box that made *them* feel comfortable.

I loved Greece, and still do. I just didn't like being told what to do or how to think. America helped me undo the damage of my early schooling and gave me tremendous opportunities for a future I could fashion for myself.

Because I no longer lived on campus, I played piano whenever I could by sneaking into empty practice rooms in the music department until someone kicked me out. But I didn't take the music so seriously that I changed my plan to become a therapist, return to Greece, and take care of sick people. At least not at first.

However, the more I enjoyed life in the States, the more difficult it became to imagine sitting in an office all day long, saying, "Next patient." I still loved psychology and had no serious alternatives to replace it, but I instinctively knew that therapy was probably not in my future. I'd get my bachelor's degree, but I might not go to graduate school.

When one door closes, another opens, right? In the midst of my indecision some friends said, "You know, you play the piano beautifully. Why don't you join a band? You could make some money this summer."

I'd never considered that; I wasn't a rock 'n' roller and I didn't have much spare time, but still the idea made sense. I checked the newspaper ads and found one from a band looking for a keyboard player. I decided to investigate and a week later walked into an Animal House that looked like it hadn't been vacuumed in six months. A guy named Dugan McNeill took me down to the basement where the band was waiting. We played a little bit and they hired me. I didn't have any equipment, but they happened to have a red Vox Jaguar organ and an Arp Odyssey synthesizer. Once I realized how many sounds it could make, that was it. My life changed. All of a sudden I was absorbed. It was like God had spoken.

The band was called Zed. Billy Melton played the guitar. His brother, Dennis, played the drums. Dugan played the bass. Bob Derickson played guitar. Everyone sang but me. They just needed backup keyboards to sweeten the sound a little bit.

We were terrible, but we thought we were great. It doesn't matter how terrible you are as long as you think you're great.

Playing keyboards in a rock 'n' roll band is not difficult. In fact, it was boring unless I did complex material by bands like Emerson, Lake and Palmer or Yes. And yet I loved being in Zed. I felt lighter, the way you do when your life suddenly works and you hadn't even known there was a problem. Rehearsals were the highlight of my day. I practiced constantly and improved both my dexterity and my musical vocabulary. Soon I could immediately copy whatever I'd heard without too much fumbling. I composed.

The lab rats got lonely.

When I graduated, in June 1976, I told the school to just mail me my diploma. Then I did something that made me sweat a bit: I told my parents I wanted to put off graduate school for a year, devote myself only to music, and see how I liked it.

Everyone thought I was making a big mistake, though they didn't say so to my face. They didn't want to dishearten me, either. My father didn't tell me to go back to school, but said, "You'll tell us if you need money, won't you?" My mother was a bit more forward. "Well, you could still play your music, if you want," she said. "Why don't you finish school and do music on the side?" My brother was getting his Ph.D. in chemical engineering, and my mother wanted me to get my doctorate so I'd have something to fall back on. At first I thought they might be right, but pretty quickly I realized I was much happier playing with the band.

I wanted to fall forward, not backward.

Besides, I had already fallen in another way. Zed always rehearsed in Dugan's basement. One day in came this gorgeous girl with blonde hair and big blue eyes. I took one look at her and went *wow*. Her name was Sherry; she was Dugan's cousin. While she hung out, listening to the band, I watched her and she watched me—and we kept smiling at each other.

After the rehearsal I talked to Sherry and she was great. I said, "You want to go out?" She said, "Okay." And that was it. On our first date we went to a coffee shop. She told me about herself. She worked at a factory that made stereo speakers. I told her about myself, and that I'd been thinking of giving up school for music.

We fell head over heels in love.

4

THE ROCK 'N' ROLLER

Sherry was my first American girlfriend, and my first love. It was puppy love, two twenty-year-old kids trying to figure out what love is and what it means. And man, was it intense. We soon rented an apartment in south Minneapolis and moved in together. We even got a gray-blue Persian cat and named him Felix.

Through Zed, I developed other close relationships. Dugan's mother, Shirley, took care of us all. She even made stage clothes for me. Shirley was a great cook who would feed half the kids in the neighborhood, if necessary. When a girl she knew had a kid she couldn't take care of, Shirley helped raise the child, and has done it more than once. Her own daughter, Debbie, got sick with a high fever when she was young and ended up epileptic and mentally challenged. Most families would send a child like that to a home, just put her away. Shirley wouldn't hear of it. She was the local Mother Teresa.

Shirley's husband, Mac, had a machine shop where he manufactured mattress springs and coat hangers. After five o'clock he'd come home, drink beer, and enjoy life. Although the Mc-Neills were poor, they gave us gifts at Christmas. I once got a check for a hundred dollars, an enormous amount of money then—at least to me. I also spent time with Sherry's mother, Barbara, a great lady to whom I could talk easily.

Between my family, Dugan's, and Sherry's, I was never alone at Christmas again.

Zed was a "cover band." In 1975 and 1976, in nightclubs and dance bars around town, we played songs by groups that had big hits on the radio and sold millions of albums. We covered the spectrum. But like many similar bands, Zed didn't last long.

I left for Archangel, a progressive group that avoided playing cover tunes. They gave concerts and already had a following. Zed fell apart; keyboard players were difficult to replace. Even today, I find it hard to hire one who's proficient, has equipment, and knows how to run it.

Archangel was also short-lived. My next band, Straight Up, was pure fun. We were the big local attraction, a "show band." We used smoke bombs and other pyrotechnics onstage, and dressed up. Think KISS. I wore black leather pants, a tight black shirt, long hair.

Rock 'n' roll, man.

My new lifestyle did not make a steady relationship with Sherry easy. When I was on the road other girls would invariably show up, willing to share themselves for the night in very creative ways. If you're young and away from home for two or three weeks at a time, it's hard to resist walking into temptation. Mostly I didn't. Maybe Sherry suspected the cheating, but it never came up. One thing is for sure, whatever happened when I was away I was still in love with Sherry. Madly in love. The problem was that such intense feelings led in only one direction.

Sherry wanted to get married and have kids. She hoped I'd go back to school and get my Ph.D. There was nothing wrong with her wanting that, except that it wasn't what *I* wanted. I'd promised myself a year to discover if music was the right path for me, and it seemed like it was. I needed the freedom to travel and create and have fun. That's not a good recipe for marriage. We were so young. What did we know about life? I began to wiggle out of the relationship, and that began a period of arguing, breaking up, making up, and breaking up again. We split and got back together so many times—everyone knows how that goes—until one day we were both so tired of the dance that we said, "No more."

I don't dwell in the past; I don't wallow in old events and emotions. I don't waste time on regret. No use going over and over the details of what already happened. I don't even keep old photos on the wall. I just let go. But even today I can remember the pain of breaking up with Sherry. Horrible. I didn't realize it would hurt that much. I was very naïve. A lot of guys, we have this attitude of, "I don't care; I'm fine. I can be without you," and then we discover later that it's not so easy.

I felt stupid without Sherry and eventually I wanted to get back together again, but she wouldn't let me. She did the right thing because our goals were different and it would never have worked. The year it took me to get over Sherry was one of the worst of my life. Sherry, on the other hand, met a nice guy to whom she is still married.

In the end I learned that it made no difference whose fault it was, who started it, who ended it: You're just going to hurt. The pain drove me so crazy that I started smoking pot just to get to sleep at night. I figured that instead of getting into alcohol heavily, why not just take a hit off a joint and go to bed. I missed Sherry terribly. I also played sad music all the time and cried; for the first time I understood the love songs I had always ignored on the radio.

And yet, I also tried hard to remember my father's lesson: Take the pain. Grab the bull by the horns. It goes away more quickly. You're done with it and you're finished. That's the objective. The more you soften the blow, the more you try to cushion yourself from feeling any discomfort—some people take pills, or drink, or overeat, or try to change the past—the more you perpetuate the problem. You keep it alive, nurture it, and give it strength. If you try to completely avoid the pain, then you'll create a monster that you'll carry with you for the rest of your life. It will always affect your behavior, always affect *you*. It only works in one direction: It becomes bigger, stronger, and drains you.

My relationship and breakup with Sherry pretty much shaped how I behaved toward women for the next ten years. I got to know quite a few and had long-running friendships that also included sex, but I never got serious. I just wanted to have fun and I was honest about it. "I'm not looking for a relationship, and I hope you're not. I don't owe you anything and you don't owe me anything. If we do this, it's what it is for tonight. If it continues tomorrow, okay, but if it doesn't, don't come to me and say I've used you." I was straightforward. I adored women, and I always saw them as human beings first. I couldn't bear the thought of the kind of pain you could cause another person over sex and unspoken expectations. I didn't think sex was so important that a brief hour or two of pleasure should cause someone pain for a month or two. The bill was too high. I thought anyone who wanted to be with me should just enjoy me and realize that owning me wasn't part of the package.

Sherry was my last real girlfriend until I met Linda Evans nearly fourteen years later. In between I didn't allow another woman to be so deeply in my life that I would be influenced by her presence or her jealousy of the attention I gave to my career instead of to her. I'm not saying I couldn't find the right woman; I just wasn't looking. I didn't have the time or the interest. I had set up my life in a way that worked and I liked it.

Linda once said to me, "I think you didn't fall in love because of how much you hurt." She was probably right, though at the time I didn't see it that way. I had studied psychology. I even remember asking myself, "Are you afraid of women now, just because you got hurt once? A lot of people get hurt. So what? Get up and do it again." And so I did. But I wanted things my way: no children, no marriage, we just hang out. Maybe I lived in denial. Maybe I threw myself into my music not because I'd have no responsibilities except to myself, but because I didn't want to experience heartbreak again. But if so, it was unconscious.

In 1978, during one of the periods that Sherry and I were only half together, I quit Straight Up and moved to Pembroke Pines, Florida, between Fort Lauderdale and Miami, to try to develop a solo project with lasers. It didn't work out. Then I moved to Madison, Wisconsin, where Bruce Lipton, a professor of cell biology, had invested a lot of money to develop lasers. The plan was to do concerts in which I played the keyboards while the lasers swirled around. Laserium had debuted in Los Angeles in late 1973, but the concept of combining lasers and music was still relatively new. I performed a couple of times in Chicago, and in some Minnesota theaters, but that went nowhere. I also did a few months of keyboard-only solo gigs—without lasers— in nightclubs around Minneapolis, playing classical pieces and

some of my own material. That's when I decided to drop the first
"i" in Yianni and become Yanni. That's also when I first decided
to get out of rock 'n' roll and get serious about my own music.

When Sherry and I split, I moved out of our apartment and asked
my sister, Anda, and her brand-new husband, Tommy Sterling, if
I could live with them. Their hospitality was critical to my survival. I had no money and couldn't pay rent. They welcomed me
immediately.

Never ones to discriminate among their children, my parents had also sent Anda to America for a higher education. But
Anda didn't take to it right away. Even though our parents
treated us equally, the times and society were stricter for a young
woman growing up then in Greece, and Anda chafed under the
restraints. We all hung around together as kids, she'd watched
her two brothers be independent, and although she was never a
tomboy, Anda wanted to be more like us. Strong, willful, and
very much her own person, Anda got to the United States and
more or less wandered off into the sunset for a while to have some
fun before returning to school to get her M.B.A. and C.P.A.

Anda and Tommy lived in a 1500-square-foot, two-bed-
room, one-bathroom house on Ewing Avenue in Brooklyn Park,
a middle-class neighborhood just north of Minneapolis. Not
only were we literally on top of one another, but if you jumped
up and down on the floor the whole place rattled. I wanted to
concentrate on writing and recording, so I built a studio in the
unfinished, unventilated, unheated basement. I threw down
some carpet on the cement floor and used the weight of the
equipment—keyboards, amps, speakers, mixing console, patch
bay—to hold it in place. The heat generated by the equipment
provided the only warmth.

I'm not really sure you could even call what I had a "studio." I didn't have any money and I didn't know anything about electronics. I built it all from scratch using logic and intuition. I stripped and soldered every wire. I solved problems through trial and error. But I loved it. The learning experience was profound because I was on my own. It was just what I'd always dreamed of in school in Greece. I found my own way.

When I was done I looked at what I had assembled. Honestly, I wasn't really sure why I had gone through all the trouble except that I really enjoyed listening to what I improvised, and the equipment I'd cobbled together would reproduce it better than my cheap cassette recorder. Then I thought, Okay, now be creative.

By then I'd begun to come up with a sound of my own. I'd roll tape and record myself playing things pretty similar to the stuff I do today. I had already written "Butterfly Dance" and I probably had begun toying with the idea of "Marching Season." The piece was so difficult—I say this in my concerts—that in the beginning I couldn't play it with both hands at the same time. When I recorded it, I played the right hand first and then the left hand, and kept practicing until I could perform with both hands what I heard in my head.

I made many discoveries in that basement. Day in and day out I honed my engineering and producing skills, recording and working with guitars, vocals, drums, bass, keyboards. I learned how to mike instruments and bring sounds to life. And most important, I realized that no matter how small-time the machinery or the studio, creativity does not depend on the equipment but on the ability to focus.

Eventually my sister and Tommy got divorced; Anda moved out while Tommy and I stayed—for seven years. Tommy and I are still good friends and he is my sound guy on tour. I'm lucky he was also a heavy sleeper and so easygoing. He never once complained about the noise, and we never once raised our voices to each other. Sometimes I'd wonder: Where can I find a girl like that?

Every day Tommy would get up early and go to work. I would get up later and go to the basement. I'd made a commitment to stay there all day, no matter what. If I didn't feel like writing or playing, that was fine, but I couldn't go upstairs and watch television or talk on the phone. I had to stare at the keyboards and the concrete walls. Sometimes I'd talk out loud, just to keep myself company. I'd say, "Okay, you stay in this room. You can play music or not, be bored or not, but you are stuck in this basement a minimum of eight hours a day, just like the rest of the world when they go to work."

My mother used to tell me that whenever I did something as a child, I was totally committed to it. If I loved something, it was that and nothing else. I was tough on myself because I feared being a lazy procrastinator and the inevitable result: being mediocre or second best. I always went the extra mile. I required at least eight hours of effort each day, and I usually went for more. It wasn't unusual for me to lose ten or fifteen pounds while recording.

I wasn't being a martyr. I was simply learning how to reach the levels of focus I needed to create the music. There's a reason why monks go into the mountains and sit for long periods of time. Time is the key. When I wasn't good at finding my creative space, it could take me a week to get there. As I got better, it took five days. Then one day. Then only a few hours. Nowadays, with years of experience behind me, I can get there in twenty minutes.

One day I was so caught up trying to work out a problem that I continued to think about it when I drove to the supermarket, and I nearly got into a terrible accident. It seems I'd keyed into a zone and stopped registering cars as cars. The intensity of that moment scared and thrilled me. The more I tuned out the noise, the more clear my thinking process became. I just had to promise myself never to do that again while driving.

I wrote lots of music and refined older songs that had for years just floated around in my head, untitled. Now they had names: "Butterfly Dance," "Marching Season." One song, "Farewell," was written when I finally accepted that Sherry and I were through.

The writing came easily; the hard part was wondering if anyone would like the result. This much I did know: Despite my technical shortcomings and the steep learning curve, music was it for me. There was so much pleasure associated with writing that I thought that no one else, no matter what the job, could be as happy as I was working in that basement. Every day I would get a rush from writing something new, solving a problem, finding a different sound. It didn't matter to me that I had almost no money, that I was on my own without a safety net. I knew that I could wind up spending years trying to become a successful musician only to find myself older, going nowhere, and having to start another career. But so what? I'd decided to take the risk, and either I'd succeed or else.

My attitude was that if I wasn't discovered one year, then I'd be discovered the next—and by then I'd be ten times as good as the year before because all I would have done in the interim was polish my music. You do good work for a long-enough time, I believed, and you'd get noticed.

I just had to keep at it. Other people could quit after a week; I didn't care. I could take the pain.

In 1980, I recorded my first album, *Optimystique*. My basement studio wasn't good enough so I worked at Cook House Studios in Minneapolis. Their bread and butter was advertising jingles and commercials, not rock 'n' roll. I knew the head engineer, Jerry Steckling, from the local music scene. He'd been hired by Tom Paske, the studio manager and part owner, to update the facility. Jerry had a lot going on during the day, but the place was usually empty at night. When I told him I had always wanted to do a solo project, he said, "Why don't you come in? I'll put up the money for the studio costs and you can record your material." Later, Tom told me, "I went home at five o'clock anyway, so what did I care? Jerry was on the line for the money and I knew he'd work it off or whatever."

Jerry spent $6,000. The instruments were a grand piano and synthesizers. I used Ernie LaViolet, the drummer from Archangel and Straight Up. The album took most of the summer to record. Tom Paske, who has since become my business manager, confidant, advisor, and one of my closest friends, says the first time we met I started right in by telling him about problems with the equipment. "Yanni said we needed a new Lexicon because the reverb we had wasn't good enough," says Tom. "The piano wasn't good enough. The mikes weren't any good. I believed him. I didn't know anything about gear, but I knew these guys knew a whole lot more than the guys who were just doing jingles during the day. I wanted to have a good studio."

Skinny and towering at six foot six, Tom looks like a cross between Sam Elliott and the Marlboro Man. Sort of a cowboy with the boots but not the hat, Tom's a very intelligent free spirit who likes to ride his Harley. In conversation, he appears not to be looking at you, but behind those half-open eyes his mind races a million miles an hour and catches everything. It took us a while to become friends, but these days we call each other Stan and Ollie, though there's no rule about who is whom. He also likes to call me when I'm on vacation in Greece and ask if I'm any whiter, fatter, or balder. I get back by saying he'll always be ten years older than me.

Back then we occasionally hung out, or as Tom tells it, we "had a few laughs." Sometimes we went to dinner or met at a late-night place, drank coffee, and smoked cigarettes. Mostly we talked on the phone a lot—now especially, since we live in different parts of the country. Tom is intellectual, into conceptualizing and problem solving. He's also very calm, and I immediately liked his dry sense of humor and his no-nonsense approach to life. He spoke the truth even though it sometimes sounded cold-hearted.

The first time we had a meal together, at one of those $1.99 breakfast places across the street from the studio, he suddenly asked me, "How much money did you make last year?"

I had made only a few thousand dollars. Maybe he asked because I'd been complaining; I don't remember.

"Whatever it is, it's what you deserved to make," he added.

We weren't close yet and I wasn't sure whether or not to be pissed off at the question and the implication. But something struck a chord and I told him what I'd made because I understood that Tom was really telling me that I had to accept responsibility for myself.

"Look in the mirror," he said. "Don't blame the government or the economy. Don't point at anyone else. It's up to you."

I decided then that I *really* liked Tom. We both subscribe to the philosopher Arthur Schopenhauer's thesis that human beings always do what they want to do—and then invent reasons to explain their behavior. (Schopenhauer is frequently referred to as a pessimist who inaugurated an emphasis on the will in modern philosophy.) I believe we're responsible for everything that happens to us. For instance, if I'm walking under a building and a brick falls and hits me on the head, it's my fault. I should have sensed that a brick would fall. Get out of the way. Don't pick the airplane that's going to go down.

I know that attitude is insanity for most people, but that's the way I live. It's just what works for me. Even if I'm crazy, this approach prevents me from blaming others for my "mistakes." It also supports my belief in mind over matter, in my ability to take pain, and it may ultimately lead to a healing effect. [Scientific research shows that you can heal yourself, from mending a broken bone faster to fighting off cancer.] But it takes faith. In order for me to have that kind of faith, I must accept responsibility for what happens to me. So I've taught myself how to have a sixth sense, an instinct, and I listen to it. So far it hasn't led me astray.

Maybe I just don't like the idea of fate. I don't want to feel as if I'm walking down the street one day and it's just the luck of the draw that I get cancer. That may be the truth; it *may* be random. It may be due to my genetic makeup, something I have no control over. I just don't like the idea that "There's nothing you can do. What's the sense?"

This is why I am always so positive. Even if we have no control in life, what's the point of believing that? I'd only get depressed. Do I want to be the guy who believes that nothing makes a difference? Why be a pessimist? Why wake up in the morning angry and pissed off and helpless and let anxiety permeate the entire day? I might as well kill myself because the game would already be over.

Taking responsibility gives me a sense of control.

The truth probably lies somewhere between black and white. *I think we have much more to say about what happens to us than most people believe.* And I know there are things I can't do anything about. But too many people I know are unaware of or afraid of their personal power, and they give up before they try. Believing that I *can* do something empowers me. For me, there's no logical alternative.

In those days Tom was one of the few people who didn't think I was crazy for trying to have a career as a musician, even though my material was nothing like the popular songs of the day. He understood that I was a strange kid who worked his ass off; that I went into a basement and when I came out I had a bunch of music—good music, though not necessarily his kind of music. One reason I'm still so close to Tom is that he's unwaveringly straightforward and he has faith in me.

As for *Optimystique*, it was an unusual album and nobody had any idea what to do with it. I'd been so focused on making the album that I never thought about the next steps. Jerry sent the tapes out and tried to get a record deal, but the responses were no, no, no, thank you very much, and no. The problem? It was keyboard music. Electronic. We got the hint. We floated a thousand copies on tape and vinyl ourselves and sold them around town. But otherwise the album just lay there, dead in the water.

Chameleon was an up-and-coming local group I'd first heard about when I was in Straight Up. They did kick-ass rock 'n' roll covers with a Def Leppard or Aerosmith feel, and some original material. Sometimes I'd run into the band at a river festival where twenty groups played. After I left Straight Up, the drummer in Chameleon told me they were looking for a bass player. I said they should check out Dugan McNeill: "He's a maniac onstage," I said. "You might like him." They hired him.

Tom Paske helped Chameleon with financial advice, and when they were ready to make their first album they came to Cook House, where they wanted some help in the studio. They listened to a tape of *Optimystique* and asked me to produce the record. During the project I became closer with Tom Paske, who began to hang around the studio more often after hours, and with Chameleon's drummer, Charlie Adams, who asked me to contribute some keyboard work to the album. (Charlie became my drummer when I went out as a solo performer.)

After we finished recording *Chameleon* I helped the band put on a very successful concert at the Guthrie Theater in Minneapolis, a venue not known for rock 'n' roll. I also performed with them there as a onetime deal. Then Chameleon went on the road and I went back to the basement.

A couple of weeks later, Charlie called and said, "Yanni, I miss your sound. I got used to you playing with us so now the songs sound empty. Come out on the road with us."

"I was on the road too long," I said. "I don't want to do it again." Besides, in the upper Midwest, "the road" meant freezing temperatures, getting stuck in the snow, staying up all night driving, and sliding off the highway into the cornfields during an ice storm. The road meant staying up late, wearing yourself out, and sleeping in places you'd rather forget. Oh—and a working band had to play nearly all year round to make ends meet.

Charlie wouldn't give up. He called again and again. "Hey, come on; it'll be wild. We're really popular." And they were. Chameleon drew crowds from Minnesota to Wisconsin, from the Dakotas to Illinois, from Nebraska to Iowa. "We're going to do more original material," Charlie said. "I need some help. Come out, buddy, come and help me."

"I've done the band thing," I said. "I want to do my own music."

"Look," he finally said. "Why don't you just try it for a month. Just a month. Think of it as a mini-vacation. There are women everywhere out here. It's a party every night. If you hate it, fine. But if you like it . . ."

How could that life *not* sound great to a twenty-six-year-old? So I let Charlie seduce me. I went out for a month—and stayed for four years.

Chameleon was Dugan on bass and lead vocals, Mark Anthony on lead vocals and keyboards, Johnny Donaldson on guitars, Charlie Adams on drums and vocals, and me on keyboards. Dugan and I began to co-write much of the music. We played heavy-duty progressive stuff and material of mine, like "The Sphynx." We'd also throw in a couple of popular tunes—maybe a ZZ Top cut—and even the *William Tell Overture* at very high speed, with Charlie Adams going upside down on his two-axis revolving drum set. I even sold a few copies of *Optimystique* at the shows. The Minnesota music scene was thriving then. Prince was beginning to take off. With ballrooms scattered all around the state we could draw anywhere from 500 to 2,000 kids a show.

At first we toured with five guys in a station wagon, followed by a truck that carried all our equipment. But soon, with bigger crowds and Tom Paske advising us, we began grossing more and more each night, and bought an RV and a semi. It seemed so *big time,* and we never slowed down.

I spent so much time onstage that I finally got used to being in front of an audience without being nervous. I learned once and for all how to be . . . well, sexy onstage: Wear black leather pants, boots, and a tight little T-shirt—a far cry from all-white—have a good body, move your arms and legs a lot, throw your hair, play the keyboards upside down. It's not that I checked myself out in the mirror and went, "Oo, I am sex-y," but if the girls in the audience thought I was, who was I to argue?

I also learned invaluable lessons about light and sound and how to arrange songs for a live performance. I worked on timing, when to talk, when to play, in what order to play the songs, and how to get an audience excited when they seemed bored to tears. I watched the crowd, what made them tick, how they danced, drank, did drugs, brawled, had a good time. I couldn't stand kids getting drunk and punching each other, but it was a fact of life.

One lesson I had already learned in Straight Up was the importance of the drum solo, when to call for one and how long to let it continue. One night there was a power failure during a show. We said, "Ernie: solo." The whole band left the stage while Ernie wailed. When the power came back on we were all in our van—getting blow jobs. The roadies came running out: "We're on again!" Ernie had been going for fifteen minutes and was about to die! So were we.

True to Charlie's promise, life with Chameleon was wild. Women were always available. It was and still is very easy for a musician on the road to pick up girls. You have access to everything; you're admired and adored. You can be with almost anyone you want.

I liked to choose my companions rather than the other way around. I'd watch from the stage and if I saw somebody I wanted, I'd walk up to her on the break and ask, "What's your name?" Then I'd say, "You look very nice, Mary." If she smiled, I'd say, "Hey, what are you doing after the show? There's a little party back at the hotel. You want to come over?" That was it. The seduction had already taken place while she watched me play. She knew I liked her because I approached her, and most of the time she'd come with me. If I got turned down it didn't make any difference because there were so many other possibilities. But I was never a pest; you could get rid of me easily. All you had to do was look like you weren't interested and I was gone, gone, gone.

After the show, if the party wasn't in my room it was in another guy's. (Usually there was a party in *every* room.) There were more girls than any of us could possibly be with, sometimes five times as many as there were guys. That went on just about every night, and I say the more, the merrier. I was very promiscuous. And very creative. We had a lot of fun. Remember, we knew nothing about AIDS, and it was a very permissive time. Women could have one-night stands and it was no problem at all. In fact, most of the women I met liked one-night stands. As soon as I set out the conditions they'd say, "Yeah, great. Me, too. Don't worry about it."

I wouldn't lie to a woman, or promise more than I intended to deliver. She knew we were going to have fun that night only, and that was it. I was very clear, so I never felt guilty.

It was rock 'n' roll.

Sometimes, after a girl would show up at the hotel I'd discover that she seemed a little lost and wasn't sure she wanted to be there. In that case I would only talk to her, not touch her. I figured the least I could do was show her some warmth and try to encourage her in her life. I'd tell her what I liked about her and make it easy for her to talk to me.

Nor would I get anyone drunk or high so I could get her in the sack; I wanted to know that I could do it on my own. The alternative seemed degrading to both partners. Besides, the more you *don't* push, the more you get what you want—at least in my experience. I knew that if I treated someone correctly, the next time I saw her she'd be more than happy to be with me again because she trusted me.

The reason girls want to be with guys in a band is probably the same reason why rock 'n' rollers want to be with groupies: Sleeping with someone new, someone you think is hot-looking onstage, or sexy in tight jeans and a halter top, is a challenge. For me it also had to do with burning off energy after a show, fighting loneliness, and handling the boredom of relentlessly traveling from town to town.

In each town I had a girlfriend or two. Not *real* girlfriends, just girls I knew. Or someone I'd just met. I didn't mind having sex with a woman I'd known less than an hour. I was young, they looked good. Nothing else to do. Let's have some fun. There was no judgment, and I never felt guilty. You're just driving down the highway and you're lonely; you meet someone who eases the boredom a little bit for the night. And the next day you get up and do it again.

However, I discovered something important about myself during this period: I had a great time, but it was just something I did; *it wasn't who I am.* Take my father: He was a banker; that's what he did, but that hardly describes the man. I am actually very particular when it comes to women with whom I want a continuing relationship. Meeting and being with someone is about so much more than a nice body. A mind goes with it all. The women I met on the road were real people, not inflatable dolls. But to be perfectly honest most of the time these encounters were a disappointment. More often than not it was pretty dull. And maybe they felt the same way about me. Just because somebody looks good at the nightclub doesn't mean she'll look good in a motel room with her clothes off. And equally as true, maybe when I pulled off my tight T-shirt and leather pants I wasn't any prize, either.

I did make some good friends. There was Kelly, who I adored. I met Allison when I was with Straight Up; she was sixteen and a knockout. She wanted to get me in the sack. At sixteen! I kept going, "Uh, get away from me, you're too young." I ended up talking with her, and over the years, we became close. Well, little Allison grew into a stunningly gorgeous brunette with pow! pow! everything. Fun, easygoing, great soul. When she was old enough we finally went to bed. Then she wanted to have a steadier relationship and I didn't, but in between boyfriends she'd always call me. That "relationship" lasted years. I've had a few women like that in my life.

I also had other means of escape. I smoked cigarettes, drank a bit, tried drugs. Cocaine was the craze for a long time, but until I got into Chameleon I had avoided it. The first time I tried coke it may not have been very good, because I snorted a line and nothing happened. I couldn't figure out what it was supposed to do.

I soon found out. In rock 'n' roll there was cocaine available every night. Everywhere. All the time. As much as you wanted. People who had it and had money liked to hang out with bands, so they always brought coke with them. Local dealers just showed up. Rock 'n' roll was a magnet for that kind of stuff. I snorted it for maybe a year until one of our "friends" said, "Hey, try this." This? "Freebasing." I thought, Hey, what's the big deal with smoking it? What's the difference? Well, there's a *huge difference*. You might as well be shooting up. It's an amazing feeling. Up like a rocket. And then down like a rocket, too. A horrible feeling.

I freebased for a little while but quickly realized I had gotten in too deep. Nobody had told me my heart could stop or that I could die, but I could tell I had a serious problem from the way I felt. One night, while everybody partied in the living room, I went into the bedroom and tried to sleep, but couldn't. I took a Quaalude and still couldn't sleep. I was too high on coke and, at the same time, lost in the emotional and physical depression of coming down. I remember thinking: If I had feet in the back of me I'd kick my ass all the way to Greece. This was not why I came to America. This was not what I wanted out of life. This was not why my father and mother sold their home, so I could sit around and do coke.

That was it. I walked out to the living room, into the middle of the party, and said, "Okay guys, I have an announcement to make: This is the last time I'm going to ever do this."

They all laughed uncontrollably. "Yeah, yeah. Sure. Come here, do another line."

I didn't.

The next evening, there was coke in the nightclub dressing room. It pulled at me. I could hear it saying, "Oh, you'll feel great." I began to get that temporary rush of euphoria from anticipating the high. Then, just as quickly, I shut down. I played it smart. I made sure I had a very clear, strong memory of what it felt like coming down.

I never did coke again—and the only reason I've told this story is to show that it's possible to get over this crap. That's the most important part of the story to me.

I recently quit smoking the same way. What did I take? Nothing but the pain. No gum or patches. Cold turkey. Grab your own shirttail. Just cut it out. It's the best and quickest way to be free. I have a habit of quitting habits overnight with just one decision, and it's worked for me.

Except for the cocaine, I never let myself go too far. I participated not because I was forced to by peer pressure but because, frankly, I like to play with fire and experience all I can. To avoid things because we're told by someone else not to go there doesn't seem like living, in my opinion. The key is to pick the right fire to play with. You can't play with them all. I got close enough to wave my hand through, and to feel the heat, to get singed but not burned. Fortunately I didn't need to stand in those fires to feel alive, and I'd seen enough to keep me at a safe distance. The guitar player in one of my bands—not Chameleon—would drink a six-pack of beer, drop acid, smoke pot, and get onstage. He'd play really well, though I don't know how the guy put one foot in front of the other. He'd sweat like a pig, and every once in a while he'd fall down. Yet the kids would go crazy. The higher he looked, the more they loved him. Eventually the drugs affected his perform-ance and his life, and he almost died. I tried talking him out of it, but that's a decision we all must make alone.

I've never been high or drunk onstage. Not even half a glass of wine—except one time, when I was with Chameleon. I got my green card and four years later applied for naturalization. I studied for the test, and while riding between gigs in the RV, I'd ask the guys in Chameleon questions from the book. Nobody knew anything. "Aren't you guys Americans? Didn't you go to school? What did they teach you in high school?"

One morning I passed the test, was sworn in, and became a citizen. That night, during a break in our show, we all celebrated. Tom Paske said, "Hey, come on, have a shot of tequila."

"I can't now," I said. "After we finish."

"No, come on. Have a shot. You're only going to become an American citizen once."

One shot led to another, and I got more bombed than I wanted to. I walked onstage really drunk, drunk like I needed to lie down kind of drunk. As I sat at the keyboards to play the opening song of the second set, I heard the national anthem. I immediately jumped up—and got woozy again. Unbeknownst to me, the band had prepared a surprise. A guy dressed like Uncle Sam walked onstage and announced to the packed night-club: "Yanni has now become an American citizen." Everyone cheered. Uncle Sam gave me a big phony certificate. On the flip side it said, "Now that Yanni has become an American citizen, he is eligible for every paternity suit. . . ." It was a big to-do. I was really bombed and could hardly play. I don't remember much, but Paske said it was hilarious.

Those years were incredibly fun and just as dangerous. There was promiscuity, drug abuse, and alcohol abuse. If you had a very strong upbringing and a very focused mind about what you really wanted to do, you could survive. Dugan didn't do any drugs; he's clean to this day. Charlie and I were lightweights. We never wanted to get completely unconscious, but we saw guys who needed to be, and we don't know if they're still alive. I mean the people who get up in the morning and have a glass of straight vodka just to start the day. They have a lot of pain inside. I never had that pain. I was lucky. I liked life.

I was Ulysses, wanting to hear the Sirens' song without crashing into the rocks. He told his mates to tie him to the mast and then plug their ears so they wouldn't hear the song and wouldn't listen to whatever crazy things he said.

Many men crashed on those rocks. I tied myself securely to the mast.

5

OUT OF THE BASEMENT

Chameleon eventually stopped doing cover songs and played only original music, most of which I wrote with Dugan. I was also the band's producer and engineer. Because it was free, my basement became the place to develop material, and when the time came to do our second album, we went to Cook House Studios.

I also kept having ideas for another record of my own. Whenever I got a week or two off after a month of gigs, I'd come home and lock myself in the basement. I'd already "written" the music in our RV during the hours I spent staring at the white lines on the highway. After a while I'd just close my eyes and compose. I used my shorthand notation to keep notes and got quite good at it.

I took my creative moments where I could find them. I didn't yet understand how to tap into the source at will. Like most artistic people, I was lost in this area. I only knew that once in a while stuff happened, and when it did, it all seemed so effortless. Other times, when I wanted to create, I just ended up banging my head against the wall without knowing what kind of wall it was or how to get to the other side.

I'd never played with an orchestra, but I always heard one in my head. There was no limit to the sound. I wanted to create a world blend of different instruments, of acoustics and electronics, not just a rock band with a backup violin. Nor did I want to come in from left field with some cold and meaningless electronic *whoop-whoop-whoop*. I like to begin acoustically so the listener can feel the heart and soul of the music—and the musician. Then I add the electronics to create a tableau. Beethoven would have used synthesizers if he'd had them. To mix artistic metaphors, what painter wouldn't want more colors, better brushes, better everything. In Beethoven's time, making a new sound meant making a new instrument. It took a couple hundred years just to perfect the piano. Nowadays, you just move a few virtual knobs and you get millions of sounds. When I started out I had to defend using synthesizers because they weren't considered "real" instruments. These days people don't realize that most popular music is in many ways electronic.

I don't need lyrics. Classical composers communicated across cultures and centuries beautifully without words. That's proof that it can be done. I prefer not to use words when I'm trying to move you emotionally, so you don't have to use logic to understand what you were just told. Also, my music gives you the ability to make up your own story as it plays; your mind is free to wander and create. You can use the music as a soundtrack to your emotions.

Much of what I did then, in the basement, sounded like the music I compose today. When I played it for friends like Dugan and Charlie and Tom and Tommy, they liked it, but they still said, "Electronic music? No lyrics? Will it sell?"

I wanted to find out.

Like all bands, Chameleon dreamed of landing a national record deal. Unlike many bands, we actually had a shot. We were probably one of the few unsigned groups of that time and place that played only original music. We drew so many people that we could write our own rules. If we weren't the number-one Midwestern band, then we were among the biggest. In Minneapolis, when we released our first album, we outsold *Tattoo You* by the Rolling Stones and got written up for that in the newspapers.

Almost four years after I joined, we retired our lead singer and hired Peter Diggins. He was an unknown from nowhere and we found him after lots of auditions. Great voice. Great-looking kid. A little bit of a wild child, and we had to baby-sit him some, but then again in those days everybody was a little crazy. I spent almost a year working with Peter in my basement studio, writing music for him, teaching him how to handle a microphone, slaving over the console, and recording him. The objective was to make a demo, send it to record companies, and get signed. With Peter on board, the band and I believed we could finally move up.

In truth, we had to. As popular as Chameleon was, we had begun to stagnate. We'd stayed alive in the Midwest for years, but we knew that if we couldn't make the transition to the national scene we'd fall apart. The crowds at our shows were big but not getting any bigger. We'd already played every venue, and the fifth time around wasn't as much fun. We were dying of boredom.

We got some interest from MCA Records, and their A&R

guy came to see us. Tom Paske and I also went to Los Angeles to meet with them, but before anything could happen the guy got fired and the deal collapsed.

Next, we heard from A&M Records, in Los Angeles. Actually, *I* didn't hear from them, but Dugan did. He got a phone call from our managers, telling him to come into the office for a band meeting. When he got there, he saw only Peter Diggins. Dugan freaked. Where was the rest of the band? The managers told him not to worry; there'd be a conference call with everyone, and the record company. But on the call, it was just the A&R guys, Peter Diggins, Dugan, and the managers.

What happened next blew Dugan away. The record company didn't want to sign the band, just Peter and Dugan. It's a classic story of record company folly. The Thompson Twins and Tears for Fears were popular, and A&M was looking for clones. Peter was the light guy and Dugan would be the dark guy. When Dugan asked why Charlie and I weren't included, the answer was, "They have mustaches. It's passé. They wouldn't fit in."

Can you believe it? Blown off because I had hair on my upper lip? This wasn't about music, it was about money, and it looked to me like our management was in cahoots with the record company.

Dugan considered the offer for a moment, then said no. "Our integrity and the love among brothers was more important to me than a record deal and a career—at least with those people," he said later, when he told me what had happened. He said he'd rather break up the band.

That took incredible integrity. Most people don't understand what it's like to say no to a record company. Try to imagine Dugan's temptation. For years he'd played local nightclubs, grinding out a couple hundred bucks a week; then he joined a popular band and one day along comes a serious bite from a record company willing to sign him. And he said no rather than tie his fortune to people like that.

Still, Chameleon broke up and A&M signed Peter, thinking that he was the creative force behind the band. They didn't realize—and our managers didn't reveal—that what they'd heard on the demo tape was my production, and Dugan's and my work. Peter sounded better than he really was. A&M moved Peter to Los Angeles and worked with him writing songs and in the studio, trying to do an album, but it didn't work out and they dumped him. Two years later, Peter called me out of the blue and asked me for a job. I didn't have one to give, but I still don't understand how he had the nerve to ask.

To leave Chameleon like that was a disappointment. But what was I to do? It was over. Now I had all the time I needed to pursue my own music and not worry about what anybody else said. I knew that most of the time in the record business, if given the chance, people would tell me I was bad, didn't fit in, wasn't what they were looking for, was doing it wrong. Ninety percent of all comments were negative. But I had faith in myself. I don't know why I stayed so long with Chameleon. Maybe I was like Ulysses on his way back to Ithaca, when he checked into Circe's Island and lost track of the time. I knew I should move forward, but staying where I was had felt too damn good.

Also, I was disappointed about the failure of *Optimystique* and at a stage in my life where I needed to party, to stretch, to get crazy, to let go, to unfocus. Maybe I was tired because I'd been fixated on one goal or another for so long. I'd enjoyed the rock 'n' roll life; it was carefree. In my head, I kept hearing my dad's words: "Don't forget to live." So, I lived. But after eight years in various bands I could no longer imagine myself going from nightclub to nightclub for the rest of my life, trying to make ends meet. The situation with A&M just forced me to face it and pushed me out the door into a new world.

It was the best thing that ever happened to me.

It's a cliché—but true—that life is not a dress rehearsal. You get to do it once, so do it well. I'd done my best, and now I wanted to do something else. The only problem is that when I finally reached the crossroads, I was thirty years old, and there's nothing worse than a thirty-year-old ex–rock musician who leaves the life with nothing to fall back on. You're not old, but you also don't have the unlimited energy or innocence of youth. I didn't sit around feeling sorry for myself, but I also couldn't pretend I wasn't scared that while I'd been partying, opportunities had been lost.

My spirit wasn't busted, but my equipment was. It was beat up and broken down from being on the road. New equipment would cost about $50,000—a serious chunk of change. Unfortunately, I'd just left behind my only source of income.

To my surprise, my brother volunteered to get a bank loan so I could buy the new keyboards and studio pieces I needed to record. He'd been telling me to leave the band for a couple of years and do my own stuff, and apparently he meant to back it up with action. I really wanted the money, but I was terrified about how I'd pay him back. Yorgo had finally earned his Ph.D., had gotten married, and was starting a family. How could I let him be liable for $50,000 if I wasn't totally sure I could make the payments? I'd never made more than $18,000 in one year— usually less—and as much as I believed in my music, I wasn't sure a derelict musician was such a good investment. I resisted for as long as I could—those were dark moments—but in the end I took the money and revamped the studio.

I also got a job so I could pay him back. After going to school for a month I became a licensed employment counselor for the state of Minnesota. The first day, I put on my suit and tie and reported to work. At lunch with all the other suits I looked around and thought, You've got to be kidding me. I can't do this! After I finished eating I got in my car, left, and never went back. So much for the nine-to-five.

One night, while having dinner at my brother's house, I met Sig Gesk, a friend of Yorgo's wife, Linda. Sig was an artist/designer and the owner of one of Minneapolis's top product packaging design firms. Yorgo put on some tapes I'd made and also asked me to play the piano—which I didn't normally do to entertain. Sig was impressed and he said, "Have you ever thought about doing commercials for television? Your music would be perfect for it."

"I haven't," I said. "But I'd like to. I need to make some money."

"Maybe I can help," he suggested.

That night, in bed, I decided not to take Sig's offer too seriously. Lots of people talk with good intentions while drinking during dinner but don't necessarily mean what they say. But the next day Sig called and asked me which agencies I'd like to visit first. I didn't know from agencies, so he took me to lunch instead and gave me an education. Then he made some calls to the biggest ad shops in Minneapolis and introduced me to the creative directors and art directors.

My first job was writing music for a television commercial for a shopping mall called the Dales. Everyone noticed it and pretty soon people were asking, "Who is this guy?" and I had a little business going. Tom Paske got me some contracts. Eventually I wrote music for Braun coffeemakers and British Airways commercials. The first paycheck was a godsend, a serious help.

I remember telling Sig, "What you did is amazing. I don't think I can ever repay you. Tell me what I can do."

"Don't repay me," Sig said. "Just help somebody else later when you can." He told me a story about how someone had helped him when he was younger and told him to do the same—kind of like the movie *Pay It Forward*. I've been repaying Sig ever since by trying to support people while they chase their dreams, or give them aid when they need it desperately. Each time, Sig comes to mind and I realize it's possible in ways both large or small to make a difference in someone's life.

I could have made hundreds of thousands of dollars a year just sitting around in Minneapolis, writing music for commercials. After long stretches of carrying a checkbook balance of no more than $300, if I was lucky, the money would have been a welcome change. A few ads could keep me afloat for months, and let me pay back my brother.

But then I realized, wait a minute! The money is nice, but it doesn't solve my problem. This is another detour. I want to do *my* music. If I keep doing commercials I won't have the energy or the time to do albums. Also, I'd probably buy a house, then a bigger house, and then a car and boat, and soon I'd *have* to make commercials.

That moment of clarity changed everything. I quit commercials and got back to the music. Tom Paske later told me his reaction. "You saw your opportunities, you didn't take them. You just had a one-track mind: Do albums. And that was it."

It was all or nothing. I had no Plan B.

It seems that in every culture, however tough life is and however impossible the conditions, there are some resilient human beings who find their way through, who survive and make something of themselves. Somehow they escape the horrors of where they were born. I've always wondered why *they* did it and not others. What drove them, what gave them the passion?

There are many examples from my homeland. I remember the story of some starving Albanians walking through the mountains into northern Greece, in the winter. To get lost is to die, yet they walked for forty days, braved the winter, slipped into a country where they didn't speak the language and were hunted by the police, found little jobs, sent money home, and survived. These people didn't accept their fate; they were willing to die trying to improve it.

When I finally shed all my excuses and diversions, I like to think that I became the guy who would walk through the mountains in the ice and snow and risk his life or die trying. I was completely committed to the music and the pleasure I got from creating, from discovering the rules of creativity, from being able to hear constant improvement.

In fact, I hadn't been out of Chameleon for long when I went crazy and did an album's worth of songs. I worked seven days a week, including holidays and birthdays. I hardly ate and didn't answer the phone. My parents came to visit at Christmas—only their second time in the country—and Yorgo and his wife prepared a huge dinner. I was supposed to show up, but I was in the middle of a song and didn't want to be interrupted and lose my train of thought. Whenever inspiration struck, I knew better than to let it go. When the clock neared time for dinner, I called my parents at my brother's house.

"Mom and Dad, it's Christmas and I understand you've come a long way to see us. But I'm in the basement in Brooklyn Park and I'm working on this great piece of music, and I can't stop. If I stop now, I'll lose it. Is it okay if I don't come?"

"Okay," they said. "Of course." I could get away with my

selfishness because they understood I wasn't being capricious or indulgently blowing them off. My parents knew me well enough to realize that I loved them. My parents also knew the kind of focus I maintained. When I swam, I practiced even on my birthday. If I didn't expect to celebrate my birthday, then why feel bad for not celebrating something else?

I showed up at one in the morning anyway, spent as much time as I could, then raced back to work.

When I was consumed I'd sometimes call Tom Paske at three in the morning.

"Tom? You up?"

"What time is it?"

"About ten to three. I finished the last song. It's killer. You gotta hear it."

"Over the phone?"

"It's the best work I've ever done. Meet me at Perkins in half an hour—okay?"

"What's the temperature outside?"

"About six below—you gotta hear this. Half an hour—okay?"

"I guess I'm up then, huh?"

"Half an hour."

"Ooh!"

Tom says he doesn't know why he got up, but he just did. "When Yanni was excited I couldn't tell him to wait until noon the next day. It had to be right then."

I'm still the same way. My focus on work and my lack of structure can drive people crazy. My friends, because they're my friends, tolerate it. But it's difficult for me to have a social life because my whole life is dependent on "the monster."

I didn't know it at the time, but my parents had come to

visit with the express purpose of talking me out of the music business and back into school, to get my Ph.D. When they came to my house, my father asked to see what I'd been doing in the basement. He wanted to get me alone and talk. I was excited to have the chance to show him all my new stuff. I chattered on about equipment, sounds, songs. When I played some tracks I could see his face light up. Maybe he thought it was still crazy to risk my livelihood on music, but I could tell he got it. He felt what I felt. We went upstairs without his ever mentioning his concerns about my future.

A few years later, after I signed a record deal and began to sell albums successfully, he came clean. "I was there at the family's request to convince you to quit," he said. They knew they had to pull out the heavy artillery because I'd only listen to my dad. "But you convinced me that music was the right thing for you to be doing, so I never said anything."

Even if my father had said something, I probably wouldn't have changed my mind. I'm not sure my family understood how stubborn and uncompromising I had become. I knew I could never have a regular job; it was music, no matter what. In Greek they say, *"E Tan E Epi Tas"* as part of the Spartan ritual when a soldier is sent off to war. His mother would give him a shield and tell her son to return with it, or on it. Sure, I was scared at times, worried about how to pay back my brother, anxious about what I'd do if being a solo artist didn't work out. Some nights I couldn't sleep. I had doubts. I was broke, at times disillusioned. I searched for direction. But I wouldn't live in fear. It's just not part of my personality. It's not how I was raised.

In 1985 I got a phone call I never expected. A DJ named Richard Ginsburg, from radio station WFMU in East Orange, New Jersey, was on the line, raving about my music. He told me that he had a show called *Synthetic Pleasure* on which he played lots of electronic music—or basically whatever he liked. He was always asking listeners to be on the lookout for new material. One day he got a call from a bus driver on the Todd Rundgren tour who said, "I've got a cassette I picked up in Minneapolis by some guy named Yanni and I think it's really worth a listen." Richard told him to send it in.

"I put the tape on the air, figuring to play a cut or two," Richard later told me, "but the station got flooded with more phone calls than I'd ever had—so I just let the tape play all the way through." The tape was *Optimystique.*

Richard started making phone calls to Minneapolis, looking for someone named Yanni. Finally he reached the Guthrie Theater, where Chameleon had played. They knew who I was and put Richard in touch with Tom Paske. Tom gave him my number.

When Richard called he said, "Man, you've got to get signed, this is incredible music. We play your music here all the time and people are going crazy. I've been trying to find you for months." He said he could even help sell my tapes there.

With that encouragement, Tom Paske and a friend in the construction business, Mark Macpherson, decided to buy my album from Jerry Steckling. Tom called to tell me the idea. I was all questions:

"What about this Macpherson guy? Why's he doing this?"

"What can I say? I was talking to him about *Optimystique.* He really likes it. I said if he put up ten grand, I'd put up ten grand. We'd buy the album from Jerry for sixty-five hundred dollars and use the rest to put out the album."

"Just like that?"

"Just like that. We'll each own a third. At ten dollars each we sell two thousand and we're even. Then we split three ways."

Silence. Tom filled it.

"Maybe he thinks he'll make money. I think he just likes the project."

"Has he got the money?"

"Macpherson has to borrow it. But if he says he'll have it, he'll have it."

"Don't we need a contract or something?"

"I'd do it on a handshake. But I'll write something up if you want."

I thought about it for moment. "Nah. It's up to you. I'd rather just be around people I trust than go through life trying to figure out airtight contracts."

"That's what I think. It's probably naïve but it's a better way to live."

"Naïve by design?"

"Yeah."

"Do you think we'll make any money on this?"

"Who knows? But I know this: That album's just sitting in the can. At least this way there's a chance it'll get heard."

"That's really all I want."

"Hey—maybe you get rich and famous off this deal. . . ."

"Right. I get the fame and you get the money."

"Sounds fair to me."

"You want to do this?"

"I do."

"Okay. Do it."

Macpherson's family kidded him about spending his borrowed money on an unknown electronic music artist, but Paske said, "Someday he's going to make his investment back a million times over, and then Mark will do the laughing."

Now Tom, Mark, and I owned the tape—on a handshake. We got artwork done for a cover and pressed a couple thousand more albums. Thanks to a little bit of an underground buzz we sold a few. Then Ginsburg gave out a number where people could call for it. A friend of mine, Kip Kilpatrick, knew a record distributor and he ordered four hundred copies. Eventually we got rid of them all at seven bucks apiece. We didn't get rich, but we made back our investment and more.

In the meantime, the music I had played for my father just came rushing out of me. Songs like "Santorini," which was later used as the television theme for the U.S. Open Tennis tournament for years, played at the 1996 Olympics in Atlanta when the first athletes walked into the stadium, and it is one of the most widely used pieces I've ever done. By the way, Santorini, the southernmost Cycladic island in the Aegean Sea, is an awe-inspiring place. Some think it's the site of ancient Atlantis. It's volcanic and dramatic. The cliffs are breathtaking and perfect for a romantic getaway. I do not like to describe what my songs are about, but I can say that "Santorini" is a day in the life of the island, from sunrise to sunset. It's like me sitting on the edge of a cliff watching the fishing boats go out in the morning; it's different ocean colors, the wind coming up, waves crashing against the rocks.

One day, Kip Kilpatrick called me from Seattle and said, "There's this new record company in New York. It's called Private Music and is headed by Peter Baumann, one of the founding members of Tangerine Dream. I know someone there and I think they'd like your music. If you have anything, I'd be happy to send it in."

"I'll make a deal with you," I said. "I'll make you one tape. You can send it, but you have to follow up and call me back and tell me what they said. I don't want this to fall through the cracks. I want to know if they liked it or they didn't like it."

Kip sent the tape to Beth Lewis, a woman he knew at Private Music. Tom Paske, who was acting as my manager, and I also sent a copy to another record company. Before long I got a phone call from Peter Baumann. "We'd like to meet you," he said. The trip east cost $500—my last $500. I called Richard Ginsburg and told him I was coming to town.

"Great! Fantastic!" he said. "You can stay at my house." Ginsburg picked me up at the airport, drove me to the record company the next day, and waited outside while I took the meeting with Peter Baumann.

The closest I'd ever been to New York was flying through JFK on my way from Greece to Minnesota. I felt like a fish out of water. Everything was completely unfamiliar and intimidating. I met Peter Baumann in a dark little room. He wore muted colors and was nice looking, about five foot ten, slightly stocky, short blond hair, blue eyes. Intelligent and well-spoken. "I really liked your tape," he said, and explained that he'd started Private Music because he wanted to release music he liked that was out of the mainstream. He talked a bit about Tangerine Dream. I knew the group; it wasn't one of my favorites, but I didn't tell him that. Baumann knew how difficult it was to sell "different" music and sympathized when I told him I'd been writing it for years and just sitting on it.

The other record company also responded positively, which seemed miraculous to me since I thought I'd end up sending out a hundred cassettes and get back a hundred "no thank you" notes. I still remembered how five years earlier with *Optimystique* I couldn't get arrested.

One afternoon, Tom called.

"Hello."

"Yanni?"

"Hi."

"What are you doing?"

"I just got up."

"I was just on the phone with Peter Baumann."

"How is he?"

"He's fine, Yanni. Are you sitting down?"

"Why? What? He wants the album?"

"Oh, he wants the album all right."

"Tell me."

"He wants the album—and three more."

"You're kidding!"

"Nope. A four-album deal."

"Yes!"

"Maybe you'd like to hear about the front money."

"Oh God!"

"How about forty grand!?"

"Holy shit!"

"And the money goes up for each album."

"Is this for sure?"

"It's a done deal. He probably would have gone higher. But I took it."

"I'm gonna call Mom and Dad. I'll call you back and we'll meet somewhere."

"Unbelievable!"

"Unbelievable!"

Both companies made offers. We decided to take Private Music's offer because of Peter's experience with Tangerine Dream. I thought he'd be more artist-friendly. He'd inspired me, I felt comfortable around him, and he expected to succeed. Signing with the company was the happiest day of my life. Later I heard that Peter had told someone, "I discovered the new Vangelis."

It was a lucky choice, because the other label went out of business in a year.

Tom Paske and a New York lawyer negotiated the deal. This was an enormous amount of money for me. It was the big time—and an opportunity to pay back my brother. I remember we were all convinced that the record company would make me a star. It was validation. I felt great. Maybe I wasn't crazy after all.

The money allowed me to rent a digital thirty-two-track Mitsubishi machine and re-record everything on the demo tape. I did it all in the basement and never went to another studio again. I also got some good album cover art.

But I still didn't have a title.

One afternoon the phone rang at my house. I answered and a voice said, "Keys to Imagination."

"What?"

"This is Richard Ginsburg."

"Hey, Rich, whaddaya doin?"

"I'm sitting here, just listened to your new tape. It's absolutely stunning. I've gone through it twice. I think you should call it 'Keys to Imagination.'"

"Okay, thanks," I said. "Sounds good. Nice title." I never thought I'd use it, but the more the words bounced around in my head, the more I thought it was brilliant. First album, all done with keyboards. And I was discovering the keys to imagination myself by opening doors to creativity. Yes, beautiful title.

. . .

Keys to Imagination came out in 1986, and while it didn't do poorly, it didn't sell as well as Peter Baumann had hoped. We didn't get much if any airplay because the Wave, the soft jazz radio format, hadn't yet debuted, and other stations didn't understand what I was doing. Also, I didn't tour to support the record. All in all, it was a very humble beginning.

That summer I went back to Kalamata for the first time since 1974. My parents had come to America in the years in between, but I had not been home. I had stayed away because I needed to find myself and to get used to the idea that America was my home. But I missed Greece and couldn't stay away any longer.

My return moved me more than I had expected. I visited my old school and the church, went to places where I'd taken my first girlfriend, found the spot on the beach where I had had my first kiss, and stood on the dock where my father and I had said our good-byes.

Then one day I got some news: *Ad Lib* magazine had given *Keys to Imagination* an award as best New Age album of the year. I didn't consider myself a New Age artist even though, at the time, New Age was electronic music, and only later did it evolve into something else. If anything, I was a contemporary instrumental artist, but this was my first album and first award and I wasn't going to argue. I left Kalamata and went to Japan, where the magazine was published, to accept.

A week later, Kalamata was hit by a 6.3 magnitude earthquake that virtually destroyed the town and the memories I'd just visited. I'm not normally superstitious, but I couldn't help feeling that Kalamata had waited for me to come home before it went away. Later, I wrote "Standing in Motion" about the earthquake— about surviving and persevering—and dedicated the *Out of Silence* album, which I began that fall in my basement studio in Brooklyn Park, to Kalamata. The dedication reads: "To the town of Kalamata, which stood strong and waited for me one last time."

I, too, had waited, learned through trial and error, accumulated wisdom and experience, had many women and little money, and focused on a succession of goals. With the release of *Keys to Imagination,* the old Yanni had been, if not destroyed then at least transformed, and a new Yanni emerged. I now had the chance to be the Yanni I'd imagined myself to be for so long—as well as the Yanni I couldn't yet imagine. All I had to do was *do* it.

6

NOT NEW AGE

2:00 A.M.

"Gee, I wonder who's calling at this hour?"

"Your favorite Greek."

"What's up, Yanni?"

"I was talking to Peter . . ."

"I know, he wants you to move to L.A."

"What do you think?"

"I wouldn't live there on a bet!!"

"I know."

"Smog, crowded, phony. America's armpit."

"How do you *really* feel?"

Silence.

"You know I gotta do it, don't ya?"

"Why? You can't write in Minneapolis? We got audiotape, you know. Electricity."

"The music *business* is in L.A."

"Great. Lawyers, contracts, flashbulbs . . ."

"So you don't think I should go?"

"Nah. You gotta go, but it sucks."

"Look. I could write fine just where I am. But nobody's gonna hear my stuff. If I could go to L.A. and figure out the business side, maybe my stuff could get heard."

"And that's what matters, I know."

"Hey. If I can get my music out there, if I can get people to *hear* it, it's gonna hit 'em right between the eyes."

"I think I hear a little arrogance."

"Confidence. No, actually I'm not that confident. It's vanity."

"Do we need to get you a bigger mirror?"

"No, a bigger microphone. Look, I admit it. I want everybody in the world to hear my stuff. I want them to love it. You think I want to write this stuff and just play it for myself?"

"Okay, okay."

"Peter says I need to do this. He'll help me out. I think I gotta go."

"Okay."

"I'm going then."

"Okay."

"I'm gonna do it."

"Okay. Bye."

"I gotta do it."

I moved to California in 1987 also at the urging of Sam Schwartz, a powerful movie music agent who'd heard my albums and wanted to get me started scoring pictures. "Come on out," he'd said. "You'll be great for the movies." I thought he could be right, and I moved not only for that opportunity but because I'd begun to feel too safe in Minnesota. The record deal allowed me to compose and record to my heart's content in my basement studio, but I wasn't being stimulated or challenged enough. I wanted to put a little more jeopardy into my life. I had this vision that being in Los Angeles would introduce me to a lot of intelligent and experienced folks; some of the best people on the planet in show business would be there, as well as great weather. I loved the idea of leaving the Midwest winters behind. To me, it had always been just a matter of time.

Tom Paske had advised me against going. We didn't argue, but he didn't believe the move was necessary. I'm sure he worried that once exposed to a fast-talking, self-indulgent lifestyle, I'd lose myself to the superficiality and be distracted from or at least be less driven about my career. But I knew it was time to keep working hard, not party. I'd just been through years of rock 'n' roll and I didn't need that anymore.

I suspect that Tom also didn't want to lose a friend. We'd grown close. I reassured him that our connection was very deep and our friendship didn't depend on seeing each other all the time. He was my brother, part of the family, unshakable. Even our business relationship had never been about money, but, as Tom said, "I'm in this for the ride. What a great ride!" Yeah, crazy ride. He got to be in Minneapolis and deal with everybody in California, New York, and, later, everywhere in the world. He got to stay in his office, make everyone come to him, ride around in his Jeep, sleep in his own bed, smoke cigarettes, and talk to a Greek kid who thinks he's a star. Many times I would say to him, "Tom, I don't know how you get away with it, but I'm just glad to know there's a human being on the planet like you who does."

Tom is tough and straightforward, a man who doesn't waste words, so he doesn't often reveal emotional vulnerabilities, but I knew he felt things deeply. When I'd visited Greece the year before, we had said our good-byes in the airport parking lot and I saw tears in his eyes.

I flew to Los Angeles and rented an apartment for a month at the Oakwood complex in Burbank—home to traveling professionals, single guys, and soon-to-be-divorced husbands tossed out by their wives. Then I went house-hunting and found a little place on Willow Glen, near the top of Laurel Canyon, in the Hollywood Hills. Peter Baumann, who in the meantime had moved his offices to the West Coast, stuck his neck out and guaranteed the house loan to the bank. I took that as a sign of his continued faith and support.

Back in Minneapolis, I packed my stuff, hired a truck, and drove to Los Angeles in the brown 1979 BMW 320i I'd bought a few years earlier from Yorgo for $9,000. To keep myself occupied, I decided that the drive would be a good time to quit smoking. The idea of two days and nights without a cigarette seemed horrible; if I could make it, I could do anything—and I did.

At the new house I hired a construction crew to convert the master bedroom into a recording studio, and helped out when I could. I lifted equipment, sanded wood, installed insulation. The studio was more elaborate than my Brooklyn Park basement. I turned a walk-in closet into a soundproof isolation booth where one person, maybe two, could play and sing. It was also big enough for half a drum set. I put the studio speakers where the door to the master bathroom had been, and to use the facilities I had to cut a narrow pathway through a linen closet and enter sideways. I slept in a guest bedroom on an old mattress that came with the house and was probably the former owner's spare. A couple of springs poked out at the foot, but I didn't care.

I put my piano in the living room.

Those were the days of no distractions. I had few friends and, as for women, I saw Allison now and then, and some other girls from Minnesota who'd moved to Los Angeles or who occasionally came through. No one local. Mostly, I was a monk. I lived in the studio and lost track of the hours. Sometimes I'd go in and everything worked; other times I could stare at the walls and come up with nothing. I don't mean that I was waiting for inspiration to strike. Inspiration doesn't arrive from somewhere else and hit me over the head. It's all inside. I am responsible for it. When I *give up* control, the music comes. I was still learning through trial and error that any other approach simply destroyed the moment. Only when I let go did everything flow effortlessly and the music become available in abundance. Only then did I experience so much physical pleasure that I became ecstatic. I felt alive, bright, aware. Everything was clear and clean and in focus.

Writing a piece of music is like giving birth. I am the channel for a powerful emotion inside that wants to come out, and when it's ready there's no stopping it. Sometimes I didn't eat for days, didn't make or take phone calls, cut out all other input. I had no problem being alone. I think it was Gandhi who said, "Jail is only horrible for people who can't be by themselves." Silence is not the enemy. In silence I get to think and discover. Being alone is how I recharge. I uncover truths about myself, I get over frustrations, I heal. When I'm alone is when the magic happens.

Though I mostly worked, I also wanted to enjoy life. The house had a baby-sized backyard and a hot tub under a tree. At first I used it quite a bit; being outside reminded me that I was cheating winter. When I left the house it wasn't to party, haunt nightclubs, or even go to the movies. I went grocery shopping, bought clothes, got my hair trimmed, went to the bank, ate pizza at Coyote's, got the car washed.

If it sounds like Los Angeles life could be boring, it was, but I didn't notice. Although I wanted to be there, I also had Paske's skepticism about the place. I didn't know Los Angeles and didn't want to. I was into my career. This was my shot to create my dreams. I just wanted to become better and better at my craft because I believed that if the music was good enough the people would find it. And that's *all* I cared about. One night I left the studio about 1 A.M. and called Tom. He'd become used to the phone ringing at any hour.

"Tom. What's goin on?"
"What's up with you?"
"I started the new album."
"The new tape recorder must have showed up."
"Yeah. It's in. The new studio's up and running."
"Great. What else?"
"I got a cleaning lady."
"Don't tell my wife."
"I know. I'm in the big time."
"You're going L.A. on me."
"Did you ever notice how if we're going to clean a room, we start in one corner and then go step-by-step around the room, dusting this, straightening that. Then we see how it looks when we're done. And it always looks terrible anyway."
"I'm depressed just thinking about it."
"Well that's not how she does it."
"Who?"
"The cleaning lady."
"Really."

"She sees the whole room. She knows how it's gonna look, in her mind."

"And you know this because?"

"I took the time to watch."

"Okay. She sees the big picture in her mind."

"Yeah. The big picture. It looks like she's wandering around, picking up stuff at random. But she's not. There's no wasted effort. The whole process just flows. When she's done it looks great."

"And the point is?"

"The point is—and see if you can get this—that's what it's like for me in the studio. That's how I write. I don't start with the drums then go to the bass and on and on. I don't build it one part at a time. First I see the whole song at once. Then I try to hang on to it. If I can do that, all the individual sounds fall into place."

"Has the cleaning lady got any albums out?"

"No, asshole. She gets to start out with a room, a finite space. I start with nothing. I have to get to a place where the big picture will come. That's the trick."

"Art transcends science. Just ask Schopenhauer."

"Oh, really?"

"Well, it isn't like somebody looked in a microscope and said 'Golly. Look, an electron.' No. Somebody had a flash and figured out it had to be there. From out of nothing. Then everybody scurried around until they found it."

"You're telling me Einstein wasn't just flying around at the speed of light watching mass turn into energy?"

"You've discovered the Grand Unified Cleaning Lady Theory of the Universe."

Silence.

"You're not getting it, are you?"

"No."

"I'd kill for a cigarette."

"That I can understand."

"Bye, Tom."

"Bye."

I had made some quick money scoring a couple of pictures—something for HBO and two ABC Movies of the Week. I did them back-to-back and earned $120,000. It helped cover the mortgage, and I also bought a new tape recorder that cost $80,000. Easy come, easy go. I knew that Sam Schwartz—who had since become a close friend and helped me navigate the Los Angeles maze—could get me more work, and he wanted to, but once again I realized (and could tell that I was beginning to sound like a broken record) that all this side work was distracting me from my albums. I told Sam I had to stop—temporarily, of course—but I knew I probably wouldn't return until I established myself and had more time to spare.

I also had a lot to learn about the business.

I thought the record company signs you, develops you, and sells you—and all you do is create the music. I thought the record company was going to make me a star. I knew Peter Baumann was trying, and he promised me that as soon as something broke, the company would jump in and support me. That sounded nice, but I kept asking myself—and Tom—this question: How would I get that break without support in the first place? I don't mean to make too big a deal of this; that's how it has usually worked in the record business for new and veteran artists alike. There's little time to grow an act. It's even worse today. Like a flop movie, if you don't make it right away, you're gone. I was luckier, but I was sometimes impatient. Frustrated.

Rather than let it make me lose my hair or go gray, or make my face cave in, I would talk it through with Tom. We spoke every day. I don't believe it's smart to repress feelings. Tom was the calm voice on the other end of the line. He was together and didn't rattle when I vented about the difficulties of trying to kick off my career. He encouraged me but didn't pander. I could call day or night and he'd say, "You want to talk for two hours? Fine. What do you want to talk about?"

Those talks helped me keep my goals in sight and not become bitter in the process. That's key. It was also fun. I thought, "Let's show them."

When we finished talking I went back into the studio.

I don't want to characterize those days or myself as unhappy. I didn't have time to be unhappy. I was too busy in the studio, learning, composing, solving problems, inventing new techniques. Any anxieties I felt I channeled back into the work. Realizing my dreams had always required an uphill battle, starting with swimming. Besides, how many people got the chance to do what I was doing? I felt tremendous validation because I'd made it happen with hard work and single-minded focus. This is what I lived for; how could I complain?

Plus, one fact always gave me hope: Though I had a very small audience, the people who liked my music *really, really* liked it. They were serious. They sent letters to me and to the record company. I'd meet fans who were just beside themselves, and Peter Baumann would run into people who said, "You've got a lot of people on your label, but Yanni, he's on a different level." That kind of reaction made me believe there was more out there for me; it helped deflect my fear of not being discovered. I just needed to do something. I had to find a way to get the music out.

To support my new album, *Out of Silence,* I put together a small band and toured, playing the new music as well as selections from *Keys to Imagination*. Although I'd written, as always, with an orchestra in mind, I couldn't afford one, so I reproduced that sound in the studio with my synthesizers. But because I wanted to play everything live onstage, and not against tape, I needed three keyboard players and a drummer on the road.

Charlie Adams had moved to Los Angeles about six months after Chameleon broke up, and he joined the band first. Watching Charlie play is spectacular entertainment. When he hits a drum it's like poetry. I also hired Joyce Imbesi. She's from San Francisco, and we were introduced through a friend. I admired her dexterity and her ear. She also did her own jazz-oriented stuff.

The final keyboard player was John Tesh, the former co-host of *Entertainment Tonight*. Tesh was a fan. I heard that he wanted to meet me, so mutual friends put it together; one afternoon not long after I moved to Los Angeles, he came to my house—as Tesh the *Entertainment Tonight* reporter. I didn't know that he was a musician until he told me. We hit it off and he invited me to his place in Marina del Rey, where he lived with his then-wife Julie, to play beach volleyball. After the games we'd usually have drinks and dinner. John was funny and enjoyed making people laugh. A couple of times I got pretty bombed and spent the night at their place.

One day Tesh called to ask what I was up to.

"I'm going down to Orange County to do a radio interview."

"Want me to come with you?" he said. "We'll have fun. We'll have a drink on the way down and chat."

"Okay, sure."

In the limousine Tesh surprised me. "I don't know how to say this," he started, "so I'll just say it: I'd like to play with your band. I've never been onstage for a live performance and I need the experience. It'll be really good for me and I'd learn a lot."

My face must have revealed my uncertainty.

"I'd work my ass off," he insisted. "I promise you're not going to be sorry."

I'd heard John play—beautifully—and he was very gung-ho about convincing me to give him a shot. But still . . .

"John, you've got a job," I said. "Do you realize how much we'll be rehearsing? *Every* day, including Saturdays and Sundays. How are you going to do that and still do *Entertainment Tonight*?"

"Don't worry," he said. "I've already thought about it. I'll do *Entertainment Tonight* in the morning and rehearse with you all night if necessary. I'll be fine. The show knows my passion is music and they'll cut me some slack." He was right, though the producers may have been peeved at me for pulling him away. Tesh even moved out of his house for a month and rented an apartment close to our practice space in Burbank. We worked hard and long, sometimes ten hours at a stretch, because I was just learning how to stage the music live. Tesh was excellent, a fast learner, intelligent. It didn't take long for me to show him a few things.

One afternoon we were walking on the beach and he asked, "Do you think I'll ever make it? Do you think I'm good enough? Should I continue with my music?"

Of course he wanted his own career. Who doesn't? I said, "Absolutely. Just do your own thing." I later helped him get his first recording contract with Private Music.

Tesh was in the band for only one tour. We went to maybe twelve cities around the country. Private Music wanted me to play "selected clubs" and Peter Baumann pressed hard, but I said no.

I'd already done that trip with Chameleon and I knew it didn't work. I wanted to play theaters—at least 2,000-seaters—and said I'd risk it. Everybody told me I was crazy, but I insisted that my sound was too big for small spaces, and even if only four hundred people showed up, I'd give them the best show they ever saw. You've got to start somewhere, and I wasn't going to start in nightclubs, where I'd already been. It was the right choice.

Our first date was in Dallas, in front of almost 2,000 people. I wore my usual black leather pants and a tight top. Tesh was really nervous with beginner's jitters. It hadn't occurred to me that he'd be frightened because he was on TV all the time, in front of millions. But I'd forgotten that it's not live TV; if you blow a line you stop the tape and roll again. Fortunately, Tesh was prepared. He'd brought a bottle of Pepto-Bismol and slugged it down just before show time.

Honestly, we were all more or less in the same boat. I may have been onstage many times, but this was my first bona fide tour. Before one show, trying to get over our nerves, Tesh, Charlie, and I found Joyce's camera lying around. Someone had the idea that we should all pull down our pants and have a roadie take a picture of our butts, and then see what happened when Joyce had the film developed. I think she was at home with her parents, looking at all the concert photos, when she came across our three amigos. Surprise!

Baumann came to Dallas and after the concert he ran up and hugged me. He seemed fairly impressed. Perhaps his expectations had been low because he'd never seen me perform and because I hadn't bothered to explain the show to him beforehand. Still, it was important for me to prove to Peter that I had my act together, and I was gratified by his reaction. Maybe now he'll have more faith, I thought.

Though Baumann was happy with what he'd seen, Private

Music didn't go any more out of their way to support my next tours. One time I had to twist the corporate arm pretty hard. I said, "I'd like you to back me up to the tune of a hundred thousand dollars." If the tour didn't work, I could take a hit for a couple hundred grand, but if I lost any more I'd go belly-up. Then I made the deal too good to turn down. I said, "If I lose money, no matter what happens, the most you'll be out is a hundred grand. Even if I lose a million dollars. And if I don't need it, I won't use it."

What could they say? I was their top-selling artist. They grudgingly gave me a check, figuring they'd never see the money again, that I was just another musician with his hand in the till. The begrudging part bothered me. What I wanted would be good for both of us, but their attitude insulted me.

That mistrust was beginning to characterize my relationship with the record company, often putting me in the position of saying, "Fine, I'll do it myself. Thanks." And most of the time, in one way or another, they kicked and screamed: "This ain't gonna work."

I didn't want to hear it. I had big dreams. I was in a fighting stance. The more I wrote and toured, the more ambitious I became. I wanted people to talk about my albums, and I wanted to sell millions. I wanted to play to SRO crowds in 20,000-seat arenas. I wanted a big sound and great lighting. I wanted to leave people floating on cloud nine after the show. I didn't have enough money yet to get anything more than rental lights and the PA system or the right musicians, but I could imagine the day when I could say, "Okay, we're going to have two months' rehearsal. How much will that cost?"

"A million dollars."

"Good. Let's do it." And be able to.

When the tour ended, one of my greatest pleasures was to

return that check—uncashed. We were in the midst of some other business when I told Ron Goldstein, a smooth record executive who always lands on his feet, and who was then president of Private Music, "Oh, by the way: I've got this for you." I opened my briefcase and handed him the original check.

He said, "In my twenty-five years in the record industry, I've never seen this."

After that, Ron trusted me more. He understood that I wasn't just out to get what I could.

My next two albums were *Chameleon Days* and *Niki Nana*. Record sales and concert attendance slowly climbed. But even as my audience steadily grew, most people still had no clue who I was or what I did. I don't mean that they thought I was a hairstylist or a Greek celebrity chef instead of a composer; I mean that even if someone knew my name and my profession, he or she often had no idea what my music was about.

There are a couple of reasons why. To learn about me, they had to find me. To find me I had to somehow get their attention, which was another uphill battle. I had realized as early as *Optimystique* in 1981 that I would have a hard time getting anyone to notice instrumental music, and I was prepared for that. We lived in a rock 'n' roll era. You couldn't find me on MTV or on any radio stations except the Wave. They played instrumental cuts, though now it's mostly what they call "smooth jazz."

I was in a box. All I could do was continue to write, record, perform—and push wherever I could. But exposure is an obstacle course that requires proper advertising, tour support money, creative marketing, and word of mouth. I figured if I did my part then the record company should do theirs, especially since my sales kept growing. When I brought up the subject, Peter Baumann was always encouraging, but it was tough to get him to put his money where his sentiments lay.

And money alone couldn't do everything.

The difficulties of my quest to be heard were compounded by my music being called something it isn't. When I recorded *Optimystique,* my songs were called "electronic" because they were performed with synthesizers. Unfortunately that wasn't considered "real" music. It was thought of as rubber music. Cool. Repetitive. Techno. Droning. Mine wasn't anything like that, but because I used synthesizers I got lumped with that group.

Next my music was called New Age, a label meant to conjure visions of artists who say "Ommmmm" a lot and use the ambient sounds of tree frogs, crashing waves, and waterfalls to enhance meditation. That's never been me either; it's just not what I do. Ironically, I'm criticized by the real New Age people for being way too intense. Had I been willing to accept being a niche artist, I wouldn't even mention this, but that was never my goal, and anyone who listened to my music had to be pretty dense not to realize that it never fit any prefab definitions. Was I angry? A bit. I knew that I was an odd duck. I just wanted to write the music that I enjoyed and reach people who might enjoy it, too.

These days this stuff bothers me much, much less—not at all, actually. But when I lived in Los Angeles and was eager to get my music out to as many people as possible, my emotions seesawed. I'd be pissed off one day, not dwell on it the next, then my blood would boil until I'd focus on more important things.

One thing I never had a problem with was people hearing my music and deciding it wasn't their cup of tea. I don't like all kinds of music either. What bothered me was the New Age label scaring away people who might like what I do. I didn't like it when, because of a label on a record store bin, or a review, someone could say, "No, no, I hate that crap," without ever hearing me.

This much I know: It's very difficult to lie with instrumental music. You're asked to describe an emotion, but not with words. Words you can fake; anyone can say "I love you." Try to communicate "I love you" without words; if you've never felt love then there's no chance in hell that you'll accidentally choose the right notes to describe the emotion.

Instrumental music works on us subconsciously. If it doesn't move you emotionally it's meaningless. The music has to give you goose bumps. It's not something you understand intellectually, you just *know* it. That's what I love about instrumental music. It bypasses logic; it's not something you analyze. You enjoy it or you don't.

Whenever I talk to the press, inevitably I'm asked the "New Age question." I've always responded by saying that New Age is not a musical term but a philosophical point of view.

It's quite simple, really.

Some critics and journalists understand and leave me alone. Others make fun. I don't remember the first time I heard someone call me "Yawnee," but I can take a joke. Sometimes I even call myself "Yawnee." I like the *New Yorker* cartoon of a dentist asking a patient in the chair, "Yanni or Novocaine?" What's wrong with people using my music to get away from pain? If you think about it, it's not a bad thing. Do I mind people making fun of me? No; I think it's cool. It's fair game, particularly in this culture. There's no one sacred here.

Sometimes what was written just made me laugh out loud. One of my favorites is the reviewer who wrote about my shoes. He came all the way out to my concert and ended up talking about my shoes. Now *that's* funny.

The bottom line is that I like what I do. If it sounds good to me, it goes out. If it doesn't sound good to me, I erase it. Will everybody like what I like? Absolutely not. That's impossible. As soon as you put your art out there for people, someone will say, "Because it is blue, I love it," and, for the exact same reason the next guy will say, "Because it is blue, I hate it." Once you understand that, there's freedom in the creative process. Otherwise, your creation is just a reaction to criticism. You won't be able to let your mind run and say, "What would I like to do today?" Instead, you'll hear a little voice in the back of your head: "You must get it under four minutes long, and have a good rhythm, and get some lyrics." That's enslavement.

In the beginning, like most people who aren't used to the press, I was a little taken aback by some of the responses; they seemed so unrelated to what was really going on. Then I realized they had *nothing* to do with what was really going on.

It took me a few years until I was able to get it and say, "New Age, Schmew Age, who cares? How do you like this *song?*"

I've never taken shots at critics because what is there to respond to? I'll say it now: *Critics are always right.* Anything they say is correct. If it's art they're writing about, then everyone has the right to a response.

Before my career took off, I watched an interview with a famous sitcom actor from a show I loved. When the guy told the story of how he'd once gotten a bad review for some performance and became so terrified that he wouldn't even go out shopping, that stopped me in my tracks. I thought, Why would you do that to yourself? Think of how many people enjoy what you do. Why would you let a review potentially ruin your life?

No one likes rejection and I'm no exception. But if you're an artist, you must *expect* rejection. It comes with the territory.

Be prepared for it. Your reaction to rejection is what's important. If it overtakes you and fills you with self-doubt, fear, and insecurity, then it can be very destructive.

After listening to one of my albums, my aunt Sofia said, "I don't like any of the songs that have drums. I prefer the gentler pieces." And guess what: She was right. That's what she likes. I don't take it personally, and that attitude is what gives me my creative freedom. Today, I call it the Aunt Sofia Principle.

Just because critics like you doesn't mean you'll sell albums, and if they hate you it doesn't mean that you won't. When did you last go to a critically panned movie and have a great time anyway? The media has its opinion, but any artist who depends on being a media hit is lost in the long run. Believe it or not, the media is a tiny audience. Loud, but tiny. You've got to show your art to the public. They decide. In that sense, the opinion of my neighbor the garbage collector is just as important as any critic's.

Sometimes I'd like to say to a reviewer, "If you think my music is boring, great. Now let's go to your house and you play me the music that you think is not boring." And maybe when he does that I'll go, "You listen to this?" I'm certain we'd both have a good laugh—and connect as human beings.

If I have any complaint it's that there are rock critics, jazz critics, classical critics, but not many *music critics*. A job requirement should be that you've heard a zillion different types of music and are open to all of them. You should find beauty everywhere. You should listen to country & western as much as jazz, opera, classical, rock, pop, rap, grunge, and R&B. Check out Algerian music. Egyptian, Israeli, Asian. I don't write only in 4/4 time. I like 7/8, 9/8, 5/8, Middle Eastern scales, blending classical music with rock, and world culture beats. I draw from many influences.

In truth, the media missed me. They never helped me

succeed and they didn't help me fail. I've never been theirs. They didn't find me, the people did.

Sometimes being found can change your life.

In early 1989 the actress Linda Evans and her friends were sitting around at her home near Seattle, listening to my music and wondering, "What would this guy say if he knew how much we played his albums around here? We should let him know."

Because of the profound effect Linda had on my life, I've invited her to join me for this part of the book and speak in her own words.

> LINDA: *The music was so heart-tugging and soul-searching and beautiful. It was my favorite. I went to a school where a thousand people adored him and meditated to his music. They felt that it helped them attain certain levels of consciousness because it was so inspiring. One day we had the music on and said, "Maybe he doesn't know there's a bunch of maniacs up here who think he's a great guy. Let's call him! Let's invite him up here and tell him we love him."*

Linda was nominated to call for the most pragmatic of reasons: because she was *Linda Evans*. Everyone figured I would return her call. She told her assistant, Susan, "Find this Yanni guy. I think he's Japanese." Susan called Private Music and reported back that I was Greek, not Japanese, that I lived in America, spoke English, and was finishing up an album. "He doesn't like to talk to anybody when he's doing an album," Susan said, "but he'll be through in a month and then you can talk."

I knew who Linda was. When I first came to America in 1972 I remember seeing this beautiful blonde woman on TV in the dorm lounge, in a rerun of *The Big Valley*. I even told a friend about this "ungodly beautiful girl."

Years later, when I returned to Greece in 1986 to see my parents, sometimes we'd be eating al fresco, under the moon, on the balcony overlooking the bay, and my mom and aunts would *leave the dinner table* to watch *Dynasty*. I'd never watched a whole episode. Who had time? I usually said, "What are you guys watching TV for? Why don't you come out here and look at the moon and the beautiful view?"

I was wasting my breath. The show, and Linda, were extremely popular with Greeks. My mom and aunt would talk on and on about "this Linda Evans girl," so I finally gave in and watched a bit and still thought she was stunningly beautiful.

Before I actually talked to Linda, her assistant called me to ease the way. "What's she like?" I said.

"She adores you so much," Susan said, "it's going to be easy. Don't worry about it. She's crazy about your music and it won't be a big deal."

That relaxed me. But only a bit. I was no stranger to women who liked me, but a famous, beautiful woman wanting to speak to me just because she liked my music was very exciting and a nice ego stroke. It made me a bit nervous. I had no idea what to expect, no idea of what to say or how to say it. Turns out Linda was anxious too, and had almost reconsidered the whole thing because she'd never made one of these calls, either.

When Linda rang I realized that she didn't know much about me. Right away she confessed that she'd thought I was Japanese. We probably talked about the weather for the first few minutes, but soon I felt like I'd known her all my life. Linda is very down to earth. Extremely intelligent.

The conversation lasted about an hour. We spoke about my music, and then we got into life. We seemed to agree on a lot of things important to both of us: existence and existing, with how you look at life and how you enjoy the *now*.

At the end, I said, "I love talking to you," and asked if I could call her. She had sparked my interest. I loved her sexy voice. But as a guy, I tried to be a little cool—a leftover from my rock 'n' roll days.

Linda said, "Sure. Call me any time." And then she said, "If you ever want to come up here, we'd love to have you. I have a house on a lake. It's a big place, a mansion. You'll have your own room. You can come and stay, and meet these people who love you. And feel free to bring your wife, or girlfriend, or boyfriend. Whatever."

"Thanks," I said, smiling to myself. "It would just be me."

Now that I've known Linda for so many years, I can see why I was immediately attracted to her. She gives off incredible energy. She picks you up and makes you feel good about yourself, and she does it instinctively. I've watched her do it over the years with everybody from the wardrobe girl to Prince Albert.

When we spoke again, I learned that Linda had just moved to Seattle and wasn't interested in having an acting career anymore. She was fried after ten years of *Dynasty*, going every morning into makeup and shooting day in and day out. It was time for her to live.

Unfortunately, living was something I didn't have much of a chance to do. Even after four albums, I still spent most of my time on my career. I hadn't had a steady relationship since Sherry, and I still wasn't looking to find a girlfriend or a wife. But the way I felt about Linda, just over the phone, made me start to wonder.

When I care for a woman I'm very committed in my heart, but I knew that being with me could be hard on someone who's not self-sufficient and together. When I write music, I go away, and not just physically. I distance myself mentally, and that's much more difficult to deal with. You can't talk to me because I'm not interested. I don't hear anything. I don't watch television. I don't eat. I sleep one or two hours at night, then I get up and go right back to the studio. How many women can put up with that?

I felt I had to tell Linda about my life. Warn her.

"Of course," she said, the next time I called. "That's exactly what I'm trying to learn how to do. What you do naturally, that ability to focus and be creative, that's as close to God as you can get, and it's what I'm studying."

I was stunned. "But how do you know that?" I asked.

"Because I know," Linda said. "Your passion is to write music. My goal is to find the passion inside of me and inside of everybody; that's the beauty of all of us. That turns me on. It is so exciting and so powerful and so magical."

Linda was far more successful than I had ever been, and was successful for such a long time. She seemed to understand the power of her mind and how to use it to create the life she wanted. "I know exactly how you're supposed to do everything," she said, "because I did it."

When I heard that I thought, Really? Wow. Maybe she does understand me. I had told Linda about what I believed were the worst parts of me, the aspects that would drive anyone away, yet she didn't seem to mind. In fact, Linda encouraged them. She said, "Absolutely. That's the only way to be if you're an artist. It's wonderful that you can do that."

The more we talked, the more I kept looking at the phone and thinking, Who is this woman?

One afternoon Linda called me and said she was coming to Los Angeles and we could finally meet.

> LINDA: *I really liked Yanni on the phone, but to tell the truth, I was very busy in Los Angeles, so even though it was my idea to get together, I was so preoccupied that I arranged to have us meet only an hour before I got on the plane to go back to Seattle. While I got ready to go, my oldest friend, Bunky, said, "You know, that Yanni person is coming."*
>
> *"Oh yeah," I said. "Thanks."*
>
> *"He'll be here pretty soon," she added, "so get packed now."*
>
> *When the doorbell rang she said, "Do you want me to get it?"*
>
> *"Buzz him in the gate," I said, "I'll get the door."*

Linda opened the door. She said, "Hi, come in." She was beautiful. She led me into the living room.

> LINDA: *I looked at Yanni and my breath left my body. I could not believe that I had called this guy. I took one look at him and was madly in love. It was like the sky had opened. Lightning went off. I just stared at him. I didn't know what to do. I didn't know what to say. I couldn't breathe. I couldn't think. My heart was beating. I don't know how long that went on. It was probably only a few seconds, but I felt like I'd been staring for an hour. I thought, Oh my God, I never would have called him if I'd known he was so beautiful. I never would have had the nerve.*

I didn't notice any of this, of course, because my reaction was pretty much the same. In fact, I don't remember much because of how intensely I focused on her.

LINDA: *We were glued to each other. I have never had an experience like that. The main love in my life had been John Derek. As a kid I had a movie poster of him over my bed. When he and I broke up, Barbara Stanwyck said to me, "That's it, Audra." Yes, she called me Audra, my character's name on* The Big Valley. *"That's it for you. You'll never love again. It happens once, if you're lucky. Me and Robert Taylor. You and John."*

I thought, I hate that; I don't want to think I'm twenty-seven and I've had all the love I'm ever going to have in my life. Time went on, no big love showed. Then at forty-seven I opened the door and here's Yanni. It was the last thing I thought would happen.

Also, he was twelve years younger than me. Of course it bothered me. I couldn't imagine what it meant to be with a man twelve years younger. I had arrived at a point in my life where I was really happy with who I was. I was content. I had broken up with a guy I'd been with for a few years, who everybody said I should marry because he was such a good man and so honest and decent and right. But I said, "That's true, but I'm not in love. I'm not settling. I'm never going to settle." By the time I met Yanni I'd been by myself for a year and a half.

A couple of hours later I was on the plane home—and stunned. I said to Bunky, "I don't know what's going on. I have these feelings and I don't even know who he is. How can I love him without even knowing him?"

Soon, I took up Linda on her invitation to visit Seattle. She could have sent a car to the airport, but she insisted on picking me up herself. Her home then—she's since moved—was part of a private community. Set on a rise, the house looked out over Gravely Lake, and it was a short walk through the rose garden and trees to the shore. There were even a couple of balconies and waterfalls. I had my own room.

We hung out from morning until night for about a week, and spent a lot of time on the lake in a little boat drifting into the sunsets, talking endlessly. But it was never simple conversation. An energy kept cycling back and forth between us. The more intense it grew, the more we just wanted to melt into each other and become one. You can't imagine how powerful and seductive—and scary—that feeling of utter attraction can be to two people as independent as we were. It was a perfect scenario in which to fall in love. As Linda says, "It was something we couldn't walk away from, so we just walked into it."

When it came to being intimate, I didn't want to jump the gun. I was a little guarded. Maybe still playing it cool. But I wasn't thinking in rock 'n' roll terms; it wasn't like that. Not even remotely.

It took a few days, but the inevitable happened, and that's when our romantic relationship began.

7

THE PERFECT WOMAN

I very quickly realized that Linda was the perfect woman for me, and I was the perfect man for her. We were in love. We were financially independent. We weren't emotionally insecure. We needed each other, but not like, "I must see you, talk to you, hold you, and hear you say you love me every day—or else I'll come unglued." We trusted each other completely, and kept that trust no matter how long we were apart.

Sometimes I'd stay with Linda in Seattle. Other times we'd meet somewhere in the country when I was on tour. Though it must have been tough, Linda often rode on the bus with the rest of the band for a week at a time, crammed with me in the back lounge/master bedroom, over the engine.

I loved having her with me. At the shows, Linda was my eyes and ears. She roamed through the house and gave me a critique every night: This part was good, this didn't work out very well. Linda has excellent musical taste and a strong visual sensibility. She helped me immensely.

But now and then I'd say, "Linda, what are you doing here? Why don't you go home? This is crazy." We'd leave town after the concert and drive all night but get no rest because there's nothing harder than lying in a bunk bed trying to sleep when you're riding over potholes and bumps and going airborne every few miles. New York State's highways were the worst. Then we'd arrive in the next city about four or five in the morning and pull up to the hotel. Weary, we'd slip into our shoes, throw long black coats over our pajamas, and stumble into the lobby trying to look presentable. Ladies and gentlemen, Yanni and Linda Evans. By the time we got to our room we were wide awake.

The first time Linda came to stay with me in Los Angeles I was uncomfortable with how modest my home was compared to her mansion by the lake. I mean, she may have loved my music, but I didn't have a lot of material comforts to show for it. Linda didn't mind; she knew I put all my money back into my career. When she visited we rarely went out. A small place down the street delivered pizza and other wonderful meals. We ate off paper plates because no one wanted to do the dishes. To Linda's credit she never once complained about sleeping on my cheap mattress, about my mismatched towels, about doing laundry in the garage.

She even liked my crummy old car. One night we had to attend a black-tie function at the Beverly Hills Hotel. I knew everyone would show up in their Mercedes and their limousines, but Linda insisted we pull up in my ugly brown BMW. I was embarrassed but Linda didn't care. I think she wanted to teach me something. "So what?" she said. "It doesn't matter."

That night I met John Forsythe for the first time, as well as Linda's friends Mike and Mary Lou Connors—he was Mannix on TV. Linda had told me that Mike was really funny and very straightforward.

"I've heard a lot about you," he said. "I hear you're a swimmer."

"Yeah."

"What kind of swimming do you do?"

"I do the freestyle and butterfly."

"Butterfly, huh?" And without missing a beat he looked at Linda, smiled, and said, "Hey, he must be a great lay."

I wasn't about to deny it. Linda laughed her buns off.

I've always lived in the moment. Sometimes it was a little too in the moment for Linda. She'd never met anybody quite like me. She tends to be structured and likes to plan. If Linda asked me in the morning what I wanted for dinner that night, she'd be ready to go to the market, buy what we needed, cook, and serve it at a predetermined time. But I'd say, "It's morning. How would I know what I want for dinner?"

"Well, how do I buy it and cook it?" she'd ask, with just the tiniest bit of exasperation.

"We'll just see."

Maybe I drove her crazier than she let on, but Linda would take a deep breath and say, "I'd like to be more like you. I've got too much structure in my life. I want to relax more." Of course, I understood that come dinnertime I might not get anything, or not what I wanted because I wouldn't plan ahead.

By the way, Linda is a killer cook—actually, a killer *chef*. She works very hard at it. I started to gain weight.

Since breaking up with Sherry I had been afraid that if I was with any woman on a regular basis it might cause a conflict with my music. Until I met Linda I had not let anyone close enough to have to think seriously about the problem.

I'm very difficult to deal with, particularly when I write music, because as I had warned Linda, I go away mentally and physically. Music becomes God, and everything else is secondary, including a relationship. Including myself. My willingness to ignore my own basic needs like eating and sleeping and contact with the outside world—even love—pretty much justified my behavior. My parents would have liked me to come to Christmas dinner when they had visited some years before, but they understood my need to focus. When I went into the basement for three weeks and came out ten pounds lighter, my friends didn't think "creative person," they thought "he's weird," but soon they also accepted the process.

Linda was the first woman I'd met who didn't think it was weird when I went into my cave for a week.

Linda said, "Living in society is strange. What you do in your room with your creativity, that's not strange. That's real life."

I'd say, "Really? And you don't feel threatened by any of this?"

"No! Far from it: I'd like you to teach me how you get there."

Linda loved the music so much, she couldn't wait until I had a new song to play for her. She would say, "Go write it so I can hear it." Linda understood my creative process and was exactly who I needed to have with me in order to do what I did. She kept me straight and balanced; she inspired and encouraged me. Far from being bothered by it, she admired my ability to detach, even though she once told me it was scary as all get-out to be with someone who could completely turn off everything. She knew that my detachment allowed me to see more clearly, to create without judgment.

We talked about my role models: not just Beethoven and

Mozart, but Michelangelo, Leonardo da Vinci, Socrates. I admired the brilliance and longevity of their accomplishments. I also wanted to know how to reach great levels and move people. I knew that I wouldn't if I did only the minimum work required of me every day.

When you grow up in Greece you see ageless monuments everywhere you look. We still fuss over what the ancients created two thousand years ago. I thought, What could I make—it doesn't have to be music, it could be anything—that anyone would care about two thousand years from now? That question inspires respect, even for bad antiquities. Whatever the quality, it was a creation powerful enough to survive. I took that seriously. That meant a lot to me.

When I was in the studio, I thought only about the music. When I was with Linda, she was all I focused on. I didn't bring my briefcase to the beach, as they say. I didn't talk about work at the breakfast table. I didn't read the paper, either, or watch TV. Instead, we connected. We traveled, had fun being together wherever we were, and had serious discussions about creativity, philosophy, and life.

Passion defined us. We had great sex and a great love. We are both very affectionate. I held her hand all the time. We kissed often. We slept wrapped up in each other all the time. Every few days for us was Valentine's Day, and yet Linda didn't care whether or not I remembered an anniversary.

As for my previous romantic history, Linda seemed amazed that I wasn't jaded by my years on the road playing rock music.

LINDA: *Yanni told me all about his rock 'n' roll days, being admired and adored, having access to all the women he wanted. He also told me that he woke up one day and said, "Been there, done that. This isn't going to take me where I want to go." And he just stopped.*

Sometimes I thought about that after we'd been together, making love, and I'd ask him, "How can you be so innocent? How can you be such an innocent man after what you lived through?"

"Linda," he'd say, "it's just what I did; it's not who I am. It does not define me."

Linda discovered even more about me when we went to Greece to visit my parents. They adored her immediately, and the feeling was mutual. They were delighted that a strong, stable woman had finally come into my life. The wonder of it was that Linda's parents were alcoholics and she'd overcome a very tough childhood. She used to tell me that my parents were extraordinary in the way they'd allowed me to be me. More than once she said, "If I come back in another life, I'm going to be first in line for them as *my* parents. If you try to get them again, I'll beat the hell out of you. You're not getting them a second time."

"I could go to Greece and move in with them right now and be very happy," she says today.

In Kalamata, we swam often and walked all the time. One day we went into a field next to my house to photograph butterflies. I had been taking pictures of one in particular. Usually, they fly away, but for some reason this one let me get closer and closer. In fact, she wouldn't leave. I gave Linda the camera, I sat in the field, and I imagined this butterfly landing on my finger. I put out my hand and waited. She flew close, circled, then darted away. Then her mate came and they swirled together for two or three minutes. And yet I remained still until, as if she were mesmerized by me, the butterfly landed on my hand, just as I'd imagined. It was amazing. That fragile creature stole my heart, and the experience reaffirmed my belief that I could create the life I wanted.

In the afternoons, when everyone took naps, I would pull one of my father's books of Greek philosophy off the shelf and read to Linda. "Listen to what Socrates said . . ." I'd read the ancient Greek, then translate it into English. One I remember is when Socrates was asked by a younger student: "Tell me what is better: To get married and have children, or not?"

His answer was: "Whichever one you choose, you'll be sorry."

We both laughed.

I'd been with lots of women, but not in many long-term relationships. Linda had been married twice before and was far more experienced in that sense than I. She was together, intelligent, funny, witty, challenging, sexy, beautiful; she was a woman, not a girl; an adult, not a scared kid who relied on me for her well-being and her life. Yet we never really talked about marriage except to acknowledge that Linda didn't need to get married again, and that I didn't want to, as they jokingly say, "Make the same mistake once."

"Besides," I told her, "as far as I'm concerned we're already married. You're the only woman in my life. Signing a piece of paper is not necessary. I'm committed."

Eventually, the subject of children came up. I had thought about it long before and decided I didn't want any. Family and children are an extremely profound and consuming experience. You do that and guess what? You can't go in the direction that I headed. At least I didn't believe I could. I didn't want to have kids and then be one week in Japan, the next week in Russia, while the kids were home with the nanny, needing Mommy and Daddy. It

was tough enough for me to be so focused on my career in a relationship with a woman. Everyone needs attention, and kids
need lots more. You can't come home fried from the road, or
emerge from three weeks in the studio, and not want to talk to
them. After being raised by my father, I thought, If you're not
going to be a great father, don't do this to another human being.

And still . . . one night, Linda and I were lying in bed and I
said, "Linda, I'm thirty-five and you're forty-seven. Maybe you
want to have a child."

She didn't answer.

"I have the luxury of having children ten years from now if
I want to. But you don't. So . . ." And then, with absolute sincer-
ity, I said the words I never imagined I'd ever say, "I'd be more
than happy to have a child with you, if you choose."

She started crying.

LINDA: *I'd had this big dream during* Dynasty *about
having a baby that the press went crazy with. In truth, I
never really wanted to be an actress; I just wanted to have
a husband and a baby. For reasons of fate and life, it never
happened. Yanni knew that. And I knew when we met that
our relationship didn't necessarily have to be a forever
thing, and that if he wanted a wife and kids, that at my
age I was not the best choice he could make in a woman. He
said he didn't want children and that was that. But one
night, out of the blue, he made the offer and it just touched
my heart so much. Here was this man who was so freedom-
oriented and so independent, offering to tie himself up as
much as any man can. I cried and cried. I was just
stunned. I said I wanted to think about it. Then I realized
that his life was so full of going and coming and doing,
and that if I had a child, I'd be the kind of mother who*

Felitsa and Sotiri as newlyweds, strolling in Kalamata.

Mom and me.
What a smile.

Yanni: Live at
the Accordion.
(left to right)
Me, Anda,
Yorgo—and
the flocatta.
I was nine.

Barely 14 years old,
training even at night.

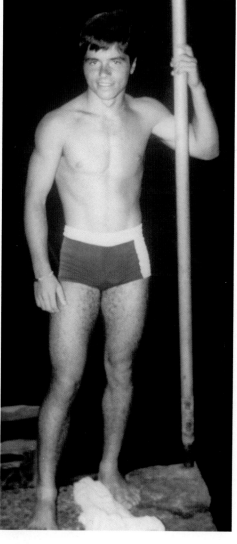

In Athens,
getting the cup
for breaking the
fifty-meter
freestyle Greek
national record.

Anda, 14½, and me,
16. Mr. Beefcake on
the beach.

The Cat Stevens years. Summer, 1974, in Kalamata.

Chameleon Days. Rock 'n' Roll. Need I say more? (*Joe Stafford*)

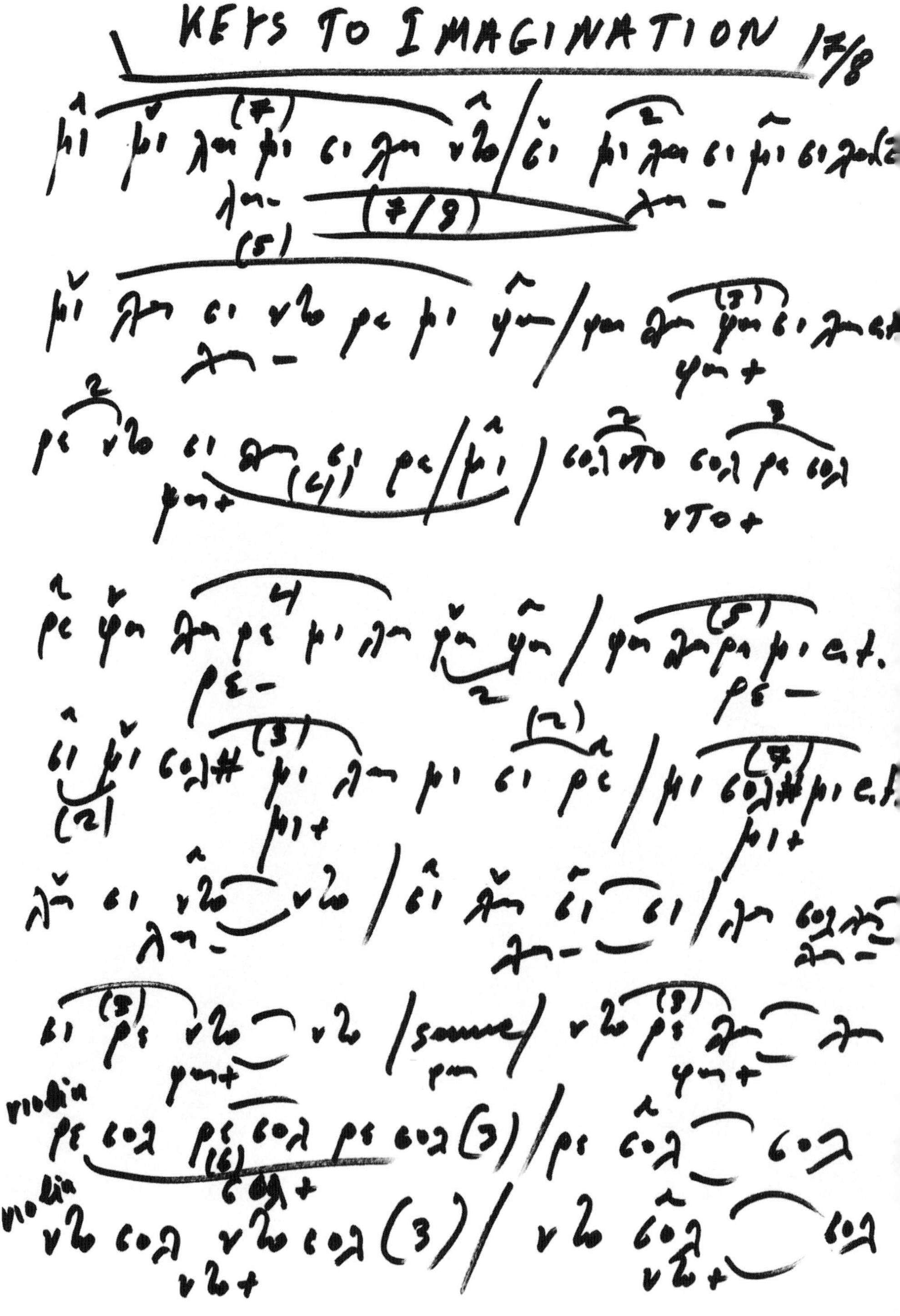

My musical shorthand.

The young couple in love, 1991.

Live at the Acropolis. (*Lynn Goldsmith*)

With my mom and dad, after the show, at the Acropolis. (*Lynn Goldsmith*)

Alone on the steps of the Herod Atticus Theater. (*Lynn Goldsmith*)

Yes, you too can be Yanni. Linda and me clowning
around before the Acropolis show. (*Lynn Goldsmith*)

Taiee and me. The bird that taught me the lessons of a lifetime. (*Linda Evans*)

Miss Butter and me. (*Linda Evans*)

The Taj Mahal. (*Kazuyuki Nagae*)

With Biptee Ram and the farmers, meeting the press. (*Kazuyuki Nagae*)

The Forbidden City. (*Degiang Ma*)

Dad and me on one of our many walks, Christmas 2001. (*Rogina*)

would be there with the child. I couldn't leave a child with
a nanny and go off with him, so I didn't know how we
would have a life together. I could have the dream of hav-
ing a child come true, but then I didn't know how I could
be with him. And I loved him so much.

Linda thought it over and said it was too late and that there were
too many things about herself she wanted to work on. I accepted
her decision.

Just as Linda gave me space to be myself, I gave her the same
space in return. I know it may seem from the way I speak about
her that she did not have a life apart from me, but that's not accurate. She'd already done Hollywood and walked away. Now
she had her school and her friends. Linda enjoyed the simplicity
of the life she had earned.

Linda is very spiritual and always on the lookout for ways
in which to improve herself. She would go on retreats with her
school and teachers for a month at a time. I wasn't into it, but I
wasn't threatened by it, either. I respectfully bowed out of
studying the metaphysical and she never tried to push her beliefs on me.

One of Linda's big goals was to reach higher levels of focus
and creativity. She'd say, "I've been going to school for six years
and I bust my ass. You just do this on your own, without anybody ever telling you, and you do it better than most of us in
school. How the heck did you arrive at this?"

I would explain, using music as a metaphor. I probably
didn't tell her anything she didn't already know, but it often
makes an impact when you hear your own wisdom in someone
else's words:

"If you *are* the music, you can write the music. If you're not the music, you're outside, judging it. Judgment and creativity are opposites. Both are valid, but they can't exist in the same place at the same time. To create, you have to become one with your creation and let it flow freely. You have to be in the zone. For me, I have to become one with the music. The instant I begin judging my creation, I find myself outside looking in, and the creative moment is gone."

Then I'd say it in another way: "Be the music. There's a truth to it. If you want to write music, you've got to be the song. If you have any thoughts about that song while you're writing it—if you say, 'That's a great song!' or 'That's a terrible song!'—you're outside; you've lost it. You're not in the creative moment anymore, you're an observer looking in. Now you can't create."

"But how do you learn to do that?" Linda would ask.

"How? By doing it wrong all the time," I'd say. "And doing it over and over again. Eventually you are just there with what you're creating. There's plenty of time for judging later."

After five years with Private Music, during which my record sales and concert attendance slowly yet steadily improved, I had the opportunity to make my dream of hearing my music played by a symphony orchestra come true.

The idea had always been in the back of my mind, but I'd never had the money to carry it off. I had to use a synthesizer to pretend there was a horn or string section in addition to my band, and it was very limiting. And I knew the dream could have a dangerous outcome. Acts like Emerson, Lake, and Palmer had tried touring with an orchestra and gone bust, canceling their shows. The highway was littered with people who had attempted to do what I longed to achieve.

In June 1990, a big radio station in Dallas sponsored a benefit concert to fight AIDS and invited me to appear with the Dallas Symphony. I jumped at the chance. It was a golden opportunity to test the water, to figure out how to work with all those musicians, and to master the technical aspects of arranging and amplifying an orchestra to make the music sound the way I heard it in my head.

I also wanted to film the show, otherwise my first experience would be just like any other concert. People might talk about it afterward, and maybe I'd get a good review in the paper, but so what? It would be dead forever. But I discovered that the cost of using only three or four cameras was prohibitive.

I called George Veras, a senior producer at CBS Sports. We'd been introduced a year earlier by John Tesh. I liked the way George had used my music on TV to open *CBS Sports Saturday* and *CBS Sports Sunday*. Other producers there had used music I'd written for the U.S. Open Tennis and the Tour de France broadcasts, the World Figure Skating Championships, and other on-air promotions. George and I hadn't met face-to-face, but we talked on the phone now and then, and as two Greeks in the entertainment business we hit it off immediately.

I said, "George, can you help me? I'm playing with the Dallas Symphony. I can't afford to film it. We're not looking for the best production on the planet, but I want a visual record of this concert. How can we do it?"

"We can videotape it," George said. "I've never done a music concert, but how hard could it be? I could get a truck and some lights, and we could figure it out." He even offered to direct. "It's gonna look great," he promised. "I can use the same guys who shoot the Dallas Cowboys games. Ten cameras."

"Ten cameras?" That set off alarms, but I told him to look into the cost. The next day he had an answer: "Forty grand."

"You got it," I said.

George asked why I'd picked him.

"Because everyone else wanted two hundred and fifty grand . . . and somehow I trust you."

Next, I went to Private Music to drum up moral support and a little money, bearing in mind Peter Baumann's mantra: "As soon as we know you have something, as soon as you have a hit in our hands, guy, we're going to put so much money into you it's going to really happen. All we need is the break."

This time I thought I finally had what he wanted. With great passion I explained my plan to play with the Dallas Symphony. "It's going to help me move beyond my New Age piano-player image," I said.

But instead of enthusiasm, Peter only had doubts. "Who is George Veras? This won't work. It's crazy to spend any money here." He passed.

I couldn't believe it. I wondered exactly what kind of break he'd meant: Somebody guaranteeing 8 million albums sold? No one can promise that. Peter was a good friend, but he also seemed like a scared kid whose pattern was to promise yes but always say no because he really didn't know what to do with me. I'd always thought that Peter knew more than I did—and maybe it was true—but if I let him talk me out of filming the show I'd be selling myself short.

I told Linda what Peter had done—or rather, not done. Linda was more than a lover and an inspiration, she was a mentor. A stabilizing and motivating force. She'd been in show business for many years and knew things that Tom and I didn't. I listened. Given the opening, a new side of Linda emerged. "Your record company is full of it," she said. As an actress who'd taken advantage of her own breaks, Linda understood opportunity when it came along. "You have twelve sets of balls. They have none. Everything doesn't have to make money right away. It's an investment. Your music will sound great with an orchestra; it should *always* be played that way. It's your calling."

What she said next surprised the hell out of me: "Go tell them I said they're a bunch of fools and I'll pay for it myself. I'd invest two million dollars in you tomorrow because I know I'm going to make my money back."

I knew Linda would have given me the few thousand I actually needed—though I'm not sure I'd have taken it. At least it was nice to know the money was there if I wanted it. It made me a bit bolder. I went back to Peter and said, "Linda thinks you guys are a bunch of fools and have no balls."

As Linda had probably figured, Peter was so insulted that he agreed to give me a little money to cover George Veras's fee.

The CBS truck showed up in Dallas and preparations began.

George Veras says that for him, "It was like a regular TV shoot. The interesting thing was meeting in the dressing room. I walked in and Yanni had his shirt off. He was wearing black pants, sitting on the couch, and smoking a cigarette. And there was Linda Evans, who I'd never met, showing him all these outfits. It was like walking into the middle of a marriage argument, or into the middle of Brent Mussberger and Phyllis George disagreeing over leads. Linda was saying, 'You need to wear this to look good.' Yanni said, 'I only perform in black. That's who I am. I'm a rock and roll guy, and that's all I wear.'

"I said, 'Hi, I'm George Veras.'"

I looked up and introduced George to Linda, who said,

"Maybe this guy knows what I'm talking about." She held up a black outfit and a white outfit. "What do you think?"

George said, "You know, Yanni, you do what you want to do. But what color is the stage?"

The stage was black.

"What color tuxedos does the orchestra wear?"

They wore black.

"Well, I'll tell you what," George said. "If you wear black when we shoot you, your head will look like a pimple on an elephant's ass. Now, if you want to do that, cool."

"Oh!" Linda said. "I like this guy!"

George said, "Why don't we do the first half of the rehearsal with you in black, and the second half in white? Then we'll come back and view the tapes, and decide then."

George is a cigar-chomping, straight-talking streetwise fighter from New York. He was also diplomatic. I liked him, too.

I'd never been shot before by a professional with a long lens camera and some lights behind me. Later, when I looked at myself on the monitor, I thought, White looks great! And I noticed something else: A white outfit changes color with the lights. It makes you look interesting. Black hair, white clothes, black backdrop. I was learning.

George had also put a light directly behind me. Every time I threw my head back, it lit up my hair, making it glisten through the beads of sweat. As we rolled the tape, the guys in the video truck said, "Holy shit! This is the money shot." George called it the Jesus shot. I don't know about that, but it looked good.

I've since gotten a lot of flack from the media for wearing white onstage. They keep looking for some mystical, spiritual significance. There is none. I did not want white. I lost that argument, but it was absolutely the right choice.

The show got a killer review in the *Dallas Morning News*. I was relieved, but I still thought we did a lousy job with the orchestra sound. I'd put the microphones as close as I could to the violins, but the musicians would get annoyed and push them out of the way. The best way to play with the sound would be to tear the orchestra apart and reconfigure everything—not that I could at the time. A microphone not only picks up the sound you want, but the sound around it. You have to isolate the instruments that make a lot of noise—drums and percussion; you don't want to put the trombones right next to the violins. A cello is very sensitive, so its microphone has to be even more sensitive. When you take an instrument that's meant to be heard acoustically, in a room, and amplify it to 110 decibels, it becomes a different instrument. Each instrument also has its own quirks and its way of being treated. I had to study each one and create a way to fasten a microphone to it, not to mention find the right microphone for that instrument, then run it through the console for its own special effects, equalizers, compressor limiters, and gates. Only then would I have a *sound*. It took me six years of trial and error to get it right. The result is an enormous power and range onstage. My concerts can be as gentle as a single violin or flute and as powerful as a full-on rock band.

When I was at Linda's house we spent a lot of time on the boat on Gravely Lake. She would drive while I water-skied, then we'd go out to the middle of the lake, turn off the engine, listen to music, and talk.

Linda liked to play my albums on the boat's cassette deck. Until I met her, I'd never been able to listen to my music with others around. I believe in it with all my heart, but I'm also shy about it. I want people to feel they can say, "Turn that stuff off and play something else." When I'm around they don't feel comfortable doing that.

One day, after Linda and I had been together less than a year, we took the boat out and put on a tape. The player had no auto-reverse; after twenty minutes it would stop and I had to flip it to the other side. I got fed up and said, "Why don't I just make us a cassette that will run forty-five minutes? Tell me which songs you like. What are your favorites?"

Linda was always very positive. Rather than say, "I don't like this song," she'd simply avoid playing it. But that day we listened to all five of my albums in one sitting. When she'd say, "Oh, I love that one," I'd write the name on a list.

Back in my studio I created an order for the songs she'd picked and put together her personal compilation. I brought the tape with me to Seattle the next time I visited. When she played it I realized that it didn't sound or feel like any of my albums. It was my music, but because of the selections and running order it had a very different sensibility.

Houseguests would say, "What is that?"

"It's a little tape I made."

"Hey, can I have a copy?"

I made a few duplicates for friends, but after about thirty I got tired. Instead, I went to Private Music and said they should release it. They said, "Yeah. Great idea." That's how *Reflections of Passion* was made. In fact, Private Music liked it so much they sprang for a music video also called *Reflections of Passion*.

THE PERFECT WOMAN

. . .

After the Dallas Symphony concert Linda and I kept talking about my frustration with Private Music. For five years I had been living in Los Angeles, with more people telling me more ways to get my music across than Greeks sitting in cafés drinking coffee beneath the stars. I sold more albums and played to bigger crowds than ever, and I'd finally worked with an orchestra, but it was all because of my efforts, not the record company's.

In other words, it was the same old story: I needed to find a way around my perceived limitations. I wrote contemporary instrumental music that everyone called New Age, and I was considered a much tougher sell, to a smaller and supposedly less accessible audience, than bands who wrote three-minute formula songs and got on MTV. I knew it was true, but that didn't make me feel any better—or any less ambitious.

Linda sympathized. She loved the music, and based on her experience as a much-adored public figure, she believed that I had an audience out there that the record company was missing.

"Great," I said. "But what do you know about the *music business?*" I asked.

"Nothing," she said. "But I still know a lot more than your record company. They have no clue."

"But I can't force them to spend money," I said. "Besides, maybe I'm not ready yet. I'm still developing. Peter says that in a few more years I'll mature and be ready."

Now it was Linda's turn to vent. "You'll mature into what? Peter just allows you to believe that he knows more than you. You've already done it! You wrote *Reflections of Passion.*" Linda thought that instead of finding clever ways around obstacles such as the New Age label, Peter was blowing me off, pacifying me.

"Your music is full of passion. When we do breathing exercises to it at the school, we end up screaming and driving energy into our heads because it gives us the feeling we can do anything. New Age music you fall asleep to."

She asked me again, "What are you going to mature into? What are you waiting for?"

The answer was rooted in conflict. Peter was my friend. We had dinner often. He'd helped me buy a house. He'd signed me, for goodness' sake. I was ambitious, competitive, and upset that opportunities had been missed and that things were taking so long, but I still trusted him. I believed in what he said despite evidence of his reluctance to take risks for me. I had a hard time admitting that maybe he was out of his depth.

Perhaps it would have been easier if, as a person in authority, Peter had been more like my Greek teachers: mostly inflexible. Hateful. Maybe then I'd have been more willing to insist on following my own instincts. Then, I knew I was boxed in. Now, I felt the same, but with less urgency because it was a nicer box. Bottom line: I could see the truth more clearly when I was twelve.

On the other hand, wallowing in negative emotions was a waste. To spend my time feeling resentful, fearful, and anxious—"Oh my God, I'm in my thirties, in the middle of Los Angeles: What are the chances I'll make it? They could drop my contract and I'd be living a nightmare, owning a house that I can't pay for, having to find a job . . ."—would just as likely cause me to fail.

The key was not to be a victim. I went inward and sat at the foot of my bed at night, running through everything in my head until the anger was gone. It's a deal I've made with myself that at the end of every day I must release, and relieve, and understand. It's a way of calming myself, reconciling everything, facing problems I may be having. Even when it's not necessary, I just sit quietly and allow thoughts to play. And I find it extremely relaxing; it's like you're in heaven. The stress goes, beauty appears. And then I can sleep.

When I'm in real trouble sometimes I'll stay up until five or six in the morning in a comfortable position on the floor next to the bed and allow my mind to fly without controlling it. I sit back and enjoy the movement. Eventually, if there's a problem, I find an appropriate course of action, and move on.

My way of handling the Private Music problem was to channel that frustration back into the music and keep doing good work, which I believed would eventually pay off. I was thirty-five, still young; many years of creativity lay before me. My most important job was to come out of the recording studio with music that was recognizably and uniquely me, whatever the cost.

Linda used to tease me about that attitude and remind me of a story my mother had told about how, when I was very little, she'd put me in my child seat and try to feed me, but I'd grab the spoon and say, *mono mu*, which means "by myself." True. I could be an independent little you-know-what. I took refuge in my faith in myself. "If I'm not discovered this year, I'll be discovered next year," I told Linda. "And if not next year, then the year after, and each year I will be better than the year before."

One afternoon Linda put dinner in the oven, set the timer, and went out on the lake with me to talk. She respected how I lived my life, and I respected how she lived hers. We had things we wanted to learn from each other and were never pushy. I knew it was in that spirit that she explained why she thought I had just been swimming in place, caught between blaming the water and buying Peter's story that I needed more practice to win the race.

The problem, she said, came down to one word: *Me*.

"Me?"

"Yes," she said. "You keep saying that someday, if you keep working hard, you'll be discovered and become famous. Well, don't worry; you will be. But you may be dead by then."

"What? No, thank you. I don't want to become like van Gogh, who died before anyone appreciated his art. 'The guy's dead now, but man, he was good!' I want to experience it. I wanted to connect now."

"If you do, then you've got to work as hard *at that* as you work at your music," Linda said. "If you want to be found, you've got to help yourself. There's no way around it. You can't just sit at home and say, 'Some day I'll be found' or 'It's the record company's job.' Maybe it is, but it isn't working. Now you have to actively seek to be found. Look at how famous I am or another celebrity is, and you'll know how much they *needed* to be famous."

"Sure," I said. "It would be great if more people heard of me, but I'm not going to kill myself doing it." Just as writing movie themes and commercials—even playing rock 'n' roll—had distracted me, I thought that becoming more involved in self-promotion would mean shortchanging the time I devoted to being creative. Without the music, no amount of marketing would make a difference.

Linda didn't buy it. She believed I'd reached the point where I already *had* the music and that without more of a push on my part I might as well accept being a niche artist and get on with life. My career, as it stood, was perfectly fine if that's what I wanted. She wouldn't love me any less if I was willing to just cruise along, my main responsibilities being to myself and the music, and the rest be damned.

Of course, the problem really went deeper, though at the time it was difficult to articulate. Simply put: I didn't like the place I was at, yet I was afraid to leave, because if everything Linda said I had to do worked, I feared the price of success.

Was that unusual? No. It's perhaps easier or more common to think of fearing failure—and I did; I'm vulnerable like any other human—but fear of success is just as real. Sometimes it's easier to love the dream than to live the reality.

For me, it came down to an apparent disconnect between my upbringing and my goals. I'm my father's son. He believed simplicity was the answer and had told me so many times. It seemed very black and white. As I now say in my concerts: "The greatest things in life—truth, creativity, imagination, love, kindness, compassion—are already inside us, and they're all free." Being happy with less is what makes a great human being, not a big house with marble floors, or everyone knowing who you are. Linda told me how she'd won five People's Choice awards and a Golden Globe, but that she'd also been in the back of a limo with her awards and been lonelier and more lost than ever.

I wanted success, but I saw it as tainted by distractions and misery. I didn't want to think too much about clothes, hair, makeup, and which morning show I was appearing on. I didn't want to need validation so badly that I'd hungrily show up at some overblown party and mug for the paparazzi. I didn't want to play the game and get lost in it. Once again I was like Ulysses who wanted to hear the Sirens' song but not crash on the rocks. It's great to have tempting and dangerous experiences, but the idea is to come out whole. And Linda knew it. She'd played the game. Then it struck me: She'd survived success. Perhaps I could, too.

"We'll see if you get caught in the game or not," Linda teased.

"I'm not gonna get caught," I insisted.

"Well, we'll see," she said, smiling. "I've felt it and it's pretty powerful. Very attractive, but full of hooks and danger. You're very clean and you could get hurt—but knowing you, you'll probably make it. We'll see."

We often had discussions about personal power and strength; we went deep into understanding one's self because, like me, Linda was very interested in psychology and philosophy. But I still wasn't certain if I had what it took to really play on the next level, and told her so.

"Remember when you broke the swimming record in Greece?" Linda asked.

"I did it, but so what?" I said. "That was a long time ago."

"No, no, no. You don't become swimming champion of your country by *accident*," she said. "Think: Where did you get that strength, where did you get that commitment?"

I'd asked myself those same questions once, but they hadn't crossed my mind in a long time. "I don't know. My arms were a little stronger, my heart was a little bigger, or maybe I just swam a little faster, got lucky. Had a quick day."

"There's no such thing as just lucky," she said. "You only swam in the ocean. You had no coach, no pool. Then you go up to Athens with all the Greek champions and you beat them? The *first time*? That's strength and power above and beyond your body and muscles.

"Something in your soul and mind forced you to overcome everything and succeed. You simply decided that you were going to break the national record. You decided you were going to beat everybody, and you did it. You did it mentally, not just physically. You believed it so much, you did it. You flew right over the water. Why don't you pull out that power again? Whatever that was, find it, wake it up, bring it out."

Linda's enthusiasm sent me soaring, and her certainty sent me even higher. "Yes, the recording industry is standing in your way," she continued. "And yes, your record company maybe doesn't get who you are and doesn't know how to sell you. But if you do it in your mind, then reality will have to conform."

"That's a very strong thought," I said. "A very tall order. Sure, sounds good. But how . . . ?"

"How did that little boy from Kalamata have the balls to do what he did?" she asked.

I got it suddenly. Faith was the engine. Passion was the fuel. This was not just philosophy; it was based on something that had really happened to me. Then I had wanted to win so badly, I would have done anything. Maybe it was the way my mother and father had managed to convince me that the sky's the limit.

Ever since I was a kid all I'd wanted was to be different. Mediocrity was death, unacceptable. Being fine and fitting in was unacceptable. I'd promised myself it would never happen to me, and something inside of me actually believed that I'd be that one-in-a-million person. Yet because I'd depended too much on Peter Baumann's good intentions, I'd paid the price for his fear and inexperience. I'd gone against my own instincts even when I could see things weren't happening. Nobody could believe in me the way I believed in myself.

I was through wondering if the problems were Peter's fault or my own unrealistic expectations, whether Private Music had messed me up or if I'd been stupid. It was pointless being mad at them for what they didn't do. I had to do it. I had to stop blaming and take back the power. I hated having any avenue of expression blocked—a result of my years in the Greek school system—but I was tired of falling back on the excuse of having been screwed, of being a victim. My swimming victory *had* meant something. My faith in myself then—innocent, unwilling to consider why things couldn't be done, certain that anything was possible—could be reawakened.

"Success happens in your mind," Linda said. "It doesn't

happen 'out there.' You've just got to accept it." It was advice I'd
have given anyone in the same situation. You make it happen.
You don't become famous accidentally. You become famous because you actively seek to become famous. It's hard work. It's a
full-time job.

"You have to get to the media," Linda said. "You have to actively seek to be on television. You have to go out and raise hell."

"What about you?" I asked. Linda worked for Clairol doing
Ultress commercials, but otherwise she was semiretired, on her
way out by choice. "If I do this I'm going to drag you right back
into the spotlight, just when you've gotten away from Hollywood. I feel bad about that. I can't do that."

"Look, I don't *need* you to be famous," she said. "I've been famous enough for both us. I know that if we do this and your career takes off, it will change things and take me back to a place
I've already left. But I don't care. It's nothing. This will be easy,
it will be sweet to watch you get your dream. It will be a joy to
do this for you."

And that's what it came down to. We never used each other,
and I would never have asked Linda to do any of it, but sometimes it seemed she had more faith in me than I did and an unlimited belief that people should know me. When I think back
on how much she *didn't* need this in her life, I realize how much
she loved me.

When we returned to the house, dinner had burned, but I'd
made a big decision. Linda had made me see there was a story to
my life, and it was time to write the next chapter.

8

———

PLAYING THE GAME

I'd always wanted to be discovered, of course, but I'd been very nonchalant about it, so it took a while to get comfortable with selling myself. Meanwhile, Linda, who didn't need to live a public life again—she would have been content, and it would have been easier, if I'd sold a few albums and she lived happily ever after with her young boyfriend, by the lake—knew how passionate I was about writing music, being onstage, and connecting with people, made getting me more exposure her new interest.

"Here's what we can do right away," she said. "Let's show up at the U.S. Open Tennis tournament." Linda had to go because Clairol was a sponsor, and she told me beforehand what to expect. "When we go in and out of the hotel there'll be forty guys with cameras, flashing in your face. Just smile and keep going. Everybody will ask, 'Who is this guy with Linda?' I'm sorry about all that, but it should be fine. And it's what we want."

I think there were more than forty photographers, but I didn't stop to count. "Linda, look over here!" they yelled. "Yanni! Let's have a picture together!" *Click-click-click,* and lights flashing in my face three hundred times a minute. Not even Linda could prepare me for that.

Paparazzi, by definition, are intrusive, and I had to learn to deal with them. Once, after a long flight, while having a cigarette outside the airport terminal, I looked up to see a guy standing twenty feet away, clicking off pictures. "Do you mind if I just smoke in private?" I asked. "I don't want you taking pictures of me with a cigarette."

"Not at all," he said. *Click-click-click.*

"Do you mind getting outta here?"

"I ain't leaving."

I took a deep breath and said, "Look, if I let you take some pictures, will you leave me alone?"

"Yeah. Sure."

At least I could put out the cigarette and stand against a nice background. "Okay, then let me stand over here. Take your pictures."

What could I do? Punch him? That's stupid. All they're trying to do is make a living. Ever since I understood that, I've had no trouble. Treat them nicely and they might give you a break one day when you need it most and not publish that picture of you with your finger up your nose. I say, "You guys okay? You got enough? Okay. Thanks. Bye." It's much better like that.

Linda talked about me on Regis Philbin's morning show, and then we decided to let *People* magazine do a cover story. I had no idea that publicity was so tough. It's easier to spend time in the recording studio than talk to the press. But Linda said it would change my life, and she was right. That story thrust me into the public eye. I was recognized almost everywhere I went.

I didn't love or hate every minute of it, but I discovered that my energy had been renewed. I had a goal, and it was getting closer.

Linda also knew clothes. I like jeans or drawstring pants and a T-shirt and was never comfortable in the outfits she came up with: wonderful suits, fine silk shirts, great pants, but I wore them anyway. Like a typical guy, I not only hated wearing this stuff but detested shopping for it. "Can we go home now?"

I listened to Linda about many things because she made a lot of sense and she never pushed me. She qualified everything by saying, "That's my opinion and you can listen to it if you want. You have great instincts." When I expressed them she was a great sounding board. A mirror.

Through it all, as a way of motivating me and, perhaps, pacifying me, Linda kept saying: "See success in your mind. See yourself on television. I know it's difficult, but *see* yourself there."

Thanks to Linda, in November 1990, my vision of being on *Oprah* became a reality.

Linda had been on the show many times, and Oprah wanted to know what she had been doing since *Dynasty*. She'd also read that Linda was in love with a younger man. Because Linda was hot and people wanted to know who the new man was, the topic of the show would be romance. Linda agreed to appear and suggested that I come also and play a song at the end of the segment.

"People are going to fall in love with you," Linda told me when the booking was confirmed. "They'll buy the album like crazy." Of course, we both knew the truth: If the music wasn't any good, who cares who Linda's boyfriend is?

LINDA: *The night before we went on the show Yanni was beside himself in the hotel room. He was so nervous. It was*

so much for him to go through. I think about how much he
learned later and how well he learned to do it, but this was
his first time out and he knew how important it was for
him. He was really scared.

On the show, Oprah started with Linda, who went over-
board. She talked me up immediately, saying, "He's so great and
so fantastic." They worked it up to a frenzy. Soon I was the
biggest thing since sliced bread, nothing short of an Incredible
Human Being. I sat backstage with a producer and said, "There's
no way I'm going out on that stage. *You* go out on that stage.
There's nobody that good!" My knees were buckling. What
could I possibly do at that point? I was finished.

The producer let my anxieties go in one ear and out the
other. "You'll talk first," he said, flatly. "We'll have a piano ready,
and if she asks you to play, you'll play a song. But keep it under
two minutes, m'kay?"

Then it was show time. Oprah called me out. I'd never been
on national television and I was petrified. It was nothing like being onstage. All the cameras and lights hit my face and I felt out
of control just knowing that millions of people were watching. I
sat there in a daze, trying to answer questions.

Then Oprah asked me to play. I did "In the Mirror," a song
I'd written about Linda because she had helped me see myself in
ways I couldn't. The song went on for more than my allotted
time, but to my surprise Oprah asked me to play out to commercial, and when we came back she asked me to play another song
that wasn't planned. She also said how much she loved *Reflections*
of Passion: "I have one in my car, one in my house, and I'm buying copies to send to my friends." I didn't expect any of that. The
show had turned into one big Yanni commercial.

"I told you so," Linda said afterward, with a big smile on

her face. "All they had to do was see who you are and hear your music."

Then a good friend of ours who was a buyer for a record distribution company called and said, "Yanni is exploding." The album was selling like hotcakes. In the next four weeks I sold three quarters of a million albums.

To be perfectly honest, it took me three months before I could watch a tape of the show, and I had to get bombed to do it. Linda watched when it aired and kept saying, "Come on, you've got to see it. You're not bad. You're pretty good, actually." But I hid.

Linda's efforts had given me a kick in the butt. To keep up the momentum, I hired Jeff Klein, Private Music's co-founder and former vice president of marketing and sales, to be part of my management team. He was a mover and a shaker, a ball of energy who had always believed in me. He went to work trying to capitalize on my good fortune.

Because *Reflections of Passion* began to sell so well, I started to pour more of my own money into my career to create the kind of sound I wanted. First, I held auditions and added a cello and three violins—real, not electric, because they're more emotional—to my band. Now the group was bass, drums, percussion, two keyboard players, a cellist, and three violinists. One of the violinists was the incredible Karen Briggs.

Karen showed up to try out and didn't do very well with the song I gave her, "Keys to Imagination." It's difficult, and as I listened I decided she wouldn't make the cut. But toward the end of her audition, I heard something in her sound and I had a hunch about her. I said, "How are you at improvising?"

"That's my main thing," she said.

Sometimes violin players need to warm up, so I asked her to improvise on "Within Attraction," a song in 7/8 time that originally didn't have violins at the end but had room for her to have fun. What she did made my jaw drop. Karen was very powerful. A volcano. I said, "Okay. Take the music home. Come back in two days and play the songs for me again." She did and I hired her.

On that tour, for the *Dare to Dream* album, I played again with the Dallas Symphony, and with orchestras in Minneapolis and Denver. I kept working hard to improve the sound quality and spent countless hours finding the right microphones and devising ways to connect them to the instruments. The shows did very well. Linda came with me and was, as always, fiercely protective. At one airport, she read a bad review of a show and just threw it in the garbage. "These people have sold out and they just want you to sell out, too."

Every artist has the possibility of doing something that strikes a chord. Some musicians have only one hit because they did something that became a catchphrase or intersected perfectly with the times. My career had not been that. My fortunes kept improving, a step up every year. Where my albums once sold 30,000 a year, they soon sold 300,000 a year, and then a million or more. Instead of 1,200 people at my concerts, there were 3,500, then 6,000, then 7,500, then 12,000. At the beginning of my career, I'd hear things like, "There are very few people who know who Yanni is, but the ones who have heard his music are fanatics. They come back every year, and bring friends."

Clearly that was true.

Something was going on. I would look out at the audience and be amazed and thrilled at its makeup. I'd see an eighteen-year-old kid dressed in a leather jacket. I'd know he'd driven his motorcycle to the show. Right next to him would be a grandmother. I'd be thinking, Halfway through the concert I'm going to lose one of those two; it will probably be Grandma when Charlie Adams does his seven-minute drum solo. To my surprise, both stayed, and Grandma stood to applaud Charlie, as well.

At Tom and George's urging, we edited the concert we'd filmed in Dallas into a one-hour show and sent it to PBS stations in cities where we toured. It hadn't been a phenomenal show, and the tape didn't look or sound the absolute best, but there were some brilliant moments and fantastic shots. It played in thirteen markets, mostly in the middle of the night, but two places, Indianapolis and Tampa, got surprisingly good results. That planted a seed in the mind of a man named Gustavo Sagastume, at the Tampa station, who would be of great help in the future.

Unfortunately, despite my career being kicked into high gear by my appearance on *Oprah*, Private Music still didn't jump in with significant support. I felt I'd given Peter the runaway hit he'd always talked about, but he didn't do much. This time, though, it wasn't that he didn't back me financially. Private Music and I were in a pitched battle of another sort. It had begun when, after selling so many copies of *Reflections of Passion*, I ended up with far less money than I expected. I couldn't figure out what had happened, so I hired some lawyers to look into it. What I discovered astounded me.

I'm about to explain a little bit about music publishing. If you get lost, I apologize in advance, but if you do, it helps make my point: I got lost, too; I didn't want to wade through pages of contractual details, which is how I got in trouble. I've made the information much simpler here, but you'll still get a taste of how I felt.

While it all depends on the individual contract, in general, a musician makes money from his record company in a couple of ways. For instance, Private Music paid $40,000 to sign me based on the demo for *Keys to Imagination*. That money was an advance against future earnings, as well as my budget from which to make the actual album. If recording costs are less than the advance, I keep the difference. If they cost more, I pay the overrun, unless I can convince the record company to advance more money.

When the album goes on sale, the artist collects a specific sum of money from the record company—it's called a royalty—for every copy sold. The royalty is usually, but not always, a percentage of the retail price. The amount depends on what the artist and his management can negotiate, which in turn depends on their leverage. Is the artist just starting out? Is he a huge star renegotiating an old deal? Is she changing record labels and getting a premium to do it? As the album sells (one hopes), the artist's royalties go to the record company to pay off the initial advance and any other costs the company managed to tag on the deal. When those debts are satisfied, the royalty goes to the artist for as long as the album sells. Have an album that sells millions, and you make lots of money. This is where I made my first mistake. My new lawyer told me that debut artists and garage bands got better royalty percentages than I had. I'd made a bad deal.

Then there's publishing income. It's more complicated, but very important. Publishing is split into two parts: mechanical and performance. The latter, which is the few cents you receive every time a song you wrote is performed live or played on the radio, and so on, is not important here.

Every song sold as a single or on an album is "published," and technically speaking it's licensed by the publisher to the record company for use. The record company pays a small fee per song, per album sold, to the publisher.

Let's say that fee is 10 cents per song. The publisher retains half, or 5 cents—the publishing share. The songwriter gets the other 5—the writer's share. If there are ten songs on an album the total cost to the record company (excluding other royalties) is $1 per album sold. If, like me, the artist writes all the songs, he splits that $1 per album with the song publisher. So, sell 100,000 albums, the record company pays the publisher $100,000. The publisher keeps $50,000, the songwriter gets $50,000. It's a good way to make a living, especially for song-writers without record deals who place their music on the albums of best-selling artists who don't write songs.

The best possible situation is to write and publish your own music and get all the money.

But often a new artist—even one who was smart enough to publish his own material—has to give away some of the pub-lisher's half (the songwriter's share can't be touched) to the record company as an inducement for them to make the deal. Call it another income stream for the label, to cover their risk by taking on the artist in the first place. Typically, this arrangement gives the record company 10, maybe 15 percent for "administering" the publishing. It can go higher depending on how naïve the artist is or how badly he wants to get signed. If you don't publish your own music, the label company can publish it through one of their subsidiary publishing companies. Or they might require it as part of the deal. There are lots of possibilities—too many to go into here. It depends on how much the artist and his manager know about these things.

When I signed my deal with Private Music, I kept my songwriter's share of the publishing pie and I thought I agreed to give the record company 50 percent (exorbitant, but I didn't know that) of my publishing half. In other words, of the total fee per song (call it 10 cents again), I got 7½ cents and they got 2½.

What my lawyers uncovered was that I'd given Private Music *all* the publishing half. I got 5 cents, they got 5 cents.

Whose fault was it? Mine. Like many artists new to the record business, I'd been incredibly stupid and naïve. I had always operated honorably, often on a handshake, and expected others to do the same. Instead of poring over my contract—it's a peculiar artist conceit: "I write the music, don't bother me with the details of a seventy-eight-page document"—Tom and I hired high-priced New York lawyers to negotiate the deal, *lawyers recommended by Private Music*, by the way. I think they did a lousy job.

Here's how. I signed my publishing deal *after* I signed my record contract. Instead of *having* to give away publishing income for a record deal, I actually had much more leverage than I thought. I was in a position to ask, "What's in it for me?" But I didn't read the fine print—or any of the print—and my lawyers, to whom I'd naïvely said, "I don't need the best deal; I don't want the worst. Get me in the ballpark," said, "This is a great deal. Take it!" I believed them.

When my new lawyer told me the news, he looked like a doctor who didn't want to tell me I had cancer. Then he gave me the *bad* news: I'd thought I'd signed a four-record deal, and that *Niki Nana* had fulfilled my obligation. Instead, the fine print said I'd actually signed up for *eight* albums.

Simply put, each of the four albums I'd promised to deliver had an option attached. It was pretty clever how they did it. *Keys to Imagination* was my first album. *Out of Silence*, which I thought was my second album, just fulfilled their option to take another album after the first. In other words, I had to do two albums to count it as one. Thus, my third album, *Chameleon Days*, was actually my second album, and *Niki Nana* was the option. *Reflections of Passion* and *Celebration of Life* were compilations, not new material, so they didn't count; that's standard. That left me owing two more albums, plus two more options.

When I delivered *Niki Nana* I thought I was finished. Tom

and I had always figured that if the relationship between me and Private Music didn't work out, they'd only be entitled to four albums and we'd move on. To be fair, Private Music had taken a chance by signing me. They had helped me move to Los Angeles and put me on a monthly retainer (to be paid back out of royalties) so I could buy groceries. Best of all, Peter was a good guy with whom I'd had a lot of fun. He'd become a friend. But because the record company had often been bigger on promises than on actual support, I wanted to look around at other companies, or at least from my position as Private Music's number-one act, renegotiate my contract. But when I found out that I owed four more albums, and my new lawyers explained why, I thought, No—that cannot be. I can't accept that. I hit the roof.

No wonder Peter had never brought up re-signing with the company. Why should he? He already had me. Boy, did he have me.

My fault again? Yes.

I felt stupid and betrayed. I'd been an idiot. How could I not have seen that? I was so angry that I went to Peter's house and confronted him. "Did you know about this?"

"Well . . . ," he said, "if you re-up with us, then we won't have to discuss the contract ever again."

"Yeah," I said, "but, did *you* know?"

I remember exactly what he said: "I know you *thought* you signed a contract for four albums."

"What is this crap?" I yelled. "Fix it! This is bullshit. How can you stand across from me and pretend you're my friend when you did that? And you've known from the *beginning*." But he wouldn't budge. I felt like punching him—and I used to deck people very well. For the first time I *knew* that Peter was not who he appeared to be. To think I'd been had by someone I'd considered a close friend made me very bitter. You see stuff like this in the movies or on TV but never think it's going to happen to you.

Peter *was* a bit of a schmuck, but I realize he wasn't evil, just scared. He wanted to protect himself against the day I might get big and leave him, the way so many musicians walk away from those who gave them their first break. But Peter was also the same guy who, when we ate dinner together, got bombed sometimes, and talked about life, and had said to me more than once—jokingly?—"I just don't want you to walk up to me one day and tell me I've been ripping you off."

Now he said, "I never thought we'd have to use this leverage with you, but it was insurance."

Unfortunately, because Peter was frightened, that day had come. It stretched into two years of hell, during which I tried to get back my publishing rights and leave the label.

It was a dreadful situation. I talked to Tom Paske, who had every right to be angry—and probably was—but as usual remained very calm. I depended on him for that. When the you-know-what hits the fan, I'd call Tom. Ninety-nine percent of the time it's the same Tom, and never a guy who says, "Whaddaya want? I just had a bad day."

When I'd complained, "I can't stand it!" Tom said, "Well, Yanni, what do you expect? He's afraid."

"Yeah. But he pretends he's my friend . . ."

After ranting to Tom for fifteen minutes I finally let it go. What was the point of stewing in my own toxic juices and killing myself? That would be a double loss: someone hurting me and me hurting me.

I also talked to Linda, who knew I had to go to a place inside myself I'd never been: I had to fight for myself against someone I cared for and loved and thought was my friend.

My eyes were opened, and a lot of my naïvete went out the window.

In 1992, in the middle of all this tension, I retreated into the studio and recorded *In My Time*. Ironically, this album of solo piano pieces is my gentlest work ever, and to this day it remains one of my favorites. Locking myself in the studio to write and record it was the only way I could hide from the acrimony. I turned off the fear. Music was my escape. My drug. It's why I'm not a drug addict, other than coffee—and cigarettes in the old days. I'd focus on the music, and the rest of the world and all my troubles would go away. Pain was my motivation, the album my refuge.

Often, Linda knew what my soul needed even before I did, especially when I was too lost in distractions to notice. One day, Linda decided to take me to meet a friend of hers named Bud. He lived on a farm an hour's drive north of Seattle and was licensed by the state to take care of wounded animals. He nursed them back to health and was able to release some back into the wild. He also took some to schools, to teach kids respect for all creatures.

One of Bud's charges was a golden eagle named Taiee. He had been shot in the wing and couldn't fly. Someone had found the bird in the forest and brought him in. The injured wing was gangrenous and much of it had to be amputated, leaving Taiee to spend ten years tethered to a tree stump by a long chain—for his own protection. He had once run off into the cold and snow and had almost died because he couldn't fly.

Linda had already visited Taiee, and she told me that no human being had ever affected her the way the eagle had. She said that the experience was so powerful that it had changed her life, and that if I had never seen a golden eagle up close, I should, because I would definitely benefit. I couldn't imagine what I could possibly learn. Okay, maybe the bird was cute, or beautiful, and it sounded like fun, but Linda said, "I can't wait for you to hold this bird."

Hold the bird?

"I can't wait until Taiee looks you right in the eyes."

"All right," I said. "Let's go see the bird."

She was so excited.

We drove her Jeep north to the farm. Bud showed us around and then introduced us to Taiee. Bud put on a glove made of quarter-inch-thick leather that extended almost up to his shoulder. Taiee's legs were tied with a leather strap.

Bud put his arm behind Taiee and coaxed the bird into stepping up on to the glove. Suddenly, Taiee let go and fell backward, but Bud held him, upside down, by the leather straps so he couldn't fall to the ground. I gasped. "What are you doing?" I said.

"Don't worry," Bud replied. "It doesn't hurt him." He grabbed Taiee from the back and righted him. The bird let go again and hung upside down. Bud pulled him back up.

"Leave the bird alone," I said.

"It's a game we play," Bud explained. "He's actually in charge. He won't stand on my arm until he wants to."

Taiee let go and fell again, and he and Bud repeated the game twelve or fifteen times, until at some point the bird stood on Bud's arm, which Bud had put into an armrest to handle the weight.

I took some pictures. As I got closer, Taiee looked at me and I stared back. Suddenly I could feel the power. His eyes scanned me like stop-animation. Side to side. Jumpy. His plumage, the colors and the detail, were spectacular: gray and white and brownish. I also noticed Taiee's talons. They were longer than my fingers. Eagles use their killing talon nail—the one in back—to grab prey. They can drive its point right into a fox's skull and crush it with awesome power. The more I looked at Taiee, the more his eyes asked me questions: "Who are you? What do you want here?"

Bud eventually set Taiee down on a rock. We walked away and talked for a while and then he said, "You've got to take him on your arm."

I've had pet birds—macaws—but Taiee was no pet.

"No, no. It's okay," I said. "I don't want to. Leave the bird alone. I came very close, looked him in the eye, took pictures. That's all."

He said, "No. Until he grabs your arm and you're holding him, you will not know."

"Do it," Linda urged.

I put on the leather glove and approached Taiee, who was still perched on the rock. "I'm sorry, buddy," I muttered. "Really, I'm sorry." I put out my arm—and the eagle walked right onto it and stood there, before I had a chance to clutch the leather straps attached to his feet. As I raised my arm to slide into the armrest, he never wavered or fell backward.

"He never does that," said Bud, stunned.

I stood there with Taiee. I realized he could feel my energy and sensed that I meant him no harm. He knew who I was and that I had respect for him. Can I prove it? No; there's no way. But I know. These animals are killers; they measure you up instinctively. They cut right through the crap, see right through to your soul, and know where you're coming from. This bird knew, and stepped onto my arm and sat there. Then he opened his one wing, wrapped it around me, and hugged me.

"I've been with him for ten years," said Bud, "and he never

did that with me. This bird doesn't trust anybody for anything for any reason."

Taiee got so comfortable with me that he tried to lift one of his legs. He kept tugging on the leather strap. I eventually let go, to see what he would do, and he perched. He stood on one leg, kept his wing around me, and relaxed. Linda took pictures.

I was thrilled. Honored. Linda said it was love at first sight—for both Taiee and me.

But what did it all mean? Here was one of the most powerful predators in the skies. He'd been shot and tied to a tree stump for ten years. If Taiee had been a man, would he still be who he used to be? Would he know his essence? Would he still act regal? Would he retain his self-respect? Put in Taiee's position, how much would any of us have changed?

The bird hadn't changed at all. He was still king. He was in charge, in control. His spirit wasn't broken. Taiee reminds me of great men like Gandhi and Nelson Mandela. You can put them in prison for years, and when they come out they're still Gandhi and Mandela, with their spirit intact. Now the lesson was clear: No matter what happens in life, never lose sight of who you are.

All of my songs are about that spirit.

I thought of how, when we're still young, we have all these great dreams, then society comes and slaps us in the face and suddenly most of us change our tune, abandon our dreams, get scared, forget who we are and what we wanted to do. But it doesn't have to be that way. We don't have to lose sight of ourselves, or sell out. I had sold out stupidly, thinking that somebody else knew more about what I do than I did. I'd gone against my instincts. I'd second-guessed myself into a corner.

I should have kept focused on the dreams I had when I was younger, when I believed in everything, before life started putting up roadblocks and walls, before people told me I couldn't do what I wanted to do. Those people had already sold out and couldn't stand the fact that I resisted. They said I'd be an old man with no money, needing help for the rest of my life. Why didn't I get a real job like everyone else? I'd come a long way on my vision of who I thought I was, and the eagle Taiee confirmed it.

On the way home I started to cry.

In the summer of 1992, in the midst of my problems with Private Music, Tom Paske and Tommy Sterling came to visit me during my vacation at my parents' home in Kalamata. They live on the bay. It's just gorgeous. The house hangs in the air so that when you're on the balcony, about seventy feet up, you can't see the ground and you're suspended over the water.

It was probably four in the morning. We sat on the deck looking at the Milky Way, talking about what we'd accomplished— and the future: That winter I would begin to tour America and play with a different orchestra in thirty-three cities. Then Tommy killed his cigarette and handed me a picture of the Herod Atticus Theater at the Acropolis, in Athens, that he'd cut out of a magazine. The Acropolis is not actually a building but a place that encompasses the Parthenon and other ancient structures.

"What about playing here?" he said.

"Yeah, yeah, yeah," I said. It's not like I hadn't thought of it. To perform at the Herod Atticus is the dream of every Greek composer or playwright or dancer. It means you've made it. But it's easier said than done. "Great place," I said, "but they don't just give it to anyone. They're very strict. The Bolshoi or Pavarotti, okay. Or maybe an ancient Greek tragedy."

I'd been there as a child. The theater was built around A.D. 100 by Herod Atticus, a Roman. When you walk in, you actually feel like you've traveled 2,000 years back in time. It hasn't been modernized; the facilities are minimal. But the theater is amazing. It can hold 7,000 people, yet it's very intimate. The seats go almost straight up in front of the stage; you feel like you can touch the audience. Plus, it's acoustically beautiful.

From the stage you can also see the Parthenon up the hill and to the right. When it's lit at night, it's awe-inspiring. I knew that with the right preparation the setting would make for a spectacular concert.

"It's really a nice idea," I told Tommy. "Someday we'll do it, but I don't think I can do it now. At least not right away."

I stood and stretched. The sun was coming up and I needed to get some sleep.

9

FOR THE GODS

In My Time was released with the record company's usual modest expectations. They'd have been happy to sell a couple hundred thousand copies. Instead, the album earned a Grammy nomination and has since sold over 2 million copies.

I spent the early part of 1993 on an American concert tour, playing with a different orchestra in each of thirty-three cities because it was more cost-effective than transporting my own ensemble from state to state. Although the shows fulfilled a long-time dream, frankly they were often pure torture. The schedule was grueling: Each day I'd rehearse for four hours in the afternoon with a new group, perform the concert that evening with musicians who had barely learned my music, sign autographs for an hour after the show, drive all night to the next city, give interviews the next morning, and start all over again with a new orchestra.

Most of the musicians were surprised by my material. They

thought it was going to be mellow New Age stuff. Some came in with an attitude like, "We're going to play some crap today and make some money." Others asked, "What is management doing sending us to play this stuff?" But those cynical smiles disappeared as soon as they saw the sheet music for songs like "Standing in Motion," "Nostalgia," and "Santorini," and the challenging nontraditional time signatures. I had to win them over, orchestra by orchestra, night by night, and many rose to the occasion. Their reward was the kind of ecstatic applause they rarely got playing classical music.

The experience was also an incredible training ground for me. I learned to understand an orchestra's personality, its attitudes, protocols, do's and don'ts. I had to learn how orchestras functioned, what made them tick, and how to anticipate their problems in order to get them to do what I needed.

To help promote the tour, Tom and George and I put together a thirty-second television commercial culled from the best video footage of the Dallas show we'd taped three years earlier. We discovered its potential almost immediately. Nederlander Concerts had booked me for a week at the George Gershwin Theater on Broadway, with a New York orchestra, but we'd sold only half the tickets before sales slowed to a trickle—maybe five a day. Jimmy Nederlander called me, freaked out. Even though buying TV ad time was expensive, and most everyone thought it wouldn't work, we tried the spot. We had no choice. We were up against the wall.

We ran the ad like crazy, and to our amazement sold out every show. From then on, we made whatever deals we had to with promoters in every city to get the ad on the air and keep it on the air. Even after the tickets were gone, we kept running it because the spot was a great way for people just to *see* me. It was a revelation. It was my MTV. Every time the ad ran, another person who thought I was a space case said, "That's Yanni?" and learned the truth.

Even before the tour started I'd made up my mind to find a way to play at the Acropolis and film and record the result. The idea was too tempting to pass up. Not only would the story of the hometown-boy-made-good returning to perform at this great monument be quite powerful, but if I could combine the lessons of making the Dallas video, the impact of our TV ad, and the experience I'd gained on the current orchestra tour—and set it against a backdrop that had once been at the center of civilization—the mixture of the music and the location would make an album and video explode with energy.

First, I settled my battle with Private Music.

My new lawyers advised compromise, but I'd had enough of the runaround and I told Peter Baumann, "Good-bye. I'm going to Greece. You want to sue me for the next four albums, okay, you can find me in Kalamata and sue me there. See how far you get. No way I'm giving you another album." Tom added, "He'll be there until the time on the contract"—seven years, standard under California law—"runs out."

Baumann couldn't have that. The seven years were about up, and Peter was in the middle of trying to sell the company to the worldwide music conglomerate BMG, which would certainly think twice if Private Music's best-selling artist wasn't included. Ultimately, he had to negotiate.

Here's what we did: I got a better royalty retroactively on my existing albums, with clauses stating that I'd get a boost when and if an album went gold or platinum (all eventually did), and I agreed to give them the albums *Dare to Dream* and *In My Time* to satisfy my obligation. Both were nominated for a Grammy.

I could have twisted arms and gotten a lot more, but I kept telling my lawyers, "I just want what's fair. I don't want to rip them off." The tables were turned. All of a sudden, life was really great.

Peter tried to redeem himself personally. He came to see me after a concert and simply gave me back half of my publishing rights, meaning our arrangement would be as I had originally intended. A couple of years later I had enough money to buy out his remaining percentage, as well as the whole publishing company, including its other properties. To his credit, he didn't try to rip me off by upping the price five or ten times. He could have. Peter knew how badly I wanted it.

Buying 23rd Street Publishing was one of the best investments I ever made. It's now worth twenty times what I paid for it.

Peter did what he did with the contract out of fear that I would leave him. The irony is that *he* sold Private Music to BMG and *I* stayed. He sold the publishing company and I bought it.

In the end, I had to forgive Peter and move on; that's the ultimate freedom. I don't know how anyone can live a life of hate, although I'm sure there are people around the planet who have been through wars and seen atrocities and violence and ugliness who could give me a million reasons. I don't deny their pain, but I still don't believe hatred is the answer. When you hate, you're enslaved. When you release your hate, you're free. But hate won't just disappear on its own; we have to choose to be free of it. Can we? I think so, one by one. I choose to be hopeful because it feels good and does good. Maybe I'm naïve, but I can't wake up in the morning as a pessimist and still get out of bed. Peter and I wiped the slate clean and I was a free agent.

I called George Veras. "Do you know the Herod Atticus Theater?" I asked.

"Yeah. I used to go to it when I was a kid."

"I'm thinking about playing there with the Greek National Symphony Orchestra," I explained. "Can you go to Athens and check out the TV station? I want to use their broadcast equipment to save money."

"I'll check it out," George said, "but I don't think it will work because their equipment is not so great."

In March 1993 George visited ERT, Greece's national TV station in Athens. He also surveyed the Herod Atticus Theater, made a drawing with camera positions, and consulted a lighting director he'd used at ESPN. "I hate to tell you this," George reported, "but not only won't the station's equipment work, but these guys don't have enough experience to light and shoot."

Again, the question that had begun our relationship: "Well, how can we do it?"

George had once subcontracted equipment from a British guy, Joe French, and he said he'd ask for an estimate. Joe said the whole package, including importing everything from England, would be $200,000. It wasn't easy getting stuff into Greece in those days, and nobody had ever done big-time TV there, but I meant to try. George began to sketch out a budget.

I called Tom:

"I've got something for you to think about," I said.
"Okay."

"The Acropolis."

Silence.

"We were talking about playing there. Remember? Last August in Greece. Tommy Sterling had the photo."

"Yeah."

"I've been talking to George. If we play there he can tape it. We do it in September, right after the U.S. tour. We'll have the band together, and the crew. We can use the Greek National Orchestra."

"I know it can be done, Yanni, but what do you get out of it?"

"We get a live album with an orchestra and a video for TV."

"You've got a point there."

"Look Tom, here's how it is. I'm not getting played on the radio. I don't fit anybody's format. MTV ain't interested, and the press only sees me as Linda's boyfriend. If we get a one-hour TV show, we bypass all of them. We get directly to the public."

"Who's gonna air it?"

"I don't know. Seven or eight PBS stations played the Dallas Symphony video. I'm hottest in those cities. Maybe more will play this because it will be better. Maybe even a network. George thinks we could do it."

"When does George ever *not* think we can do it?"

"Just think about it. Is it crazy?"

"I'll think about it."

"But is it crazy?"

"I'll think about it."

The next night I called Tom again.

"What's going on? I hear you talked to George," I said.

"Yup. You guys are really psyching yourselves up on this Acropolis thing."

"Well, we're kind of on a roll. You always said it's easier to keep feeding the flame a little rather than have it go out and have to start it up again. Let me ask you this. How much money do I have?"

"One million and sixty thousand."

"What do you think it would cost?"

"I guess about three hundred grand. Maybe three-fifty. And another fifty just to keep it together during August and September. Maybe four hundred grand, tops."

"Let's say five hundred . . . I think it's worth it."

"Well, it's TV, man. It's worth it if the tape gets on the air. Otherwise it's a half-million-dollar home movie."

"If we're ever gonna do it, now's the time."

"I know: Feed the flame."

"What do you think?"

"I think you decided to do it before you ever called. We're just looking for reasons."

"Schopenhauer."

"Later, Yanni."

The next step was to make an advance TV deal. George took the Dallas tape and our commercial spot to Encore, to pay-per-view outfits, and elsewhere, only to have the door slammed in his face. Only Gustavo Sagastume in Tampa—he'd loved the Dallas show—was supportive. "I can't guarantee you a sale," he said, "but I *can* put it in front of the PBS convention that decides which shows to use on the pledge drives. They make the final decision."

Gustavo explained that PBS picked twenty-eight shows on the basis of which ones they thought would bring in the most pledge money, and the programmers decided which shows got the best distribution during the pledge drive. WEDU in Tampa would sponsor us, and give us $60,000 *after the show was done, if it got picked,* but couldn't promise which stations would use it.

Even so, PBS was a great venue. If the show made it on and did well, it would get multiple airings. And there were more than 300 PBS stations.

I sent George to Los Angeles to meet with Private Music. Although we no longer had an official relationship, it's not so easy to leave a record company. There are strings attached, both practical—they still sold my records—and emotional. They knew me. I thought they might be interested in the project. I also didn't have the time or the inclination to go label shopping, and even if I had, there was no guarantee that another record company, where I'd have to start from scratch and light a new flame, would be any better.

George had the budget and the potential PBS sale in hand. "Let's see if they'll help us," I said. Guess what? We were stonewalled with the same old arguments. "You're crazy. It'll never work. Nobody knows Yanni in Greece. Hometown boy *there* means nothing in the United States. George doesn't direct music shows. Who cares if PBS plays it? Why are you encouraging Yanni to do this? You guys are going to get your asses kicked."

George came back from the meeting and said, "They were fine, but they're not going to help. They're not going to give you a dime, unfortunately."

What he'd said to our lawyer, Jody Graham, who was also there, was a little more honest: "I don't ever want to talk to these assholes again."

. . .

I decided to go ahead on my own. That's the absolute ballsiest decision I've ever made.

I flew to Greece in April to secure the Herod Atticus Theater. Andy Christo, from Royal Olympic Cruise Lines, whom I'd met through a mutual friend at the Greek Consulate in Los Angeles, had connections to Andreas Potamianos, a sweetheart of a man who owned Royal Olympic. He's like an Onassis in Greece, and is also president of the Greek Cruise Ship Owners Association. Andy told me that Mr. Potamianos wanted to help me set up the Acropolis concert. I thought that was very gracious. He had often invited Linda and me to his yacht; probably not because of me, but because of Linda. *Dynasty* played all over the world, and the Greeks knew Linda more than they knew Yanni. We always politely declined. In those years I went home to see my mom and dad, not to run around to islands with the jet set. Ironically, Mr. Potamianos appreciated my refusal. He later told me, "I think you have a lot of character to choose to stay with your parents."

I thanked Andy for his offer. I thought I could take care of everything myself, but I said I'd be happy to meet with Mr. Potamianos. But first, my friend Fotis Tritsis was ready to guide me through the government bureaucracy, which included the Ministry of Culture, the Archaeological Society, and others—all of whom also knew a lot about my girlfriend and almost nothing about me, except that I was Greek and a musician.

At one point we met with Theodoros Kassimis, the minister of tourism. He said, "Sure. We can arrange for you to have the theater." We shook hands. "Come in later for the details," he said. "But I will block the dates."

A few days later, I met with Mr. Potamianos at his office at

Piraeus, a port of Athens, to thank him for his interest and to tell him I had taken care of everything. Mr. Potamianos ushered me into his office. He was in his late fifties, a small-built man with white hair and a sweet face. I knew he could be tough when needed, but he acted very gently toward me.

"How are you, Mr. Chryssomallis?"

"Fine."

"How are you doing with the concert?"

"Thank you for your interest," I said. "That's why I came here: to tell you I don't really need your help. I think we're okay. I appreciate your even thinking of helping me because I realize this is not your profession." I saw a smirk on his face. He knew Greece and its famous red tape.

"Who gave you permission?" he asked, and I told him the story. "Well, if you don't mind, let me call the theater and confirm that the dates were booked."

Mr. Potamianos called a friend of his at theater operations. "Mr. Chryssomallis, yes. On the twenty-third and twenty-fourth. Right. Do you have his name on the calendar? Well, put him on the calendar. No, no, take that name off. Mr. Chryssomallis, on the calendar, now." He turned to me and said, "How many days do you want?"

I was shocked. I thought I already had two days, but figured what the hell. "Three, and one rehearsal," I said.

"So. September twenty-two, twenty-three, twenty-four, twenty-five will be good enough?"

"Yes," I said.

Into the phone Mr. Potamianos said, "Okay. Mr. Chrysomallis's name will be on the calendar for the twenty-second, -third, -fourth, and -fifth. You'll write that down? Good." He hung up.

That was my first big lesson about dealing with the Greek

bureaucracy. I had slipped through the cracks. I understood; arrangements took time. Bureaucracy moved slowly, but I needed the site quickly. Mr. Potamianos was used to this. Being a bottom-line professional, he realized that my concerts would be great for Greece. Eventually the Ministry of Culture and the Archaeological Society agreed, too.

Once I had the theater, I needed a concert promoter. The promoter is the middle man; he guarantees the performer a minimum fee against a percentage of the ticket sales. As long as the concert goes on, he has to pay the guarantee, whatever the gate receipts. If it sells out, everyone does well. He also sets up the advertising, gets tickets printed, and collects the money. In the end you split the risks: He has his costs, and the performer has to pay for the musicians, the trucks, and the rehearsal time, and so on.

The first promoter just flaked, so I fired him. I hired a second promoter, but when the time came to get the guarantee money— May first—he didn't send it. He kept not sending it, and soon it was July. I finally said, "You have one week to make the deposit or we're off." Of course he didn't do it; I fired him, too.

By then I was back in the United States and on the road, playing with one pickup orchestra after another, and burning out. At my last concert, in July, George Veras caught up with me in Cleveland, where he was visiting his in-laws. He remembers, "Yanni was slumped over. I thought, How in the hell is this guy going to perform a TV show in seven weeks? He looked terrible. He was completely exhausted."

Here's why: I'd just finished a five-hour rehearsal with the orchestra. I had one hour before doing a two-and-a-half-hour show. I had done thirty-two shows like that. I said, "I can't talk to you. I'd like to talk to you about what we're doing, but I can't."

George left.

The minute the tour finished I went to Greece to rest at my parents' house. It had become a tradition for me to go every year in August and hang out. I'd imagine the future and the chances I planned to take, accept that it would be really hard, and get ready for the struggle. It was also a way of taking a month each year to eat good food, swim, and get rid of stress and write some music. Then I'd come back to America and get hit all over again.

This time it was a little different. For some reason I felt more like a child again, the way it was when I actually *lived* with my mom and dad. As strong as I often had to be, I'm also human; I get scared and fear failure just like everyone else. Linda liked to tell me that I had tremendous stress because my dreams were so big. She also said that once I decide to do something, it is very hard for life not to give it to me. Like my mother when she prays, I'm very persistent. This time I realized I not only had to pull off the concert, but had to deliver a performance the whole country deemed worthy of the Acropolis. If I didn't embarrass myself and the family and everybody who'd be there— friends, relatives, former schoolmates, and anyone who wanted to see what I'd been doing for twenty years—I believed it would mean that I'd grown up in a significant way.

After Mr. Potamianos's help, I had moved full speed ahead with the concert plans. But without a record company's support or the promoter's advance, I had to spend my own money. Fortunately, I wasn't exactly poor anymore. A deal for the equipment had been signed. George had paid the deposit on the control truck. He and the lighting director had surveyed the site. We had travel and other production expenses. I had also been promised Greece's National Symphony Orchestra, and I signed a contract for rehearsal space.

Linda was about to join me in Greece. I spoke to her on the phone before she left and shared my exasperation about navigating the system. "You're back home," she explained. "People who go back home are reminded of all the old stuff. This is like Superman with Kryptonite. You're in the fire of your past; little Yanni Chryssomallis, the kid from Kalamata, frustrated at what he can't do. All the garbage with the schools, with feeling powerless, with being angry. All these anxieties were programmed into you as a kid, and this is your whole childhood coming back for you to own. Authority figures are in your face again and you're feeling like a victim."

With all due respect, I thought Linda was being overly dramatic, but I urged her to continue.

"Your problems with Peter Baumann were a baby test for these concerts," she said. "This is your moment. Your moment is, 'I have what I want. It's mine. Nobody stops me.' If you hold on to that and don't get emotional, you will make it happen. You're up against all the madness and you have to hold on to your dream."

I agreed with that. Succeeding in Greece would be critical to who I became and what I did in the future. Who knows what emotions were waiting to surface as the project continued. But I didn't care. I was ready to fight through them all.

By the time Linda arrived I was spending most of my days downstairs at my parents' house on the phone, talking to people in Athens, trying to get things straightened out. Unfortunately, in Greece you can't really do much of that over the phone. Plus, the country shuts down in August. At one point I realized we could book fifty shows in fifty different cities in the United States for less trouble than it took to do three shows at the Acropolis. I started to feel like all my advance work had been meaningless.

I knew I had to go to Athens.

I called Fotis Tritsis again. His uncle was a former mayor of Athens, and he and I had remained friendly since he'd introduced me around. He took putting on the concerts personally. Fotis is very strong and bullheaded and knows how to handle politicians. He's a fixer. He has an attitude. He gets things done.

He said, "Look, I'm going to try to have the government put on the shows. Then they'll be invested."

We went back to Kassimis, the minister of tourism. He clearly wanted the concerts to happen. We said, "Why don't you, the Ministry of Tourism, be the promoter?"

Kassimis agreed enthusiastically and guaranteed me $300,000 for the three nights—and this time he meant it. (Later, when the government fell and he was on the campaign trail, he continued to fight for me even though he hardly had the time.) It wasn't a whole lot of money, but at that point I'd sunk too much of my own savings into the project to make a decent profit from the ticket sales. I had to do whatever it took to produce a great album and video.

With the government on board, the situation began to brighten. Perhaps tickets would soon be printed and we could even advertise the shows.

As usual, I had a surprise coming. To print the tickets I needed five signatures. First Kassimis's secretary had to sign a paper to start the process. Unlike the minister himself, who is appointed and can lose his job when the government changes, the secretary is a lifelong bureaucrat. For some reason, I couldn't get this man to pick up his pen so we could get moving. Something was going on that I didn't quite get. Later I found out that the government itself was about to fall, and while Kassimis was on the campaign trail, his subordinates, the ones who *live* in the Ministry of Tourism, were starting not to listen to him—just in case a new government was formed and Kassimis didn't come back. No one wanted to be caught making the wrong move and being held responsible by the new guy, so I got caught in a political game.

Other problems also surfaced. In return for the rights to broadcast the concert live, one of the major TV stations had promised twenty or thirty spots advertising the show. But the day I gave them our commercial to play on the air, they said, "We don't have a deal. Get out of here."

I knew that I couldn't show my anger, so I walked away, a cool customer. If you're not cool, you're dead. Then I heard through mutual friends that the people at the station had said, "Now we've got Yanni against the wall. Now Yanni will pay."

As expected, they called back and said, "We'll broadcast the concert, but we won't pay you, and we won't give you any spots."

I nearly pulled out my hair wondering if somebody was actually *trying* to sabotage me. I couldn't figure out why, when all I wanted to do was a show.

As costs mounted, Tom Paske realized I had spent nearly all of my money except for the few thousand I sent each year to support my parents. He said that our accountant, Diane Kramer, a sweet, scrupulously honest woman who I trusted completely—she even did my taxes for free when I started out, because I was so poor—sobbed every time she had to make out another check.

I called my dad and told him the whole story, though I tried not to complain, because most everybody in Greece complains.

"It's going to be very expensive," I said. "I don't have any backing, and I'm going to use a lot of the money I've just made, maybe even what I send to you. Should I do it?"

My father is a great judge of character and situations.

"I've told you about Greece," he said, "and now you're finding out. You left here very young, so you don't know how things really work. But you don't have a choice. You've got to continue and do the shows."

"Yeah, but we're also having a little problem because the station flaked out on their deal to play my commercial," I explained. "Now I have no way of advertising the show. How am I going to sell tickets?"

"Don't worry," he said. "The Greeks love you. You'll sell out all three shows."

"How can you be so sure?"

"Because I know the Greeks love you."

I didn't know if they loved me, but I did know that word of the concerts had leaked out months before and the people seemed interested. "All right, Dad," I said. "Thanks." I was reassured. A little.

As with any country, Greece is a land of contrasts. There's beauty and ugliness. Harmony and conflict. Attachment to the past, hope for the future. Yet Greece is an amazing place. Gusto for life is part of the national character. The people are hospitable. They may not have a lot, but they know how to make the most of what they have. There's an old saying that applies to the Greeks: They live a richer life than the money in their wallets can buy. From cabdriver to garbage collector to ministry official to professional, everyone is a king.

Abroad, Greeks tend to be very successful, yet at home there are many problems. Life in that society can kick your butt. The system, as set up, sometimes doesn't function very well. Greece, it's safe to say, is going through a period of adjustment and transition. In my opinion, it's time for Greeks to accept responsibility for past mistakes and believe in themselves again. It's time for the country to begin seeing itself as a modern nation and member of the European community.

I absolutely adore Greece, and I'm proud of my heritage. Part of the problem I had setting up the Acropolis concerts is that I was still an unknown quantity. I am Greek, but that didn't give me a free pass. I'd been gone so long that my own countrymen didn't know me or what I believed in. Still, I knew I was honoring my country, not only with my intentions but with what I'd already accomplished. And if some little kid from Kalamata can do it, then anybody can. I just hope that the kids growing up there today will have the same thirst for achievement that I did, because that's the only way significant changes will be made.

In Athens, I lived in my hotel room and spent every day on my two phone lines—often at the same time—playing production manager, fireman, diplomat, artist. I never got a full night's sleep because I was always up calling America at 3 A.M. Athens time. I smoked like you wouldn't believe, and probably ignored Linda more than I'd *like* to believe. Yet she was a great woman to have around. When I went to bed with her at night, she never whined, "You're dragging me to all this and . . . how long is this gonna go on for? My friends are telling me . . . and now I'm sitting here in goddamn Athens. What the hell?"

I needed her support. A few weeks before the shows I got the news that Greece's National Symphony Orchestra couldn't play the dates. I couldn't believe it. I'd had my heart set on being a Greek in Greece using Greek musicians to show the world the kind of talent that exists in the country. Suddenly, I had to scramble again. I only began to breathe easier when I found out about an orchestra available in Piraeus. I sent my conductor, Shardad Rohani, to work with them. I called George Veras, relieved, and we took a moment to think about the future. "Shardad knows a guy in London named Siegel who's the agent for all five orchestras there," I said. "I'm thinking about doing a European tour. Not this year, but next year."

George was on his way to Oslo for CBS. "I'll stop by in London and meet the guy if you want me to. I'll give him a tape of Dallas and my phone number."

Shardad returned from his first rehearsal shaking his head. "I have bad news for you. I cannot work with this orchestra. You cannot play with them."

"What do you mean?"

"Their instruments are not up to par," he said. "They were arguing with each other during the rehearsal. They're not at the level that we need."

"Shardad," I pleaded. "You've played with every cockamamie orchestra in America, good, bad, and indifferent, and made it work. You're a great conductor."

"They're not ready," he said. "They're not even *near* ready. You cannot work with them. It's impossible."

Suddenly, I didn't have a symphony orchestra again.

Linda tried to keep me straight. "Don't get disappointed," she said. "Keep your eyes on the ball. You're doing great."

For once, I wasn't having it, and I let her know. "I'm doing great? I fired two promoters. I don't have an orchestra. It's less than twenty days before the show. After six months of preparation all I have is air. Meanwhile, the newspapers are going crazy about 'our Yanni' coming to the Acropolis, eight to ten million people know about the show—but we still don't have tickets. My deal with the television station for the only advertising I could hope for has fallen through. What do I have? I ain't got nothing."

I was really scared. Losing the second orchestra was a serious blow, perhaps the final blow. I could deal with a bad promoter and inept government officials. I could deal with almost anything except doing a concert without musicians to play the music. And I knew it would be next to impossible to find a good orchestra in three weeks, not to mention fly them in, put them up, and still have enough time to rehearse. Symphony orchestras don't just sit around doing nothing, waiting for your phone call a few weeks before a show. You've got to book them a year in advance.

Success seemed impossible, and just to keep going I had to force myself to remember that I thrived on the seemingly impossible. What do you have to lose? If you fail, it was impossible anyway. Besides, I'd always managed to get people to try the impossible with me because they knew that my vision was strong; nothing could stop me. Once I engage, I'm like a Spartan: I don't back off.

And yet had I known what a hornet's nest playing at the Acropolis would be, I wonder if I'd have even tried to do the shows. Many times I considered pulling out but didn't—not because of the money I'd lose, but because of the embarrassment I'd cause my family. I also didn't want to air my frustrations about the system or some of the officials. I'd made a point of avoiding that. On TV I'd tell people, "Keep your chin up. I know life is difficult here and I know the opportunities are tight. But stop complaining and fix your country. It's yours. You can do it."

But inside I felt like I'd built a sand castle right next to the ocean. You build it, then a wave comes and washes half of it away. You say, "No, it's like this," and you build it again. Then the water comes and washes part of it away again. You say, "No, I *told* you: It's like this." At times it seemed to me that the whole castle had been swept out to sea, and I was running out of sand. But I believed that if I persisted, eventually the ocean would go around the sand castle, and let my creation be.

I even started praying a lot, in my own way. Sometimes I'd wake up and stare out the hotel room window at the Parthenon in the distance, thinking of the twelve gods of Greece for whom the Acropolis was built. I'd say, "You guys brought me here. Don't let this happen. I cannot believe you brought me all the way here just to fail."

Beyond just being able to do the show, my biggest concern was to present something at the Herod Atticus Theater that the Greeks deemed appropriate. I would be attracting attention to a structure built for that very purpose: *to attract attention.* The Acropolis is the jewel of Greek culture. The ancients must have built it to remain in the consciousness of the planet forever, otherwise they'd just have gone swimming or eaten more olives. The Greeks take it very seriously. It's not the local movie theater. You have to hold yourself up high. I can see why they never would allow rock 'n' roll bands to play there. I didn't want to read reviews of the first show that said, "This is sacrilege. Why did we let these guys put up lights? This ain't no disco."

Instead of sitting around going "Poor me," I found my

spot on the floor at the end of the hotel bed late at night and let the fear and frustration engulf me until it faded away and left me asking the only important question: How am I going to fix this?

I called George Veras first. George has a lot of faith in me and his work ethic is amazing. He's a doer. He has tremendous, unending energy. Nothing is too big for him. There's no panic, there's no disappearing act. There's only action. I'm a workaholic and he's probably the only other person I work with who gives me a run for my money.

George said, "We'll find an orchestra. You take that half of the planet, and I'll take the other half. Let's talk in a few hours."

George said he'd call the Los Angeles and New York Philharmonic orchestras first, and he'd phone everywhere else in the country as well. I called all around Europe: Vienna, Budapest, Zagreb. I remember wondering, What's the area code for Bulgaria? The Zagreb Symphony Orchestra was close by and, to my surprise, ready to come. But before I made the deal, George called with a lucky break. He'd phoned Siegel in London to see if any of his five orchestras were available.

At first Siegel had laughed and said they didn't play my kind of music, but George said, "Look, I don't have time. Do you have an orchestra? Can they come? I'll have Tom Paske call you if you do."

To George's surprise Siegel said, "The Royal Philharmonic is available."

The Royal Philharmonic?! "I'll have Tom call you," George said.

George phoned me while I had the Zagreb Symphony on the line. He laid out the situation. I turned to Linda.

"Should we spend the money to bring in the Royal Philharmonic from London, or get somebody cheaper?"

"Don't even think about it," she said. "Get the Royal Philharmonic."

"Well, it's two hundred grand, Linda," I said. "Plus airfares. I don't know."

"It doesn't matter," she said. "How does this sound on the album cover: 'Yanni with the Local Symphony'?"

The Zagreb Symphony was very disappointed when I turned them down, but when you can get London's Royal Philharmonic . . . I made the deal with Siegel. Next, I had to get sixty people to Athens, not to mention my own band: my old friend Charlie Adams on drums, Karen Briggs on violin, Michael Bruno on percussion, Ricc Fierabracci on bass, Julie Homi and Bradley Joseph on keyboards.

Other expenses included per diems for everybody, food for everybody, and transportation for everybody. George called Olympic Airlines and made a quick deal: fly in the Royal Philharmonic and their equipment for sponsorship on the videotape. He didn't tell them that we had no guarantee that the video would be any good or ever be broadcast. Then I had to find hotel rooms for everyone, but there was some sort of medical convention in Athens and no place to stay. With one day's notice we convinced the owner of a new beach resort hotel that hadn't even opened yet to put up the Brits. We paid to clean up before and after.

We had two days to rehearse. When our trucks and equipment arrived at the practice hall I'd reserved, they wouldn't let us in; the place was booked. By whom? A famous Greek composer, and he was *that very day* rehearsing with the National Symphony Orchestra I'd once been promised. It was just another reminder that a signed contract didn't mean jack. Couldn't someone have just been honest and said, "We promised you the rehearsal space but we can't give it to you," instead of waiting until the day I arrived?

I had to find another hall quickly. It was a miracle that I did. The room was no bigger than a hotel suite, and made entirely of cement. We put up a couple of lights and some drapes on the walls to kill the sound, but the buses transporting the orchestra got lost and wandered around Athens for the first three hours. I focused on staying calm. I surrendered my anger, and my role as victim, and just thought, "This is my dream. This is how it's going to be. I'm going to do it."

Besides, I had the best orchestra. They finally arrived, and we packed everyone into the room and did two or three run-throughs. Thank goodness for professionals.

I had to get the tickets on sale. Despite all the money spent and the fires extinguished, I didn't really *have* the Herod Atticus Theater until the box office opened. If a better offer came along, the government could cancel the shows at any moment and I couldn't do anything about it.

With the orchestra finally secure, I made a chess move of sorts by holding a press conference with Minister Kassimis at the Grande Bretagne Hotel. As luck would have it, the government had dissolved and at the exact same time, Andreas Papandreou, who would become the next prime minister of Greece, was giving *his* campaign press conference at the Intercontinental Hotel. I shrugged my shoulders and thought that maybe two reporters would show up to see me. Wrong. I had more media at my press conference than at any other I'd given in the country. I was flooded with reporters and cameras. Even better, the media was on my side. Nobody took a potshot at me. This forced the government's hand, and the tickets went on sale.

My father was right. Huge crowds filled the streets trying to get tickets, and they sold out in one day. Now it was a happy time. I didn't need the Athens TV station or their advertising. Instead of allowing them to broadcast the show, I gave it to their competitor, and there was nothing they could do about it. When they found out they'd been cut out entirely, I got a call from a guy at the station. "Hi, Yanni!" He was so bright and upbeat that I could hear his cheesy grin. "I'm the new guy who's dealing with you. The old guy was bad." He was the third guy, by the way—they had double-crossed me twice already—and it felt like the new guy was getting ready to do it again. "I know we're not broadcasting the concerts, but I just wanted to make sure you'll be appearing on Roula's show like you promised."

Roula Koromila was an old friend and one of the most popular personalities on Greek television. I said, "If the station owner calls me and apologizes for all the crap you guys have given me, then I'll show up on Roula's show like I'm supposed to. Otherwise, I'm canceling now."

"Come on," he said. "Don't penalize all of us here just because the previous guy was a *malakas*," which means a jerk-off.

"I can't do it, sorry—unless the owner calls."

"That's impossible."

"Well, then, it's impossible for me to be on your show. Goodbye." I hung up the phone and went to dinner that night with Linda. But first I called Roula and said, "It's nothing personal, but I'm not coming on the show. It's not because of you, but it's because these jerks . . . ," and I told her the whole story.

"Serves them right," she said. "They've been driving me crazy, too. Good for you."

Frank Sinatra was correct. Success is the best revenge.

. . .

I could finally concentrate on the music. Good thing it was second nature to me after having played the songs again and again during the American tour. At the dress rehearsal the Brits were great. They looked terrific and had a classy air that you could almost taste. They hammed it up and gave me great performances.

But I wasn't out of the woods yet. During the lighting rehearsal we discovered that the supply truck with diesel fuel for the generators was mysteriously empty, and the driver had left the site. George went to a gas station and got another truck. Stuff like this happened at every turn. Everybody wanted a little money here and there. Everyone had their hand out: gimme, gimme.

We also had to be very, very careful around the antiquities. All of my people were insured, but none of the locals were. Needless to say, "Oops" is your least favorite word around monuments. There is no oops.

My crew got crazy because—guess what?—when someone said they'd deliver gear by seven thirty in the morning, he wouldn't show up until four in the afternoon. And when he did arrive he'd have only half of what was promised. When someone came to me, I always said, "Do not complain. It doesn't help. Just fix it. You don't have the equipment? I don't care. Don't tell me how they screwed you. It's not important. They've screwed me. They've screwed everybody in this room. Just take care of your end. Fix it. How? I don't care."

We made up tour T-shirts that read: We Came, We Saw, They Lied.

With that mantra in mind, I left the dress rehearsal feeling as confident as I could. I was certain other stumbling blocks lay ahead, but we finally seemed to be heading in the right direction.

My family came to Athens for the performances. They were very centered, and I tried to emulate their calm. I was once again reminded of my parents' love of music and life, and how they'd also given me that gift.

I had a huge suite at the Intercontinental. My bedroom was on the right side, and on the left was a smaller bedroom where my mom wanted to stay; she'd come with two of my aunts. One evening, before the first show, Tom and George and I sat in the living room making plans and talking over the day's problems. Perhaps my dad was with us as well. All of a sudden we heard beautiful sounds coming from my mom's room. Everybody went, "Shhh—what's going on?" I walked over, opened the door a little, and peeked inside. On the table was a candlelight dinner, and in its glow I saw the three women gazing out the window at the Parthenon, singing like birds.

My relatives were happy about what I was going to do. In fact, it would never have crossed my mom's mind that it could not be done. Whenever I've attempted the impossible, if Mom is around I have more faith than usual. I know it's not going to rain, the wind will die down, the show will go on. She's very religious and knows the power of prayer. She can focus. I've talked to her about this. "What do you do when you pray?" Turns out she's like me when I write music. Trancelike. Surrendering. She goes to the same intense level, and miracles happen.

The next day, Guilio Proietto, the comptroller of Private Music, showed up. He is slightly rotund, energetic, and has a good heart. Guilio has always wanted to do the best for me. He was excited about the Acropolis show and wanted to make a deal for the album and video then and there. Tom negotiated with him by the pool at the Intercontinental Hotel and ended up with a promise, based on a handshake, nothing signed, of a few hundred thousand dollars when we handed in the album. We also cut a deal for the video and took a small advance against a much larger back end. Our risk was that they might hate what they saw and say, "What promise?"

The day before the concert, the second promoter I'd fired sued me in such a way that I wasn't supposed to know about it, and therefore I wouldn't show up in court. I'd lose the case, and he could stop the concert. Fortunately, some people who worked for me got wind of the lawsuit. I hired two big-time lawyers, the kind of guys who defend the prime minister, and won. The promoter claimed I had damaged his reputation, but he didn't have a leg to stand on. One thing less to worry about.

I worked until about ten minutes before the show, handling random situations and the tiniest details. I could be a general or a grunt when I had to, and be perfectly happy as either when tasks had to be taken care of—an attitude that always inspired my people. Then it was time to go on. My mom, dad, and Linda walked into the theater. Everyone stood and applauded. I hoped they were very proud. A few minutes later it was my turn. I was finally about to embark on my rite of passage, the test of whether I could go home again and be accepted, appreciated, perhaps even admired.

I took a moment to pray, then ran onstage, bowed, and walked to my place between two banks of keyboards. It took me a moment or two to catch my breath. The orchestra was already softly playing a rhythmic pattern. I put my hand up for two bars, then brought it down and we broke into the majestic "Santorini." There is a moment not too far into the song when things get quiet and I should be able to hear a pin drop. When we arrived there and brought the volume down, I heard applause. It was my first indication that everything might work out after all. I exhaled. Twice.

I usually can't see the audience from the stage because I am lit with two spotlights. But when the light moves to someone else, I can pick out faces. Because the seats at the Herod Atticus are so close, I could see my parents and Linda sitting right in front of the stage, at almost the same height as me. My dad looked very cool. My mom had a big smile. Linda looked gorgeous. I felt goose bumps. The audience loved the music; they loved me. I could see in their faces a reflection of my own pride. It was heaven. There was so much coming at me at once. I surrendered to the moment. I didn't analyze it. I did not try to stand outside myself and watch as if someone else were having the experience. Just standing onstage I knew in an instant a million truths about myself. It was my moment and I ran with it.

Linda had earlier used the metaphor of Superman and Kryptonite to describe the forces at work surrounding my return home. Now, on the Herod Atticus stage, I knew I'd defeated my weakness and fears. Perhaps even a few of the teachers who had pushed me around were in the audience. I realized in an instant that after the show my life would never be the same again. This *was* my rite of passage. I didn't have to prove myself in Greece again. It wasn't because of the money and success that I hoped would come. I'd been transformed. I would survive and emerge on the other side, alive. I was free.

Afterward, Linda cried and said, "You'll never have a sweeter moment than the first time you outrageously make your dream come true." She was right. Focused will is incredible. If you have a dream and you don't give up no matter what obstacles come up, then life's problems will fall away and you will get what you want. It happens. It works. Some people experience it naturally and some people don't believe that power exists, but it's in everybody. We're all capable if we have faith and passion.

The first night I felt very uncomfortable speaking English to a Greek audience, so I used my native language. George Veras understood, but afterward he gently scolded me. "You've got to do it in English, Yanni, because this is going *all over the world*." For the second show I spoke English, but in Greek I also said, "Tonight I feel like our ancestors are here with us. We're at their most sacred place, and their energy is here." I meant it. I could feel the rush.

By nature I'm an artist and by schooling a psychologist. The people I admire are not necessarily musicians, but all are original and independent thinkers: Christ, Buddha, Socrates, Leonardo da Vinci. Michelangelo had enormously focused creative energy and greatly inspired me. I felt connected to them all. Maybe it's just because of human genetic heritage, or maybe it's simply a matter of tapping into that creative stream. That probably sounds mystical, but I don't see it that way. To me it just is; it's matter-of-fact.

Tom Paske told me that Peter Baumann had shown up at the control truck during the performance. He heard the concert. He saw the audience. He experienced everything. All he said was,

"How much must this cost?" He looked at the golden goose but it still just looked like a goose to him.

We laid a couple of goose eggs ourselves. During the first show half our lights went out because one of the rented generators ran out of fuel. It was our own fault. When the generators were delivered, no one thought to ask, "Is there enough gas in this thing?"

That night we also had a cameraman up the hill at the Parthenon. Even though we had clearance from the Archaeological Society, the guard on duty kicked him out, saying "You're not supposed to be here." He meant, "Give me a hundred bucks and you can stay."

After the show George walked into the dressing room and I asked what he thought of the show. "Oh, terrific. You were fabulous," he said, as one of his crew shot the conversation for the documentary.

"So, did you get some great shots of the Parthenon?" I asked.

"Well, I hate to tell you this," he said, "but the lights were not on."

After all the hoops we'd been through, they hadn't lit the monument?! I'd been too busy on stage to notice. "They weren't?" I asked. Stupid question. Smarter question: "Will it be lit tomorrow?"

"You bet," George said. "We'll get it lit or we're not going to play."

Afterward, my emotions careened from exuberance to exhaustion. Back at the hotel we high-fived each other and got to work watching the raw footage, critiquing, adjusting, and inventing fixes. My clothes—as well as Linda's and my parents'—were quickly cleaned and pressed. For continuity's sake we had to wear the same outfits every night.

The next day the reviews came out. Miraculously, not one paper gave us a negative review. Instead, they embraced me. I was grateful—and relieved.

The next night, an hour before the show, the Parthenon was still not lit. George called Kassimis into the truck and said, "You see that? Yanni is not going on the stage until that thing is lit."

Kassimis led George and a group up the walkway to the top of the hill, where he confronted the guard, who shrugged and said he didn't have written permission. No payoff, no lights. Typical. I'd instructed everyone to pay no bribes. Kassimis told the guard who he was and gave him a piece of his mind, and we got permission on the spot.

The third night we didn't videotape—I just couldn't afford it— but since we had the truck I wanted to record the show just in case. The Philharmonic's union guy tried to charge me for another performance. I kept saying I was only going to use one recording of the shows, and that the equipment was there so we might as well roll some tape. "Well, that's the union rules," he said. "Every time you record, you've got to pay."

The orchestra people found out about it and they all banded together. "Let the guy be," they said. "When we get home we'll deal with the union. Let him record."

I ran around, shaking hands with the Royal Philharmonic. I ended up connecting with them all. They were champs. They stuck it out for me.

During the third show I relaxed a bit and allowed myself to enjoy the music. I forgot all the details and the problems and the headaches. During a song called "Acroyali"—sort of a bouzouki thing, when I play solo—I actually started tripping. I could feel the notes and the silences between the notes. I could see the imperceptible flicker of our stage lights. I tried to open myself to my ancestors and the energy they'd left behind, and I think I did.

I noticed Shardad to my left—he's a little proper, and sometimes I tried to loosen him up him by making faces—then I looked past him and saw the Parthenon in the distance, ablaze with light. My God, I thought. Suddenly I was just a little boy from Kalamata, playing his keyboard. This is real! This is the truth! I felt my dream had finally come true.

Perhaps the most moving moment for me came at the end of each show. I don't mean the encores or the applause. It's a custom in the Greek theater that no matter how much they love you, clapping is always more polite than enthusiastic. But if the audience approves, they will say *axios*, which means "worthy." I kept hearing them call out the word. *Axios. Axios.* Now I knew I had given the people something to be proud of.

That night we went back to the hotel and celebrated with a meal of hamburgers, French fries, mustard, ketchup, and mayonnaise. We mixed the condiments into a special sauce and added horseradish for kick. When the video started to play, the family cheered joyfully. George Veras later told me the room sounded like being in the Dog Pound at Cleveland Stadium.

Linda and I rarely fought, maybe once every couple of years. But after the third show, we did. It was my fault. I was so caught up in the excitement and intensity, and being yanked this way and that by the cast and crew, taking pictures and the like, that I was dismissive and I didn't spare a second to meet some of her Greek friends that she'd invited backstage.

Linda was hurt and crying, really bummed. I apologized to her that night in the hotel room. I think it was the only time I ever saw her like that.

The next morning George and some of his staff took different planes to America. Each person hand-carried a few of the show's audio- and videotapes in orange CBS News bags. We didn't want to take any chances. There were no copies.

I slept late the next morning and then posed for three days of photos at the Acropolis, sometimes changing clothes in the guard's kiosk or in broad daylight behind an ancient column. I couldn't wait to get home, not only because I was exhausted, but because as much as I'd enjoyed the whole experience and felt the incredible triumph of having pulled it off against seemingly impossible odds, I hadn't really listened to the tapes. I didn't know if I had recordings I could make into an album, or footage I could shape into a video. I was eager to find out.

It all hit me when I finally got into my studio and I had the line cut on video, and tried to lock it to the forty-eight-track music, which was unmixed. I began looking at the images that George had shot and hearing the potential of the music. That's when the goose bumps hit. I thought it would blow people away.

The music had sounded spectacular onstage. The challenge was to get that same sound in the studio when I mixed the album, keeping in mind that on the video the music would mostly be heard through small television speakers. When you record in a studio or any room there's a natural ambience, a signature sound. But when you play in the open, with no enclosure—even a band shell—the sound dissipates and what you get on tape feels dead. My task was to electronically create a "room" to hold the sound. That's where two decades of putzing around with equipment and recording techniques paid off.

I also had to repair stray noise in the orchestra: clicks, bumps, and coughs picked up by 125 microphones. In a very quiet spot on "Until the Last Moment" somebody changed a page of sheet music, bumped the stand, hit the microphone, and it fell. If somebody plays a bad note, for that moment you dip the volume and add the note using a synthesizer. But the other sounds . . . to get a flawless-seeming performance was like colorizing an old black-and-white movie. Meticulous work, often one note at a time.

Because I mixed while looking at a cut of the video, I noticed that when the camera focused on someone playing, they seemed to play louder. It's an illusion, because of your eyes' connection to your ears. I put it to good use and exaggerated certain sounds when a musician's body language emphasized the physicality of his or her playing. I wanted people to see the strain of a trumpet player blowing his horn, and the arc of the bow moving across a cello's strings. I wanted the viewer—and listener—to understand one thing: *This is real, this is live.* Every sound that's made, someone had to make it then and there.

One day Tom called.

"Where have you been?"

"I'm in the studio mixing. I haven't been answering the phone."

"For six days?"

"Yeah, they just drop food off inside the door. I haven't seen anybody or talked to anybody."

"How's it going?"

"I don't know. I'm still on the first song. Maybe I'm making it better. Sometimes I think I'm just jerking off."

"Going a little slow then."

"If I can just get through the first song I'll probably get on a roll."

"Well, I wish I could help but . . ."

"I know."

"How's the smoking going?"

"Don't ask."

I worked for about ten days just on "Santorini." I thought I had it down, but I wasn't sure. Linda and her best friend Bunky came to listen. I synched up the song with a line cut of the video and said, "What do you guys think?"

Their jaws dropped: "My God!"

Great. But the next day I decided I didn't like the sound at all and I started again from scratch. It took another week before I was happy.

The next time I spoke to Tom I said, "I don't know if anybody else is going to like this stuff, but I'm going crazy. I think it's wonderful."

I worked with the usual total disregard for my personal well-being. I spent three months fiddling, coming out of the studio only to sleep—and not that often. I was a multitrack producer with a one-track mind. I hardly ate. I still appreciate the friends who left food on my doorstep but didn't want to interrupt, so they faxed me that it was there. When the album was finally done I'd lost fifteen pounds, but I was ecstatic. All that had changed over the years was the size of the chances I took. This time I had come home from Greece with some tapes under my arm and had spent nearly every penny I owned. But I'd bought myself a chance to get out of the New Age record bin and exceed what the critics insisted were the limitations of my music.

Next, I had to do the video. George had taken a rough copy to the PBS convention and we were waiting to find out if we'd made the cut. In the meantime, I wanted the best-quality sound and the best-quality picture, and I didn't care what it cost. I was prepared to edit and edit until we got it right. Whenever George objected—he wanted it right, too, but was used to working faster—Tom would say, "Just do what the kid wants. Leave him alone. He's fine. He'll do it."

Linda was in the edit bay as well, almost every moment, giving the project heart. She wouldn't hesitate to pull George and me aside and say, "Guys, these are pretty shots, but where is the feeling? Where is the emotion? You didn't put enough of your mom in; let's get shots of her reactions and your dad's." I followed her instincts almost unfailingly. On matters of art I respect her opinions. Linda gave that video the something extra that helped it rise above. She is somehow in tune with the public, and if she likes something, I'm willing to bet that most people will, too. I take her very seriously. She was also my cheerleader. She empowered me and showed me that my music was meant to touch people.

Gustavo called with the good news: *Live at the Acropolis* had been picked twenty-sixth of twenty-eight shows at the PBS convention. The biggest stations didn't want to play it because they weren't sure it would work, but secondary outlets picked it up—often they served the same major markets—and we knew we'd get national exposure in about 50 to 60 percent of the country. I had to deliver the show to the network by February 1, 1994. I thought we would make it, but the gods were not through with me yet. George had only a few days to spend editing before he had to leave for the Winter Olympics on January 30. In the predawn darkness of January 17, the Northridge earthquake hit Los Angeles.

Linda and I were in bed at my house, but it felt like we were on a boat. Fortunately we were okay. I don't have a phone in my bedroom, but because of the many calls we received from people making sure we were still in one piece, I brought one in. Half an hour later I hit my head on a nightstand, reaching for the phone on the floor, and drew blood. The building we worked in fared better than my head and was one of the few editing houses in the city left functioning.

On the last day we had to work, George and I sat on the curb outside the studio, somewhere in Burbank, at sunset. Cars raced by and I smoked a cigarette. I was fried. I'd been hunched over in the dark for almost a month. I'd lost more weight. After all we'd been through, in a moment of insecurity, I turned to George and said, "Do you think this is going to sell?"

"Sure," he said. "At least a hundred thousand copies."

I hoped he was right. But in my head I replayed a conversation I'd had earlier with Tom Paske, in which I worried that I could end up with the most expensive home movie of all time, *one that no one would ever see.*

The whole Acropolis project from reception through promotion, had cost me about $2 million, including the money we got from the Greek government and the advance from Private Music. I didn't have to use the money earmarked to support my parents, and I had $30,000 left in the bank. I thought I had more. Tom didn't tell me the actual figure for years.

But what was the alternative? When you want something badly enough you take your chances, knowing that at any moment it could be "Lights out! You're out of money." The record company drops you. The contract is gone. The tour is canceled. You live on the edge. It was all or nothing. You make a hundred, you put the hundred in. If you make a thousand, you put the thousand in. If you make a million—you get the idea.

Then I remembered something else I'd told Tom. "I don't care what it takes because I am so tired of not being able to show people what my music is like. This is probably the best and only chance we've got to bypass everybody who's stood in our way. We have to take it."

Live at the Acropolis debuted on WLIW in New York on March 5, 1994, as part of PBS's semiannual pledge drive. The album had come out the month before. I wanted to make sure people knew to watch, especially because PBS was not exactly a "network" and often local station managers called the advertising shots. We knew they didn't have big budgets, so we asked them, "What would you do if you had the money?" They told us and we placed ads in *People* and in every regional edition of *TV Guide*.

The reaction was phenomenal. The pledge drive phones rang off the hook with callers asking, "Who is Yanni? *What* is Yanni?" Station WLIW normally raised $10,000 a drive; that first night they raised $45,000. If people saw the video before going to bed, they'd stand outside the record store the next morning before it opened, to get the album. George called me and Tom, and said, "You're on a rocket ship."

To be honest, I couldn't imagine how people could not get caught up. No one had seen or heard anything like this show. The sound was great, even through little speakers. And the way George Veras shot and directed it was not only brilliant but original—at least back then. People stopped changing channels in the middle of surfing: "I was just clicking through and—wait, what's that?"

Two weeks later the big PBS stations changed their minds and put on the show. The results were even better. The album and video raced up the charts. *Live at the Acropolis* eventually raised over $14 million for public television and has since been seen by over half a billion people in sixty-five countries. The tape itself is more than ten times platinum. The album has sold over 8 million units—and still sells.

I guess the gods were with me after all.

10

GOING GLOBAL

Once *Live at the Acropolis* broke through, my career really took off. I sold a ton of albums and videos and, although making money was not the primary objective, I can't deny that I loved how investing in myself had paid off handsomely in more ways than one. Yet even though my standard of living improved, I continued to plow almost every dime right back into touring, promoting myself, improving my studio, and keeping the momentum going. I'm not the type to simply cash in and retire. I couldn't go backward. As Tom Paske put it to me: "If you're Yanni and now you can play this music in front of another billion people, are you going to do that or are you going to limit yourself to another concert in Smallville?"

My new question was, What do you do when your dreams come true? My answer was: Find new ones. I placed all my bets on myself and told my team, "Let's ride this rocket around the world."

It started with another late-night phone call to Tom, during a U.S. tour.

"Tom. What's going on?"

"You tell me. How's the tour?"

"The tour's fine. I've been thinking."

"Why does that scare me?"

"This is serious. Listen . . ."

Silence.

"I was thinking we should take this show around the world."

More silence.

"I know, I know. But think about it. If we're ever gonna do it, now's the time. We're up and running. George is getting the video played all over: South America, Asia. It's the power of TV. If that video plays, we can draw a crowd."

"Expensive, man."

"Hey, you always say, 'It's easier to keep the flame . . .'"

"I said that? I thought you said it."

"Never mind; it got said. You say it all the time."

"I was lying. I do that sometimes."

"Be serious for a minute. I think this show and this music will connect with people in any country, any culture. Just look at the orchestra; it looks like the lobby at the U.N."

"What happened to the beach? You promised me and George we'd 'cash it in' and go live on a beach."

"Maybe I lied."

"I think it's gonna cost a lot of money. Maybe two or three million. It's risky."

"I know."

"No beach, huh?"

"Just think about it."

. . .

I couldn't take London's Royal Philharmonic on the road, so I had put together a thirty-two-piece orchestra of my own, in addition to the incredible band and musicians I already had. We were a tight-knit blend of different religions and musical schools of thought. I didn't take that lightly. I didn't want to let these people go. I had given them my respect and earned theirs in return. I wanted audiences to see us and what we could do. I kept saying, "I don't care if only four hundred people come, those four hundred will walk out of the show saying, 'I've never seen anything like this in my life.'" I had faith. I knew I could take my music to the most remote place in China, where they'd never seen a foreigner, and listeners would enjoy it.

We'd already had some interest from Australia and Mexico, but first I toured the United States with the Acropolis show. We put on sixty-four shows in forty-nine cities over seventy-seven days. Meantime, George made multiple international TV deals and sent the *Live at the Acropolis* video to many of the friends he'd made around the world while televising events for CBS Sports. One, Dennis Muddle in Australia, gave it to John Quayle, then-president of the Australian Rugby League. He loved it and offered me $100,000 to perform at a nationally televised gala dinner to kick off the 1995 Rugby League season.

We also cut another thirty-second TV commercial—using Acropolis footage—only this time I insisted we run it on *60 Minutes*, a show for people who think. Professionals will tell you that it takes maybe five impressions for an ad to make an impact, but at $270,000 for half a minute I bet on one airing during Christmastime. My instinct was that when the usual Toyota or Mercedes spot came on, everyone would glaze over.

Same with the razor blade commercial. But then my ad would start and be so unexpected that viewers would be hit right between the eyes. Tom said, "Well, okay, Yanni, it's your money!" I admit this was a roll of the dice, but he supported me completely. I think we both wanted to see if we could disprove the predictions of the powers that be and maybe drive them a bit nuts.

The next few weeks our sales spiked considerably, selling more units than during any previous week since the release of the album.

When *Live at the Acropolis* hit, BMG, the company that had swallowed Private Music, wanted to re-sign me. I was too caught up in the whirlwind of touring and expanding my audience to think about a new deal. Besides, I hardly had time to focus on the new music swirling around in my head.

However, having given BMG a hit album, I figured that the new management might finally trust me, and we decided they ought to give us some money and PR support to help me tour all over the world. What was good for me would be good for their catalogue sales. Tom and George wrote up a marketing plan and scheduled a meeting with the BMG executives in New York. My team explained my commitment to play everywhere. "If you care to participate in any way," they said, "we can *really* open up our market."

First, George presented our plan to play Mexico. Tom remembers, "We were all sitting at a table, maybe seven or eight people from our organization and five or seven from theirs—and they started ripping us like we were morons. 'This will never work,' they said. 'You'll never get this done. In fact, here's *your* timetable. Look here: You were going to have an article in the paper by this date and it's already passed.'"

"Sometimes trains don't run on time, either," Tom said, apparently between clenched teeth, and got so mad—which he *never* does—that he was ready to go over the table at the guy. George held him back.

Then Heinz Henn, BMG's vice president and head of marketing, turned to Tom and said, "I'll tell you what: If you sell out the Auditorio Nacionale in Mexico City, I'll make you president of BMG South America."

At that moment I'm sure my entire team had the same thought: Okay, so you don't want to give us money. But don't also bet *against* us. That's just stupid.

"Fine," Tom said, and everyone walked out.

Not long after the meeting we did a press conference in Mexico City. Jaime Mijares, who convinced me to play Mexico City, had seen *Live at the Acropolis* and was a big fan. He worked for a big liquor distribution company and arranged for them to sponsor the show. He coordinated marketing and promotion in Mexico for me, including a three-day publicity trip. We started running our killer TV ad. I was on all the major radio and TV shows. The biggest were hosted by Pedro Ferez. He's got morning drive–time radio and 6:00 P.M. TV. We were booked on the morning show for fifteen minutes, but he kept me on for almost the whole hour. We really connected. Then he had me on the TV show that night. He's the Larry King of Mexico. Jaime and Pedro have since become good friends of mine.

Out of nowhere we had a gold record in a month, and when we played in November 1994 we sold out *two* shows at the Auditorio Nacionale. (In 1995 we went back and sold out three shows, and in 1997 we sold out *five*—still the most by a non-Mexican artist.) Afterward, Tom made up a business card for

BMG's Heinz Henn. It read: "Tom Paske, President BMG S.A."
He sent it to Heinz with a pair of SRO tickets.

Earlier, in July 1994, after my U.S. tour wrapped in Atlanta, I
met with Danny O'Donovan, a concert promoter with tremendous international experience, to talk about what it would take
to mount a world tour.

We hit it off immediately. Danny is British, proper, soft-
spoken, and never loses his cool. Even when he's really mad, the
most he'll say is, "We'll talk tomorrow." Danny had spent many
years in Asia, especially Japan, and could handle the language.
He'd promoted concerts for everyone from Frank Sinatra to Diana Ross to Michael Jackson, had managed artists, was a world-
class negotiator, and had the power and patience of a diplomat.
It wasn't long before I nicknamed him Winston, in honor of
Churchill. Danny said I could go global, and for the next few
months we brainstormed the big question: How?

Danny convinced me that before playing a note I should do
a promotional tour of Asia, where my sales and exposure were
minimal. I'd just do interviews and press conferences. "There are
lots of countries where you can make a lot of noise in a short
amount of time," he said. "You can generate goodwill, make
friends, and expose your name and your music. Once people actually meet you, they will be able to put a face and personality to
the image and say, 'So *that's* Yanni.'"

Danny also said he'd use the trip to beg every promoter he
knew to give us a venue and a concert date.

In the meantime my team did their best to get the *Live at
the Acropolis* video played and the album released in places like
Japan, Korea, Taiwan, Hong Kong, Thailand, Indonesia, Singapore, Malaysia, the Philippines, and more.

Danny and I left together for Asia in January 1995. "It was very difficult at the outset," he remembers, "but in the end I set up almost the entire tour myself, using local promoters less as promoters and more just to make local arrangements.

"For example, I went to Florence Chan in Hong Kong and said, 'Look, Florence, how long have you known me? Did I bring you Frank Sinatra? Did I bring you Diana Ross? Did I bring you Michael Jackson? I need a date for Yanni.'

" 'Who's Yanni?'

" 'Don't worry. You know me. I wouldn't be here and ask unless this was a good thing.'

"One by one they did me the favor," Danny recalls. "However, I had trouble in Singapore. Even though I dealt with the biggest promoters, there was no venue available, so we moved on. After our trip, out of desperation, I got on a plane and went to Singapore. It was Chinese New Year's Eve, and I wanted to take a look at the Singapore Indoor Stadium. I was told, 'Are you kidding? It's Chinese New Year. Nobody's working.' I went to the stadium anyway, walked around the building, and checked the doors. All locked. Then I saw a window and knocked on it, just to see if anybody was inside. Sure enough, this guy comes out of an office and opens the door.

"I said, 'I'm terribly sorry to trouble you, but I'm a concert promoter trying to get a venue and I really want to find out if this building is suitable and possible.'

"He said, 'I'm the general manager here. Actually we're closed today, but lucky for you I popped into my office to get some papers.'

" 'Would you mind if I came in and took a look-see?' I asked. He let me in. It was big, about an 8,000-seater. I said, 'I have an artist named Yanni. It's his first concert in Singapore and I need a venue.' I told him the date I needed because by then I had the rest of the tour in place. He looked in his diary and said, 'We have a show in the day before, and we're loading out that day. Perhaps if we could make some arrangement with them to bring in extra crew, we could load them out faster and you could come in.'

"Long story short: We got the date. We put it on sale. We got channel 12, in Singapore, to do the promotion. They aired *Live at the Acropolis* and it was a smash. Before we knew it we had sold out. I went back to the general manager and said, 'Can we sell behind the stage?' We added another five hundred seats, which were really dead seats. We still had such a demand for tickets that when another date became available, I grabbed it. In the end, we sold out two shows—seventeen thousand people—and broke the stadium record. We did more business than Elton John. More than Phil Collins. More than Janet Jackson."

Afterward, the local newspaper wrote: "In January [1995], we didn't know who Yanni was. Now [in March] he's the hottest thing in town. How did he do it?"

Danny could work miracles of other sorts, too. I'd discovered that even if we landed in some remote, humid Asian capital and had less than an hour to unpack and meet before going to an important dinner, he could show up fresh and immaculately groomed, wearing a perfectly pressed suit and tie. Even I can't do that.

In February 1995, I kicked off my Pacific Rim tour in Australia. We had the rugby league sponsorship, and *Live at the Acropolis* had played on TV. Unfortunately, BMG had managed to sell only about 400 albums in the whole country, and the Australian record company reps had told us not to even bother coming over. "Yanni doesn't sell here," they said.

We thought, Are you kidding? We went to Australia for the

rugby dinner concert and turned it into a five-show tour in Sydney, Melbourne, and Adelaide, a gold album, and a gold video. Next thing I know the BMG guys were in a bar with their arms around me, taking photos and congratulating themselves on their first gold album in six months.

Later, during a private celebration at a restaurant on the beach, George reminded me—just as Tom had—how I had once told everyone, "When this is all over we're going to retire and sit on the beach." Clearly that wasn't going to happen, so I secretly arranged for the waitress to gather some sand and put it in a Tupperware bowl. Later, I mailed it to George in New York, with a note reading: "Here's your beach."

Sometimes we weren't as smart as we thought, and made naïve and costly mistakes. For instance, we believed that the road crew that had moved us around the United States could also take us around the world. After all, it's not too much farther from Australia to Hong Kong than it is from New York to Los Angeles. Or so we thought.

Danny O'Donovan remembers, "I was in Los Angeles working on the Asian tour when I got a call from Tom, in Minneapolis: 'They're in Australia, our guys have to move the tour freight to Hong Kong, only it's going to cost a million dollars! Help.'"

Danny made some calls, generated other scenarios, phoned Tom, and said, "If you do it like this you can save five hundred thousand dollars right away." Then he came to Australia to make sure everything went off without a hitch. "That's when I found out the way they were operating," Danny recalls. "Basically everybody, including the orchestra, had been booked into the equivalent of Four Seasons Hotels, in every city in Asia! These were some of the most expensive hotels in the world. I said, 'Do you guys know what's going on here? This is crazy. I've toured the world with Frank Sinatra and everybody, and they don't put orchestras and crew in the Oriental Bangkok or the Regent Hong Kong.'"

Danny saved us some serious money, but he never minded getting into the trenches himself. In each city he would deliver leaflets about the show to various hotels and pay the bellmen to slide them under the doors of every room. It was a tremendous education, a crash course for me in how a real promoter operated, in how to do things the right way.

Playing throughout Asia was a revelation that made me remember those nights when I was a child, lying in bed, twisting the dial of my little radio and listening to the world. I felt a connection wherever we went. Whatever the audience—Malaysian, Filipino, Chinese—they all responded. One comment I heard again and again meant a lot to me: "Your music reminds us of our music."

All at once my beliefs about the universality and transparency of what I was doing instrumentally were validated. What's more, unlike in the United States, where I had many fans but no reviews, I got great feedback in Asia. Why? They were more open to new ideas.

Everywhere we went we sold thousands of albums. The Pacific Rim tour lasted from February through March and a few weeks into April. We played eighteen shows in nine countries and finished with two sold-out shows in Hawaii. Again, it helped that Danny had somehow gotten my picture on the cover of the magazine that goes to all the Honolulu hotels. Afterward, Tom, George, Danny, and I met at the Turtle Bay Hilton on Oahu to review events and plan new ones. Danny went off to set up visits to Japan, Korea, Europe, and Mexico. I took a break, wrote, and thought about what I'd just experienced.

Before I went to Asia, that part of the world had been like the blank space on an ancient map, mysterious, the great unknown. When most Americans think of Asia, especially Southeast Asia, they picture Vietnam: a jungle with a bunch of soldiers, guns, explosions, poisons, and adversity. Other images are just as clichéd. In truth, the entire region is tremendously beautiful; the beaches and the oceans are gorgeous; the cities are alive. There are so many cultures, so much diversity.

But this isn't about East versus West. My tour showed me that there is no *one* East or West. Can you really compare Thais to South Koreans? The latter are called the Italians of the East. They love their music. They're boisterous and strong. Thais are gentle and sweet, and wear big smiles. Asians are no more alike than Americans.

I had landed first in Singapore. When I got off the airplane I was humbled. I didn't feel like saying, "Hi, my name is Yanni, I'm from Greece, I grew up in America, let me tell you how life is, let me tell you how you should be and what you guys are doing wrong." Instead I made sure that my eyes and ears remained wide open. I absorbed and asked questions. I wanted to learn everything I could about the local customs and the cultures. I wanted to discover what made the people happy. How did they celebrate? What did they eat and drink; how did they sleep? What was cute, what was funny to them, how did they dress? How bad was the poverty? How outlandish were the riches? How could I help?

I knew there'd be many religions and attitudes toward life, and different definitions of right and wrong. Their way of living might not be how I chose to live—or would choose to live—but if I let these encounters scare me rather than allow myself to feel and taste them, I knew I'd rob myself of the opportunity to enrich my life and perhaps change myself for the better. That opportunity is exactly what I was looking for. Instead of just watching the world on cable TV, I wanted a firsthand sense of the planet.

From May through July I toured America again, playing in forty-six cities. According to *Entertainment Weekly*, mine was the sixth-highest-grossing tour of the summer. By the time we wrapped up in San Juan, Puerto Rico, I'd played in front of more than half a million people.

I visited my parents in August, and in September I traveled to Kyoto, Japan, where I'd been invited to perform at the Toji Temple as part of a special event called Oto-Butai, which takes place every few years to celebrate the temple's birthday. The Toji is a revered site, one of two great early temples in the city, and is the burial site of Kukai—now known as Kobo Daishi—the monk who brought the Shingon sect of Buddhism to Japan in the ninth century.

I was sponsored by Japan Airlines and arrived a week early to set up. I got to know the head monk, Mori-san; I remember finding it curious that he loved to smoke cigarettes, but so did I at the time, despite my on-and-off struggles to quit. We didn't speak the same language and had to work through a translator, but we connected so strongly that I felt like we were brothers.

The monks held a tea ceremony to welcome me. Tea in Japan is nothing like tea in Britain, where you sit at a table or on the couch, sip a beverage with milk and sugar, and munch digestive biscuits. At the Toji Temple we sat on tatami mats on the floor while the monks undertook an elaborate ritual. I imagine that they expected me to appreciate it politely, like most Westerners, but not to care very much about the art and intricacies. Instead, I showed respect and a great interest in their ways. The cups were large, almost bowl-like, and one had to turn the cup in a certain way before drinking. I asked lots of questions: How do you drink it? How do you hold the cup? I asked if I could be taught these rites and be part of the ceremony.

The monks opened up to me. They were eager to show me the temple and monastery and places where only high-ranking monks—and never women—were allowed yet they did let Linda accompany me everywhere, as well as my translator, a Japanese woman, who at one point exclaimed, "This is so shocking. I can't believe I'm in here!"

I visited the burial ground, as well as rooms the emperor stayed in when he visited. They even urged me to try on some of the emperor's clothes, particularly a jacket fashioned with gold thread and worth maybe a quarter of a million dollars.

Impressive, yes. But even more affecting was Mori-san's humility. He would come into my dressing room only on his knees. Every day he'd pick flowers from the garden and create a special arrangement for me, and light incense. He even tried to tie my shoes. I said, "No, no. Please get up." But far from debasing himself, he was honoring me, and his actions moved me in the same way as those of the eagle Taiee.

Mori-san also led me to a room at the monastery and said, "This is your room. Any time you want to come and write music, you can stay here. *Anytime, for the rest of your life.*" The walls were covered with symbols of eagles.

On the evening of September 9, after several days of rehearsal, I performed in the courtyard with the Toji Temple lit up behind me. Five thousand people attended and millions more watched on Japanese TV.

The stage was under the open sky. Overhead, clouds loomed. I knew that if it rained the concert would be over. Forget the danger of electrocution; the instruments' microphones were so sensitive that even a five-mile-an-hour breeze could be heard blowing by. Before the show it began to sprinkle. I closed my eyes and "saw" the rain go away. My musicians echoed that faith. In the orchestra I could hear whispering: "Don't worry. Yanni will go onstage."

Suddenly the rain stopped. We did the whole show. When I got to "Niki Nana"—the encore—it began to drizzle again. We stopped. On camera I said, "If this rain would let us, we'd like to do one more song for you." The skies closed and we did the song. After we bowed off, it began to pour.

Mori-san gave me a gift before I left: his watch. Plastic with a black and orange strap, it was yet another symbol of his simplicity and humility. I wore it for three years, until it literally fell apart. He could have given me a string and I would have done the same.

On the plane home I remember thinking that I am who I am because I have faith in myself, and it has always been the possibility of emotionally rewarding experiences that has encouraged me to gamble on myself; those experiences have made all that I do worthwhile. I cried when I left, and when I thought of Mori-san I knew I would miss him.

From Japan the tour moved to Europe. We played Holland, Germany, England, Italy, and Belgium. I did eleven performances in ten cities, finishing in London, where we taped my show at the Royal Albert Hall.

Danny O'Donovan had preceded me to London to set up the date, but when he spoke to one of the city's top promoters, Barry Clayman, he was told that I couldn't possibly fill all 6,000 seats. Just before starting the U.S. tour I'd asked Danny to become my personal manager, and he demonstrated how perfectly he fit as one of my "generals" (with Tom and George), when he told Clayman,

"I tell you what. Not only is Yanni going to fill the Royal Albert Hall, he's going to do it twice."

"You're crazy," said Clayman. "You can't even fill one show."

Danny said, "That's why I'm going to do two shows, so that everybody in London will look at the paper and say, 'Yanni—two days. Who is this guy?'"

Clayman was closer to the truth than we cared to admit. Hardly anyone knew me in England. When we came through passport control at Heathrow Airport, my publicist Dione Dirito was asked, "What do you do?"

She said, "I'm a publicist."

"Oh yeah? Who do you publicize?"

"Yanni."

The passport officer gave her a blank stare and said, "You've got a lot more publicity to do. Welcome to London."

We all about died laughing.

But by then, Danny had blanketed London. He had promoted in the city for years and knew all the hot spots. He put my face on buses. He put ads in the Underground stations. He put me everywhere there were people who, even if they didn't know Yanni, would make the connection.

We'd also had trouble getting *Live at the Acropolis* played, so Danny called a friend of his, a big TV director involved in a pop series called *Cue the Music*, and got him to air the show. Then Danny did the extraordinary. We were concerned about filling the box seats at the Royal Albert Hall because many of them are held by season ticket holders who wouldn't automatically come to the show. Danny sent every season ticket holder a *Live at the Acropolis* video.

George and his crew recorded and videotaped the performance. Actually, two performances. Danny was right: We sold out both and were the talk of London. My father attended, as did

Constantine, ex-king of Greece. To this day Barry Clayman says, "I don't know how you did that."

In November 1995 we returned to Mexico City's Auditorio Nacionale and sold out three shows. Then I took a break. I needed one. But rather than relax I went back into the studio to continue with the new music I'd been writing which was linked to even more ambitious tour plans.

At the same time, BMG asked me again to re-sign, but their desire felt lukewarm. During the past year and a half we had grown stronger. My tours had gone through the roof. I'd been invited by countries around the world to do concerts. *Live at the Acropolis* had sold millions, as had the video. My other albums had gone double or triple platinum and gold. I didn't care if I didn't have a record contract; the longer I waited to negotiate, the better off I'd be.

Finally, I had to decide: Did I stick with BMG? I had long since stopped believing that BMG was the right fit. They, and Private Music before them, were shortsighted about long-term planning. The seeds of discontent had been sown.

But I have to be fair. Although Peter Baumann and Heinz Henn and others didn't behave the way I'd hoped they'd behave, no one wished me ill. They didn't wake up each morning and say, "Let's figure out how to screw over Yanni." Deep down they all tried to help me. They liked me, even fussed over me. They were also controlling and grabbed a little more than they should have, but I believe their interest in me and my music was genuine. I know Heinz Henn fought for me. He thought I could do big things; he just didn't think I could do what *I* thought I could do. Henn said, "You can't sell out in Mexico," but it's not as if BMG didn't sell my albums. They did okay. I know I'm next to impossible to sell. I'm not on TV or radio. Critics have trouble figuring me out. I discovered that if I gave someone a video of the Acropolis show, then boom! Easy. I had to create my own MTV. I had to educate the buyers and the sellers. All I'd ever wanted was a little help.

I knew I could also start my own record label; I certainly had all the people I needed to pull it off. But in the end I opted to talk to other record companies. I asked my lawyer, Lee Phillips, to put out the word and almost immediately major labels contacted us asking for a meeting. To say the response was gratifying would be an understatement.

We got interest from MCA, Capitol, Arista, Sony, Interscope, Warner Brothers, Dreamworks, and Virgin. The last had been impressed when we sold out the Royal Albert Hall, which was near their headquarters. During the first half of 1996 I met with them all and was most taken with Ken Berry, then head of Virgin, which was owned by EMI. Ken eventually ran EMI until, as will happen, corporate juggling forced him out. I'm still crazy about the guy. Ken was class A. Straightforward. Honorable. No bull. Very bright. Very powerful. We told him what we wanted and he told us what he could do. We didn't get everything, but we got plenty. And he came in with the best offer right off the bat. BMG hung in but low-balled me, then low-balled me some more—while still wanting to meet. I refused and they raised their offer. At the eleventh hour, BMG matched and slightly surpassed the Virgin offer, but by then—the summer of 1996—it had long been too late.

In June and September of the previous year, Danny, Tom, George, my full-time promotional and marketing staff, plus

Tom's office staff, met in Minneapolis to map out the future. Tom called me with an update:

"I hear you had everybody in to Minneapolis," I said. "What's up?"

"We figured out your whole life for you. At least the next few years."

"This I gotta hear."

"Okay. First, you always tell me that your music cuts across cultures, and because it's instrumental there's no language problems. You with me so far?"

"For the moment."

"Hey, you've got fan letters from all over the world. But let's not get sidetracked. We have to assume that if we can get in front of people they'll connect with your music."

"Keep going."

"What's the best way to reach people with the most impact? Televison, right? Probably the only thing that's ever worked for us. TV, TV, TV. So here's what we want to do. We want to pick two or three different countries—cultures—and ones with symbolic or well-known monuments or places, and put the show on there. And do a composite video. What do you think?"

"Like, where?"

"Like India: the Taj Mahal. Like the Pyramids. Like those ancient ruins in Mexico, or the Forbidden City in China. Like wherever."

"And all these countries are just going to let me come in and play?"

"They might. *Live at the Acropolis* is a pretty strong calling card."

"It'll cost a fortune."

"Set the money situation aside for the moment. Obviously if we can't work that out we can't do it."

"And I want to do this because . . ."

"Hey, it's something to do. If you want to do it we'll all look into it. Coming up with the reasons is your job."

"Thanks a lot. And the whole staff thinks this is a good idea?"

"Actually, there's a pretty good consensus."

"Really?"

"Everybody thinks we might pull it off. George is sure we can."

"That figures."

"Hey, it's up to you. You're leading this parade."

"This ain't a parade, it's a stampede. Just because I'm the cow in front, all you other cows think I know where I'm going."

"So."

"Well, maybe I don't."

"You know, if we could play any of these places—say India or China—and George could get the show played live in that country, with their populations you might hit a hundred million people."

"I think it's insane. You guys have bit off too much here."

"Well, it was just a thought. Think about it and we'll talk some more."

"Okay. Good night."

"Good night. Oh, Yanni . . ."

"Yeah?"

"One hundred million people."

"It's insane."

Danny, Tom, George, and I met in Los Angeles. The plan to play at some of the world's greatest monuments or natural wonders was the first priority. Tom was right: We had fan letters from all over the world, as well as invitations to play. This was no guarantee it could happen, but it was a start. The music would be new—I had been writing when I could—but the intent stayed the same: to reach across cultures and countries.

The wish list of possibilities included the pyramids at Teotihuacán, outside Mexico City, because the location is mindblowing, fairly unknown, and we were so popular there; Table Mountain in Capetown, South Africa, because of Mandela; the Forbidden City in China, because it is spectacular and it had never been done; the Christ statue above Rio de Janeiro; the Taj Mahal, because it's considered the ultimate monument to love, and—again—it had never been done; Ayers Rock in Australia; Machu Picchu in Peru; and others.

After some fact-finding and consideration we narrowed the list to four: Mexico, India, South Africa, and China.

But why monuments?

Tom said it was up to me to find reasons. I did.

First, these places remind us of the greatness of mankind. Second, how do you get people in a world saturated by three-and-a-half-minute music videos to sit through an hour and a half of instrumental music on television? Acropolis or not, I had no illusion that anyone would be content to simply watch me play the piano. I needed something exciting that would conjure images and create a mood. The backdrop would give the show strength.

Third, I understood the power of television.

Fourth, it would just be very cool. Countries around the world had let me know that what I had done at my "hometown" monument was the way they wanted theirs to be presented. I took it as a great compliment. And I still loved the challenge of proving that my music could shatter cultural barriers and bring people together.

But unlike *Live at the Acropolis,* which took me home again, I had to remain aware that this time I'd be an outsider going into a foreign culture. I'd encounter deep-rooted ideas about their holy places, and I would have to do my best to understand. Because I would control the presentation and connect my art with another country's traditions, I had to produce an experience with the proper reverence. *Live at the Acropolis* had aligned itself with the purpose of the monument: to attract attention to an edifice designed to remain in the consciousness of the planet for as long as possible. Whichever venues I chose, I'd have to find a way to do that again.

That's a tall order. You want to do it perfectly: the right performance, the right music, the right attire, the right behavior. You have to light the monument properly; you don't want to turn it into a disco and offend anyone. I knew I'd probably face difficulties that might once again seem insurmountable, but I believed the result would be worth it because the monument itself would affect the viewer's psyche and contribute to the music. The marriage of elements would elevate the experience even for the performers, and that energy would cycle and recycle between us and the audience. At the Acropolis I had connected to something immortal in the world. Call it the brilliance of humanity.

I wanted to do it again.

Linda and I had often talked about how, once you've learned a lesson, life doesn't give you the same lesson twice. You get another one that is bigger and more difficult. I never take it for granted, but it seems as though life has always provided what I needed. I've been pushed to the limit and brought to the point where I thought I'd break. I barely made it through the Acropolis experience. I thought it was the toughest thing I'd ever done and I was elated when I survived the ordeal. I emerged grateful for my success, and for millions of new fans.

The music I'd been writing since then had a message: acceptance and tolerance. That was certainly the subtext of my band and orchestra—musicians from all over the world. Together onstage their different backgrounds, different religions, and different attitudes could move your heart.

Also, the impact of *Live at the Acropolis*, and my subsequent rising fortunes, made my team feel a degree of invincibility. Perhaps we were overconfident, but we were hungry for more.

The cost of lighting Table Mountain in South Africa was prohibitive, and there were too many potential political problems playing at Robbens Island, where Mandela had been imprisoned, so that possibility dropped out first. Mexico was very much in the mix and was the locale we thought would work out first, until it became obvious that we were being mysteriously delayed. On Christmas Day 1995, I pulled the plug on Teotihuacán when we couldn't get permission to play in time. That left two of the world's most sacred places: the Taj Mahal in India and the Forbidden City in Beijing. My decision to take the next steps was purely personal. I hadn't yet been officially invited anywhere and had no guarantees from anyone.

Nothing about mounting the shows would be easy. Calling the process *extremely difficult* would still understate the enormous mobilization of time and resources, people and equipment, political acumen and cultural sensitivity—and money, again mostly my own—needed to make my goal a reality. But at least this time my record company and Ken Berry believed in me—and backed me fully. "What a great project," Ken said. "It's a dream come true. Look, don't spend all your money. Let us help you." What a refreshing difference.

At the outset I had what turned out to be a prescient vision

of myself looking like the cartoon character Wile E. Coyote after the bomb explodes. He's still alive, but his face and body are
covered with black soot, and he looks dazed. That's how I imagined I'd end up. But I pushed ahead anyway, characteristically
biting off more than some of my friends and advisers thought I
could chew.

All I knew was that the greater the pain, the greater the
gain, and if I was sure of anything in life, it was my ability to
take the pain. Another reason for my grand ambition might be
tougher to understand, but it means much to me. I'd learned
something in the studio that was just as important outside of it:
Creativity is not linear. It's not as though if you know A and then
you know B, you can deduce C. It's more like quantum physics.
You may know A and B and end up finding Q without knowing
quite how. It's not logical. It's a spark of brilliance. A quantum
leap. You're just there.

That experience, that moment of discovery, is what it's all
about for me. Somehow I had the feeling that the journey I
was about to take, no matter how carefully thought out, would
lead somewhere entirely unexpected.

11

SACRED PLACES

In January 1996, on a crisp, sunny New York winter day, George Veras and Tom Paske met in New York with T. J. Balakrishna, the head of India's Department of Tourism. Balakrishna said I was well known and well respected in India, and he was positive we could put on a concert at the Taj Mahal. He ran it by his superiors, and through the minister of culture in India, and despite some issues to resolve, everyone thought it was a good idea that could boost Indian tourism in the same way that the Acropolis concert had helped in Greece. The suggestion was also raised that I might play as part of India's fiftieth anniversary of independence, in March 1997. Balakrishna put us in touch with Ram Kohli, in India, who ran his own tourism company. Balakrishna said that if anyone could help us set up meetings with the various jurisdictional departments, Ram Kohli could. It was a beginning.

The Taj Mahal itself needs little introduction. The world is familiar with the domed, glistening white memorial surrounded by four massive minarets on the banks of the Yamuna River, as it runs through the city of Agra, 200 kilometers south of New Delhi, in the northern Indian state of Uttar Pradesh.

The fifth Mughal emperor Shah Jahan began construction of the Taj Mahal around 1632 in memory of his favorite wife, Mumtaz Mahal, who had died in 1631, at the age of thirty-nine, after giving birth to their fourteenth child. The building, its gardens, and the massive red sandstone gateway that you rarely see in pictures took twenty-two years to finish with a workforce of 20,000. The structure, once described by the poet Tagore as a "tear on the face of eternity," has stood for centuries as a love letter in white marble to the Queen buried inside. (Shah Jahan rests there, too.)

Forget the usual red tape and politicking—all the negotiations and permissions required to get the project off the ground. The biggest obstacle to overcome was this: The Taj Mahal was a tomb, not a theater. There was no place to play. It's not as if Emperor Shah Jahan had thought to build seats, or install an outdoor electrical socket by the back door. The only person who'd ever performed there was an Indian musician playing guitar for 300 people. The Taj Mahal had never hosted a massive show with orchestra and lights. In fact, while monuments from the Pyramids to Niagara Falls to the Parthenon were regularly bathed in colored spotlights after dark, the Taj Mahal had never been artificially illuminated.

In March 1996 George went to India to survey the site. We already knew that we wouldn't be allowed to play inside the Taj Mahal—sacrilegious, and what if you break something?—or up against it. George realized we couldn't perform in front, either, because it was a cemetery, or even very near it, for reasons having to do with archaeological preservation. Our only option was crazy: to set up in back . . . *in the middle of the Yamuna River on a sandbar that periodically emerged from the waters when the river dried up between*

November and late March. Ordinarily, that fertile bit of land was used by a few very poor but enterprising local farmers to grow watermelons.

The only access would be on foot, over the riverbed and remaining water. We'd have to build the stage and seating on the sandbar. We'd have to erect two pontoon bridges to get across the river. We'd have to lay roads to get to the bridges. We'd have to erect towers for sound, lights, and TV cameras, get electricity to the site, and then bring in a 747's worth of equipment (and take it out again). To keep heavy trucks from sinking into the sand we'd have to camel in materials and lay a "roadway" of metal sheets on thick straw where the bridges ended. When complete we'd have a little city, with its own hospital and mess hall.

And all of it would have to be removable in order to leave the area as it had been before—except the roads. The local government said they wanted to keep the roads.

Anybody else would have thrown up his hands at this, shaken his head and said, "Let's go home." Not George. He thought it could be done. And needless to say, I'd have to pay for it all.

Danny, meanwhile, went to China. Even before we told the Chinese that I wanted to play at the Forbidden City, the China National Culture and Art Corporation (CNCAC) had gotten in touch with us in an effort to further develop cultural exchanges between their country and the United States. They knew what I'd done at the Acropolis and, along with the Forbidden City Society, the Ministry of Culture, and the Beijing government, they'd asked if I'd be interested in performing in China. No official had decided which venue would be appropriate, but hosted by the CNCAC, Danny toured sites. "I saw Tiananmen Square," he remembers, "but there was no possibility of doing a concert there. I went to the Great Wall, but there's no place to play with our large setup. Still, I listened a lot and was very respectful, but I had a one-track mind: the Forbidden City. The official name was 'the compound in front of the grand palace in the Working People's Cultural Palace.' I kept bringing it up, saying, 'That would be a natural place to do it.' The Chinese had their own agenda and didn't deviate a whole lot, but I planted a seed."

In June, George and Anthony Stabile, our production coordinator, went to Agra to survey the location and learn what it would actually take in money and materials to build our little city on the sand. They also met with numerous officials, bearing in mind that anyone could throw a stumbling block in front of us at any time. Perhaps an army general would need to be pacified, or the mayor of Agra. We knew from experience that eventually these needs would spontaneously arise, and that it was part of the cost of doing business.

In September, Tom and George returned to India and found a co-promoter, Venkat Vardhan. He brought in Pepsi as a major sponsor and became a key player in helping us build the facility and negotiate with the various local, state, and federal agencies. By then we'd begun obtaining permissions and finding our way around, but we were faltering, talking only to lower-level government people and tourism officials. You want to play at the Taj Mahal: Who are you going to ask? There's really nobody. Walking in, you deal with one guy and then all of a sudden another guy shows up. Fortunately, Venkat came from an old political family and he shed light on what we had to do to make the concerts happen. The Taj Mahal was under the domain of four jurisdictions: the Archaeological Society; the city of Agra; Romesh Bhandari, the governor of Uttar Pradesh; and the Indian federal government. We needed four permits, but there's no one actually saying, "Get four permits and you'll be ready to go." As Tom would say, "It's like getting a boat license in Greece."

To really get matters under way, Venkat had to be officially anointed as our guy, which meant that Governor Bhandari would have to officially invite me to perform. Bhandari wanted the concert, so we told him I could do a press conference in India so he could say, "Yanni, we want you to play."

Seems simple. But Tom and George got the runaround for about a month while I kept thinking of the Acropolis. I called Tom and said, "Get someone to say, 'Yanni, would you please come and do a concert in India at the Taj Mahal?' Otherwise, why talk to the press? We either get a fax from the governor or we're not going."

By this time, of course, I'd already sunk a good deal of money into the project—and the one in China—because to carry off an enterprise of that magnitude I needed to have a staff of more than ten people on at all times; pay for offices, flights, hotels, and surveys; retain the band and orchestra; and so on.

Bhandari promised he'd send the fax and in good faith I boarded a flight in Los Angeles, connecting in London for New Delhi. When we landed we would call George. If he didn't have the confirming fax, I'd turn around. George got the fax at the last minute, just as we landed in London. I let out a sigh of relief and Danny and I boarded the flight for Delhi.

As soon as I cleared Indian customs in New Delhi, I went to visit Gandhi's tomb. It wasn't just impulse. Long before I'd even contemplated performing at the Taj Mahal, I had promised myself that if I ever got to India the first site I would visit would be Gandhi's resting place. Now my little pilgrimage meant even more to me. Not only did I have a tremendous affinity for Gandhi's ideas, and feel connected to and inspired by him, but I knew I was about to take another big shot and get pulled and pushed in the doing. I wanted to feel Gandhi's strength. I needed it.

The tomb is actually a memorial flame in a park on a hill, with Delhi beyond, encased in smog. It's like going to the Tomb of the Unknown Soldier, but more ethereal, more mystical than being in Washington, D.C. You're in a calm zone within a teeming mass of humanity in the second most populous country in the world. I arrived at dusk. I could almost touch the smoky smell and the sounds of the city; the traffic in the distance hummed like an infinite bass note. Danny and Ram Kohli left me alone and I prayed for fifteen minutes.

Mosquitoes flew everywhere. But I was focused and didn't want to move, so I let them keep biting me. When I concentrate like that I often do it in the oddest places because I don't want people to see me. Most people think that kind of intensity is weird. Sometimes I'll do it in bathrooms, just for privacy. I definitely do it before I go onstage. In my mind I see everything being right and already successful. I see no electronic equipment breaking down. I see no rain. I see no wind. I tell life what I want.

I think that anyone who has ever walked on the planet, from prehistoric man to Alexander the Great, from Cleopatra to Mother Teresa, from Leonardo da Vinci to Hitler, is inside us— the entire potential of humanity. As Socrates said: "The perfect human being is every human being together." You're part of me and I'm part of you, and we have access, whether by spirit or through the human gene pool, to whoever has gone before. I stood there, connecting with Gandhi's spirit, because I believe the spirit is available. I don't feel we just come and go without leaving a trace.

I asked for Gandhi's wisdom to come through me, to help me understand the culture that he loved.

I spent an hour with Governor Bhandari in his office in New Delhi. Then in his late sixties, the governor was an intelligent man who'd gone to Cambridge for his postgraduate degrees and had been a public servant his entire life. His late father had been the chief justice of the Punjab High Court. Just months earlier Bhandari had become governor of Uttar Pradesh. He understood I wanted to play at India's most sacred monument and that he had to make sure I was the right person before he supported it. Even though I had his faxed invitation, my purpose in meeting him was to obtain his total endorsement.

Instead of talking about the concert, we spoke about religion, its origins, philosophy, and India's history. The meeting was . . . fun. Bhandari sized me up, trying to assess my personality and character. Was I aware of the situation's gravity? Would I honor the monument and his country, or was I some happy-go-lucky musician who smoked pot and said, "Hey, we'll have a great gig here. We'll put up some speakers, set off some smoke bombs, it'll be killer, everyone will be dancing."

Bhandari's approach didn't throw me because I had gone in with an open mind, without expectation. I believed in my goal, and that the music was appropriate, and I thought I projected that. I had recently finished writing a new song, "Deliverance," and I thought life would have never let me write that piece of music and work so hard to do it, and make it so perfect for the Taj Mahal, and then not let the concert take place. Whatever doubts I'd had vanished when I listened to that song I knew the show would go on. I felt it in my bones.

As our hour together concluded, I said, "Governor, I hope

you understand, whatever I will present at the Taj Mahal I will approach it with the greatest respect and humility. I will treat it the way I treated the Acropolis, and as if I were Indian. I hope to pay the greatest possible tribute."

Bhandari smiled at me and his eyes radiated calm and wisdom. "I am certain you will," he said.

The next day, my press conference was scheduled for 8 P.M. in the hotel's garden area. Danny arrived five minutes early to welcome the press, talk for two or three minutes, then introduce me. I was supposed to drive around the rear of the hotel, go in back of the little stage, and make a surprise entrance through the curtain behind Danny. But there were so many people, I couldn't get there. As the minutes dragged by, the media stared at Danny, who desperately tried to stretch his speech. Danny carried on about my past, where we'd been. Eventually, much to his relief, I came up the center aisle.

I announced the show dates—March 20–22—and the news that the government of Uttar Pradesh would co-host. The response was like the Acropolis press conference all over again. The world came out. I loved India and it seemed to love me. One member of the media gave me a great compliment when he said, "Not since Alexander the Great has the Indian culture been conquered by the Greeks. Alexander did it militarily; you conquer our hearts."

In December, with the support of the minister of defense—a good guy to have in our corner—the Indian army began building the roads. George was on site, surveying and planning, and he brought back pictures of old ladies banging bricks apart to make gravel and a 1950s-era steamroller crushing that gravel into a road. He also told stories of giant flies that swarmed every-where, forcing everyone to wear turbans and swat themselves constantly to keep from being bitten to death.

As expected, the river, which floods during the monsoon season, had turned into two rivulets exposing the sandbar "is-land" in the riverbed. Once the roads were in, the army built pontoon spans across the water, from the eastern and western end of the Taj Mahal. Called Crupman bridges, they're made of solid iron and can bear the weight of a fifteen-ton tank. Construction required a thousand men working around the clock, but they built them in record time, fighting nature as they went. As a story in the *Times of India* reported:

> The army men had to enter the [shallow] water up to their necks. In view of it being dirty and infested, the jawans rubbed mustard oil on their bodies before stepping in and re-moving the rocks on the river bottom, to anchor the bridge.

After heavy metal sheeting paths were laid down over straw to keep the trucks from sinking into the sand, our crew of about 300 began feverishly building. We brought in about 130 tons of video and audio equipment imported from the United King-dom. The equipment arrived in more than fifty trucks and a plane. We built four towers—some of them 60 feet high—and seating for 7,200. The stage itself was 100 feet by 80 feet, 6 feet high, and tiered to hold the orchestra and band.

If all we'd had to fight were the elements, flies, and dirty water, the operation would have been easy. But that never seems to be the case. At first, everybody was supportive and there were few problems like I'd had in Greece. But at the eleventh hour the whole thing began to blow up in our faces.

Once I'd been officially invited by Governor Bhandari and started spending prodigious amounts of money, the cooperative facade crumbled. I thought the government's permission was all it took, but Bhandari's political opponents were not in favor of the concert and used the event as a wedge to attack him. "Here's our governor giving a foreigner the Taj Mahal, our jewel, which he hasn't ever given to an Indian person. How dare he!"

Quickly it dawned on me that I'd become an unwitting pawn in a political tug of war between the progressives and the conservatives. We had sold the concert based on the goodwill of the Acropolis; a man and his music honoring a culture. The progressives signed on because they had been waiting for years to find a way to raise the Taj Mahal's tourism profile. They trusted me. They knew I wasn't a crazy rock star locked in a Bombay hotel room scribbling messages with lipstick and pulling out three days before the show. The conservatives thought my appearance would be sacrilegious.

Someone told me that my being in the middle of the political push and pull was a backhanded tribute, but all I cared about was performing and making sure no one was insulted. I'm not going to say I understood the politics in India. I only know there were too many voices, mostly dissonant and beyond my comprehension. I kept wondering why none of the "interested parties" had stood up six months earlier and objected. Had I known a political firestorm would break out, and that I would be the match, I'd have cut my then-minimal losses and opted for Plan B . . . whatever that was.

The problem was that Bhandari's opponents had waited until we were far enough along and had spent so much money that the concert had become the Event of the Year. They'd made a clever chess move by realizing that for their cause to be noticed it would be smart to pick on something everyone was paying attention to. We were it. By the time they spoke up, every newspaper, every TV station, and all the magazines had reported on some aspect of my project. We were big news.

We'd gone in with nothing but positive thoughts, but suddenly we were warriors engaged in battle. We were in survival mode and determined to keep going. With every concrete step we took, from laying a roadway to building the stage, a few more critics fell by the wayside, and we readied ourselves for the next volley. The game had become to anticipate the next move.

Tom said there was a date by which tickets had to be printed and sold, and that if we could hold on and not concede anything until then, no one could use the "Sorry, no concert" threat. And the government would look stupid caving in and not letting us play. But that still didn't mean some army general might not want to make a little extra money by suddenly charging us to get across his bridge on the nights of the show, or when we wanted to get our gear out afterward.

By January 1997, the problems coalesced into three issues. The first was lighting. Some felt that illumination would decay the ancient mortar. Of course, we couldn't play or shoot a video without lights. The next problem was sound. Supposedly our decibel level would be too high and, again, injure the Taj Mahal. Last, we were told we'd invaded the "green zone" around the site and were violating archaeological parameters.

We tried to deal with each issue, and successfully reassured Governor Bhandari and Defense Minister Mulayam Singh Yadav, who had helped mobilize the army to construct the roads and bridges. But our critics knew I'd personally spent more than $4 million. (I'd eventually spend three times as much as our original estimates for India alone.) If they couldn't stop the show, they could at least hold my investment over my head while picking my pocket and dare me to back out. If I did, I would suffer a stunning loss. Just like that.

In late January my Indian promoter called and said, "You're being sued." The main petitioners—as those who'd filed the suits were called—were a historian, a social activist, and an internationally known designer. There were also two newspaper columnists, a "celebrated thinker," and a retired bureaucrat. The local newspapers termed them "environmentalists." Three separate nuisance lawsuits had been filed in the local courts asking that the concerts be canceled because we'd violated the green belt, had caused pollution by moving men and equipment, and could damage the Taj Mahal with the lights and sound. George says it was "like all the Ralph Naders of India attacking all at once."

I didn't want to cause environmental problems, but I felt certain we hadn't. Our site was more than the required distance—300 yards—from the outer perimeter of the Taj Mahal. We'd had papers drawn up by Ph.D.s attesting that our lights could not possibly hurt the mortar. We said: Here are the bulbs we're using; these are the frequencies and the intensities. From that distance you'll have this much luminescence. Compared to what the sun does during the day, it's absolutely nothing.

Not only did our speakers face away from the monument, but I'd brought a revolutionary V-DOSC system designed by a French nuclear physicist and inventor Christian Heil that canceled sound reflecting from the rear of the speaker cabinets completely. During the concerts, the sound that reached the Taj was as low as two people talking. We measured it.

We'd even given the local mayor thousands of dollars to compensate the six or seven farmers who every year jumped over the wall and planted watermelon seeds in the "green belt." Even though they had no official right to grow, the city had always looked the other way. We bought out their entire crop—and then some.

But the lawsuits weren't really about these issues. The petitioners were angry that although the concert was expected to generate significant revenue for the Taj Mahal Preservation Fund, "the amount given to the Uttar Pradesh government was peanuts." Peanuts? We anticipated they'd get 1 billion rupees.

"It is not a question of generating a lot of money," one critic argued. "And in any event, we have been informed that the concert will generate at least 20 billion rupees."

So it was about money.

When we assured everyone that we'd cause no light or sound pollution—and also agreed not to bring motorized vehicles within 500 meters of the monument—one columnist wrote that no one was in the mood for "quibbling." Then he revealed his true concern:

> The whole concept of holding the Yanni show is wrong. If tomorrow Lata Mangeshkar and Ghulam Ali [two revered Indian singers] say they want to hold the same kind of show, can you object to it? No. So the process will go on, and inevitably affect the Taj. In any event, instead of Western music in the background of the Taj, I feel that singing *ghazals* [a type of sung poetry] would be more appropriate.

Tom and George flew to Agra and our promoter introduced them to a "fixer"—an attorney to guide us through the legal maze. He helped us file papers requiring that we be kept informed of all legal maneuvers, every step of the way, so we wouldn't be surprised by any last-minute lawsuits as we were at the Acropolis. We also moved to get the matters kicked up to the Indian Supreme Court for quicker resolution. However, India's Supreme Court is not nine judges meeting in one place, like ours; it's twenty-five men who meet in smaller panels. Our cases were handled by three judges. I authorized George and Tom to hire fifteen attorneys to work the three separate cases. The government was also on my side. The past attorney general of the state of Uttar Pradesh filed briefs on our behalf; so did the attorney general of India.

My next phone conversation with Tom had a different tone than usual. We were all getting tired.

"They'll still want more money, man," Tom said.

"No bribes!"

"I know. But every time we make an agreement with these guys another guy shows up with another obstacle."

"Look. I busted my ass for a year writing songs for the Taj and rehearsing the band and now you tell me it's not gonna happen?"

"Hey, it's three in the morning and one below outside," Tom growled. "I've been getting up and dragging my ass in here for months doing this."

"All I want to know is: Is this gonna happen?"

"If I had to bet, I'd bet yes. But right now it's a tough call."

Tom was right. But earlier we'd made a good move by deciding not to take *any* money out of India. My instinct said that even if I took $100,000 from the ticket sales, some contrary politician would say I had ripped off the country: "They say they took a hundred thousand, but they probably took five million." So, no money out of India. I wouldn't even handle the tickets. I told the Uttar Pradesh government, "You print the tickets, sell the tickets, collect the money."

Tickets for the three shows went on sale February 1 and immediately sold out. The entire $2 million gross, plus Pepsi's $750,000 in sponsorship money went *directly* to the Taj Mahal Preservation Fund. Everyone should have been happy, but some people became greedy, and we were asked to do two more shows. Perhaps "asked" is the wrong word. George was on a government plane headed for the Uttar Pradesh capital of Lucknow when state and local officials, as well as someone from the Archaeological Society, tried to strong-arm him. "Give us two more shows," he was told, "or we will shut you down." George is used to intimidation and he refused. As his payback they wouldn't give him a ride back to Agra, and he had to sleep at the airport.

I was rehearsing in Connecticut at the Foxwoods Resort— an intimate 2,000-seater. Tom called me with the news at two in the morning. I knew we could have sold out *five* more shows. We could have become the house band at the Taj Mahal and played for months. The government officials—not Bhandari—knew it, too, which is why they tried to force us into extra performances.

And they were supposed to be on our side.

I didn't mind more money going into the Preservation Fund, but not that way.

What to do? If I got angry and said no, and walked out, that would have pleased the opposition who had been trying to stop us from playing. If I refused to play, we might be shut down. I was caught between a rock and a hard place.

I called Tom the next night, and I was crazed.

"How much money are we in for so far?" I asked. "Maybe we should just scrap it."

"I don't know."

"You don't know! You mean I call my business manager and he doesn't even know how deep I'm in?"

"All the numbers are downstairs. I just don't have the energy to go get them."

"Dammit!"

"Well, dammit right back. I knew when I got the report this morning at ten o'clock. I'll know again at ten tomorrow morning. I'm too fried right now."

"I want the numbers. Call me. Maybe you should go over there."

"I've been there three times already. George and Anthony are there."

"I'm just gonna pull the plug on the whole thing."

"I'm going to bed."

The next morning Tom called me at Foxwoods. My mood had changed.

"I got your numbers. If we bail out now you're out about two million dollars," Tom said.

"Never mind that. It's not about the money. I figured it out."

"Really?"

"Just tell me: Will we run out of money? Will we go broke?"

"No."

"Then here's how it goes: You're right; we're going to play the Taj. Don't doubt it. I know we will. What we don't know is how much pain we're gonna go through getting it done."

"Okay."

"We're in this with good intentions. We're not taking advantage. We're honoring their monument. We're honoring their culture. We're not asking for anything."

"You know, I can see how people go nuts. You don't let

them sleep for about sixty days and then you run them up and down the emotional roller coaster. It's on, it's off. It's off, it's on. All the while you get them more emotionally invested until one day they flip out."

"Yeah, but it's easier if you know you'll win in the end."

"Win?"

"Yeah. There's always someone who doesn't get it, who tries to take advantage, who doesn't see the big picture. It's true in every culture."

"Yeah. But we went in a bit naïve. Again."

"We always do. But it's simple. It's gonna happen. Just get the Taj!!"

"Okay."

"It won't happen exactly the way we thought. Some people are going to chip away at the spirit of the whole thing. But we're gonna play there. I can see it."

Silence.

"One more thing. Only tell me as much as you have to. Don't put any of this bad stuff in me. I have to go in the studio. I have to psych up the orchestra. I have to go onstage, do the press, and all that. I need this to be a positive thing. Inspirational."

"Okay."

"This probably won't be a clean win. It won't go down exactly as we thought. But we're in it now and we're gonna see it through."

"Okay."

"Get the Taj!"

"You got it."

"Get the Taj!"

"Okay."

"How about China? How's that going?"

"Danny's in charge of China. He's got it under control."

"That helps."

The conversation was a reaffirmation of one we regularly have whenever I play anywhere in the world and Tom's not with me— as usual. I'll call him a few hours before the show. He'll say, "Make sure you call me after the show and tell me how it went." And I always say, "I'll tell you right now: it went great." I already know the result. It's easier if you know it turns out well.

I kept my cool and thought the situation through. I called George and said, "Just tell them we're not going to do what they say. *But don't cancel the show.* That's what they'd like us to do, but we're not falling into that trap. Let *them* cancel the show—and then let them explain to the media and the people why."

The officials backed down.

Another day we found the pontoon bridges up so nothing could go across the river. Everything had to stop because someone wanted more money.

Not only would we play live and tape the show—and shoot a behind-the-scenes documentary about the Taj Mahal and Forbidden City performances called *No Borders, No Boundaries*—but India's Doordarshan TV planned to broadcast the concert to the entire country. They brought in their only TV truck to provide the uplink for a series of press conferences, and then the concerts. Then we heard rumblings that maybe they might not televise the show—and take away the truck—unless we gave them more time for ads. Fortunately, our TV production coordinator grew up in the streets of Philadelphia and had savvy to spare. When the truck arrived he gave the driver and technicians booze and a bunch of Yanni hats—then let the air out of the tires.

By mid-March two of the three legal cases had been settled. Only the issue of light and sound damage remained outstanding. Chief Justice A. M. Ahmadi appeared to be leaning in our direction when he ruled, "In law, a petition must be on the basis of personal knowledge. None of the petitioners has visited the site. We cannot go only by newspaper reports, which fear damage to the monument by the Yanni concert. If the reporter who filed the news report had filed the affidavit in the court, we would have considered the matter."

So was the concert on or off? We had to wait. The judge gave the petitioners a short time window in which to visit the site and file affidavits based on their personal findings. Putting on a bold face, the petitioners' counsel said, "The court has not dismissed our case. If my client goes to Agra before the concert and files an affidavit, the case can come up for hearing again. The court can be convinced *even one day* before the concert, since it is a question of preserving a national heritage."

I had no idea which way it would go, but I knew the time had come to go to India. The band and orchestra and I had already gotten twelve vaccines, taken the malaria pills, and endured the stomachaches. *We were going.* On March 16, Linda, Danny, and I caught a flight for New Delhi, via London.

Our plane was delayed in London and our connecting flight got us into New Delhi after four in the morning. I was tired and hopeful that at that hour there would be no press to meet me. I came through customs expecting one or two of our people to take us to the hotel. Instead, I was mobbed by TV cameras and photographers and reporters. They descended on me, yelling. I stood there dazed while crews shoved microphones in my face. The first question totally blindsided me: "What do you intend to do about the farmers threatening to torch themselves?"

While we were in the air the newspapers had broken a story that the watermelon farmers had not been paid and were threatening to immolate themselves, and it had made the world news. I was taken by surprise, but I shot from the hip; my answer came from a deeply-rooted belief and faith in my intentions. As confidently as possible I said, "There is no way anyone will ever get hurt from one of my concerts." I really meant it.

To my surprise, the reporters dropped the subject. But on the way to my hotel all I could think was, What have I done? For the first time I felt that the project was out of control. While it's fair to say you're never in control in India, this was really pushing it; the darkest moment. All I wanted to do was honor and respect the Taj Mahal and the Indian culture. Only by committing myself to that end would anyone have faith in me. And now I was hearing about people wanting to torch themselves? Over music? What if somebody got a gun and started shooting? If people could die so that the concert didn't take place, what else were our opponents capable of doing? Until then it had been a political game with factions trying to use my concert to make Governor Bhandari look bad. Now it was a dangerous game.

India itself was crazy enough. After meeting Governor Bhandari in New Delhi in November, Danny and I had driven to Agra on what could kindly be called the highway from hell. The road was filled with buses, cars, motorcycles, tricycles, bicycles, rickshaws, camels, donkeys, goats, sheep, cats, dogs, bears, people, and, of course, cows—moving in every direction at once. The scene defied imagination. In Agra, my limo drove past houses that were really four sticks holding up a cardboard roof, with a bathroom in the street. Thirty yards away we turned into the driveway of a hotel made of marble and surrounded by lush greenery and swimming pools. Meanwhile, the guy lying under the cardboard roof had never been allowed to even *look* into the hotel. I walked into the lobby and felt guilty immediately. The contrast was unimaginable. I wanted to scream, "Here, take my clothes. Take everything I've got." It was horrific, but you can't make a dent. I kept thinking that this is not what Gandhi had in mind.

And yet, I saw no despair. None. I don't want to second-guess the Indian culture; maybe they think each life is just temporary and next time they'll come back in a better place. Or maybe the pain is hidden behind well-rehearsed smiles. Mostly I saw good energy, but I couldn't understand how the less fortunate—and the more fortunate who witnessed the squalor—could be happy. I wondered why the world allowed this to be.

Today, while absolutely not condoning it, I understand a little bit more why there is terrorism in the world, and how people could kill themselves for a cause—any cause, right or wrong—because if they live in those conditions, it would be easier to imagine. I'm not saying poverty creates terrorism; certainly that's not the case in India. But lack of education and the most basic means of survival creates a fertile ground for manipulation among the disenchanted and disenfranchised. No wonder millions are easy targets for exploitative men in pursuit of personal power or acting in the name of God. How can we have peace on the planet under these conditions? Lately, I think new generations of Americans are realizing for the first time how interconnected the whole planet is. America is my country and I love it, but I'm stunned at how little we know, and sometimes how little interest we take in the world.

I arrived in Agra a couple of days before the shows. I did press conferences, waited for the last Supreme Court case to be resolved—and with it our future—and visited the site. I had seen the Taj in pictures taken by George, and from the window of the plane from New Delhi to Agra, when the pilot did a flyby. I looked down and saw our little city, and it looked ten times as big as I had envisioned. It was goose bumps time.

Now, driving there, I thought, Okay, you're chief. People here have been working for months. You're going to be calm and cool. Two trucks full of soldiers and guns escorted my car. We drove past a cricket field filled with kids playing without the right equipment, and it reminded me of playing soccer on the beach in Kalamata without a ball. I wish I could have stopped to talk to them, but all I could do was smile and wave. They did the same in return. Later I bought them a whole set of bats and balls and uniforms.

At the Taj, the military was ubiquitous, and I was the guy they'd been fussing about for months. I greeted everyone I could with *Namaste*, respecting the culture. The area in front of me was draped off, a huge perimeter that encircled 7,000 seats and the stage. And it was all carpeted. Outside the drapes were tents and light poles.

At the main entrance I turned right and there was Anthony with dirt caked on his bearded face. I realized he'd been through hell and instantly thought of the movie *Platoon*. I was Charlie Sheen coming off that helicopter for the first time, and Anthony was Tom Berenger. He was the grizzled veteran and I was the naïve lamb with a big smile on my face, ready for the slaughter. Meanwhile everyone stared at me, no doubt thinking, Oh yeah. Sure.

But no one complained about any problems because they knew their instructions, the same ones I'd given at the Acropolis: "Don't come to me and complain, because I'll complain to you about my problems—and trust me, you don't want to know my problems." To my relief the whole crew was as finely tuned as a crack military unit.

The day before the dress rehearsal I paced in my hotel room waiting for a phone call. Tom and George were in New Delhi for the Supreme Court's decision on the final lawsuit, and I expected to hear "yea" or "nay" any minute.

Tom described the courtroom as "a musty, old, big classroom. They sit up behind these big lecterns. No wigs. Robes. There are huge legal casebooks stacked around the walls, and some chairs; it's more like a night court than anything grand. People come in and out. The lawyers are all at tables in the front. It's mostly done by brief. Only the lawyers and judges speak. It's almost informal."

I'm a confirmed positive thinker, but it was hard not to be nervous. I sipped on some vodka to calm myself. After all, now I had almost $6 million of my own money invested in the project. Virgin Records had kicked in $5 million of promotional money to cover the whole tour, but I'd still be out of pocket nearly $12 million. I'd also spent nearly two years of my life preparing for this moment, writing music with the Taj Mahal and Forbidden City in mind, recording, rehearsing, planning, calculating.

If it didn't work, I was much less worried about losing money than I was about facing everyone. How could I walk out and say, "We don't get to do today what we worked so hard for two years to do, and in fact we won't be doing it ever in our lifetime." That would've been really tough.

I was in my bedroom when the phone rang. My publicist, Dione, answered. She shrieked, "We got it!" I got on the line and Tom or George—I don't remember who—explained that the decision was "almost Churchillian." The concert could go on, but there had to be a study, as the shows were held, to make sure that nothing damaged the Taj Mahal. Any damages would be assessed afterward. I think that had the court ruled otherwise, there would have been riots. The tickets were sold. The people wanted me to play. They even wanted the Taj Mahal lit. The Supreme Court had figured that out and come up with a compromise. We took the deal.

I hung up, slid to the floor, leaned against the bed, and closed my eyes.

That night I performed a dress rehearsal in front of a packed audience of press, photographers, bureaucrats, army personnel who had helped build our city, and everybody who was anybody in Agra. When we lit the Taj Mahal for the first time in history it looked like an unbelievable jewel. We woke up birds that had never seen lights at night, and we could see them everywhere, flying through the floodlight beams. The whole city of Agra seemed to be outside, watching too. Kids hung from windows.

Virgin's president, Ken Berry, flew in from Los Angeles. When he saw the site he smiled and said, "You've got to be kidding. You guys never made a call to me—and you built this?" It was beyond his wildest dreams.

I still had to resolve the issue of the watermelon farmers. I said very simply—and dumbly—"Well, we gave the money to the government." (In fact, I'd given lots of money to the government; more than was needed.) I didn't speculate about what had happened to it, but I did say, "Give them ten grand more and let's forget about it. No big deal." (Buying out a year's crop had cost about $5,000.) But I was told, "Oh, no. You can't do that. That would be an insult." To whom? The local official to whom we'd already given the money, and who, it seemed, had neglected to distribute it fairly. The farmers expected $1,000 apiece but got only $500—less than their crops were worth, they believed—and they were pissed. That left me with millions riding on a few thousand. Most of all I was concerned about the farmers' lives. But my hands were tied. Insane.

I'd learned from the Acropolis that personal contact is everything. You can't do it by phone or by sending a representative. When it gets bad, you've got to show up. I decided to meet the farmers. I held a secret gathering at the hotel before the concert. Their representative was a wizened, sweet-faced little man in his eighties named Biptee Ram. He seemed awestruck by the surroundings, but not as awestruck as I was by his demeanor and serenity. This was not a man who would light himself on fire.

"Were you thinking of torching yourself during my concert?" I asked Biptee.

"No, of course not," he said. "I'm not crazy."

And that was that. Later I learned that the news report wasn't true. Instead, an opposing political group had said *they* would torch themselves on behalf of the unhappy farmers if money wasn't forthcoming. They threaten that a lot in India.

I assured Biptee that I didn't know anything about where his money had gone. Biptee smiled the smile of someone who might actually know the answer to my mystery, but instead he said, "God is great. Whatever money I don't make this year, I will make it next year. God will give us a bigger crop next year." Whoa. He took me over the edge right there. I thought, Where do I pay my money?

I asked if he and the other farmers would meet me at the site, and then I invited the media to prove that everything was okay. The meeting went really well.

The day after, Biptee showed up early, on his own, at my dressing room door and waited respectfully until I arrived. He said he wanted to perform a brotherhood ceremony with me that involved exchanging flowered necklaces and painting a dot in the center of the forehead, representing the third eye. (It's referred to as a tilak, *tilaka, bottu,* or *bindi.*) We also hugged. All I could think was that in the midst of all the madness, I meet a guy like Biptee and come away realizing that there is hope for the planet after all.

After the shows I secretly brought the farmers back to the hotel, through a rear door into my room, and gave each one an envelope with money in it. I wanted to make sure that Biptee and the others would be okay. And I never told anyone I did it— until now.

On opening night, I stood behind the black drape, where the audience couldn't see me, and looked not at them but in the other direction, at the Taj Mahal. The orchestra had already begun playing, but I was mesmerized by the glistening building, lit at night, a breathtaking white marble poem to lost love, and all I could think was, I caused this to happen.

My emotions were . . . relief is not quite the right word because I still had to perform. Let's just say my insides flip-flopped between feeling peaceful and being filled with anxiety. Soon I would go live on Indian TV before 200 million people. But I couldn't think about that. I had to focus instead on my dream come true. I'm at the Taj, I thought, and I'm going to play a song called "Deliverance" and another called "Love Is All."

Before the performance we had a brief Hindu prayer service, with candles. Everyone who had been involved in making the concerts happen was there, religious or not. We all kneeled and prayed in our own way. Next, Romesh Bhandari gave a little speech. He said, "The good things in life don't come easy, and this didn't come easy." Later, he told the press: "I am a big fan of Yanni . . . This show should have happened a long time ago. It will be good for Agra."

I walked onstage but said nothing about what I'd been through. Also, I wasn't taking any chances. Each night after the shows, someone from our team took the audio- and videotapes, stuffed them in a carry-on bag, and flew immediately from Agra to New Delhi, then boarded a midnight flight out of the country. Even Ken Berry acted as a courier.

The concerts were magnificent, a wonderful personal reward for everyone's hard work. I especially loved that we were broadcast nationwide. Not only had millions of citizens never seen the Taj Mahal lit, but many Indians had never actually seen it at all.

Before playing "Love Is All," I explained to the audience my motivation for appearing at the Taj Mahal in the first place; I described what had been in my heart all along: "Of all the forces that are exerted on us over our lifetime, at least for me, love has been the most powerful of all. As our population increases, our planet becomes smaller and smaller. It's therefore very important that we all learn how to love and accept each other. Whenever that's not possible, let us at least learn how to tolerate one another. I learned that very valuable lesson early on in life, because of changing cultures. I moved from Greece to the United States. And to this day, people ask me, 'Are you Greek, or are you American?' First, I'm a human being, just like all of us. And then I am Greek or American, or Chinese or Indian. We must come to understand and realize that there are as many ways to live life as there are people on this planet. Twenty-five hundred years ago, Socrates said that the perfect human being is all human beings put together. It is a collective; it is a we. It is all of us together that make perfection. The next piece of music is about that. I would like to dedicate it to Shah Jahan, to the Taj Mahal, and to the architects and engineers and sculptors that loved the pieces of marble into this architectural wonder of beauty that we call the Taj Mahal. And also, I would like to dedicate it to all the people in India who loved this concert into existence, thus enabling us to send a very powerful and much needed message around the world, a message of love, unity, acceptance, and tolerance."

The musicians were all affected by the majesty of the venue, as well, and I got performances out of them that I could never get in the studio. The Taj Mahal and the Forbidden City aren't the local nightclub. They played like they never played in their lives.

During "Love Is All," my flautist, Pedro Eustache, played the *doodook*, an Armenian instrument. The song, which was written specifically for the Taj Mahal, opened with me on keyboards creating a bedding, a background sound. Then I motioned in Pedro on the *doodook*. The sound was haunting, gorgeous. I had to watch him because there's no rhythm. We had to be one; I had to feel when he was going to change direction and follow him, and vice versa. But when I looked at him he was crying. I suspected why and asked him about it later.

A few years earlier Pedro had lost a young daughter. The moment at the Taj was a cathartic experience, a chance to talk to his child. It couldn't have happened at a more perfect place, a mausoleum built by Shah Jahan in memory of his wife. It's the spot where you honor people you have loved and loved ones that you've lost. Pedro's loss, his love, was expressed in and by the monument. It truly is a white marble poem to a lost love.

When I decided to play at the Taj Mahal and the Forbidden City, I had thought that China would be difficult and India would be easy. I was very wrong.

What I learned about India is how many different opinions there are on just about any subject, at any minute of the day. Everybody has a voice, and they're all pretty loud—and they mostly disagree. This is good in many ways—very democratic—but it makes it very difficult to accomplish much. Everything's scrutinized over and over and there's lots of arguing.

But I would not change my experiences in India for anything. I learned the lessons of a lifetime. I ended up loving the Indian people, with their smiles, and absence of despair in the midst of a very difficult existence. Meeting people like Governor Bhandari, Venkat, Ram Kholi, Biptee Ram, and many others showed me that there is hope for their country. It is impossible for anyone to visit India and not be changed forever.

Danny O'Donovan had years of experience in Asia and had successfully arranged my Pacific Rim tour. He found that the Chinese could be difficult, but they were also honorable to a fault.

They kept Danny at the conference table for hours, going over the smallest details, but when they were settled, that was it. Their kind of honor is the kind I like, the kind considered naïve in the West: They do what they say they're going to do. Yes, they're businesspeople, but they deliver what they promise. China went like a dream.

Unlike India, in China only a few officials spoke English, so it took Danny's special temperament to handle the "long and arduous" process, right down to the numerous faxes every day, scribbled with minutiae. "At times," Danny recalls, "it was as exciting as watching paint dry."

Danny had to travel to China six times for meetings. Finally, in August 1996 he signed a letter of intent agreeing that we'd tour the country, as well as play at the Forbidden City. The next month, Danny and George flew to Beijing to assess the logistics of filming and performing, and got a nice little surprise. They happened upon a dingy old gymnasium next to the Forbidden City. Drawn in by familiar music, they wandered downstairs. There, working out to a bootleg tape of my music playing on an ancient cassette deck, were figure skaters. "It was unbelievable!" says George. "The power of the music reaches everywhere."

In December 1996 I went to Beijing for a press conference. I said, "My goal is to connect with people emotionally all over the world. I take life's experiences and translate them into music—music that hopefully creates an impact on the listener," and announced my tour: two shows in Shanghai, two in Guangzhou, one at Beijing's Capital Gymnasium, and two at the Forbidden City. The last was the toughest and most gratifying to secure, a dream, really.

I returned in mid-May 1997 to begin the tour in Shanghai. Even as we arrived, our Chinese liaison, Chen, asked us to do one more show in Beijing, at the big arena. The first had sold out immediately, as had all the others. I understood. They needed another show to defray costs, and we agreed as a gesture of goodwill.

China itself was a surprise. I expected a country full of bicycles and rickshaws, and lots and lots of people. I anticipated a rural and undeveloped country, even in the cities. But instead of a couple of big buildings surrounded by shacks, in every city I visited I walked into a metropolitan construction explosion. There were a hundred skyscrapers being built simultaneously. I've never seen more cranes in one place anywhere. Very impressive.

I realized my expectations of China had come from the media, and from the subtle influences of governments positioned against each other, when the people themselves weren't against each other at all.

In fact, the Chinese made quite a fuss over me. I went through the airports very quickly, thanks to the government. In Beijing there were no passport controls; they simply took us and our bags to the incredible Palace Hotel, where I stayed in the apartment suite French prime minister Chirac had occupied just the day before. I even had a live-in butler. Although I didn't need that kind of service I realized I'd insult him if I kicked him out. Newspaper stories called me a "musical messiah." Well . . . thank you, but I don't think so.

After getting settled I had a two-hour sit-down with the Ministry of Culture's second-in-command. A few people sat with us in a simple room, with paint peeling off the walls. We talked about many subjects—they really just wanted to see me in person, as usual—and what surprised me most were questions about the music business. One of the strangest was, "How much money do you make off your albums when you sell them?" I wasn't expecting that, but they were trying to learn.

It is difficult to know China, and impossible on a single trip. But what I experienced was positive and I chose to stay open to that. The alternative, that we should be suspicious, is not for me. I wanted the Chinese to understand that I was a guest in their house and wasn't there to tell them the sofa was the wrong color. I wanted to show their kids that Westerners aren't so bad, and I discovered that the Chinese people don't hate us at all. They are mostly just curious, as anyone would be about anyone else.

One result of the entire *Tribute* experience was that I began to believe that the world would be such a much, much better place if all kids, maybe when they're ten, could leave their homes and countries for a year or two for a worldwide educational field trip. They'd go to different countries for a month each, and hang out with kids in each new culture. I think that would make it much more difficult to be aggressive toward each other later in life, or to be convinced that it's okay to go kill people on the other side of some imaginary line because they're the enemy, the bad guys. Instead, the experience would open their minds to each other and maybe the world would have a better chance of being at peace instead of hunkered down, bombs in hand, ready to throw.

This reminds me of a story I once heard about Buddha walking through the forest. He was told, "Don't go that way. There's a fearsome guy in there who's killed three hundred people. It's very dangerous."

Buddha went anyway and approached the guy. The warrior took his sword and swung at a nearby tree, cutting off a thick limb. Incredible. Very difficult to do. Buddha picked up the limb and gave it back to the warrior. He said, "That was impressive. Could you just put it back on the tree now?"

Destruction can be incredible, but not nearly as much as creation.

Linda and I absorbed as much of the culture and sights in Beijing as we could between shows, but most of the time I was busy with the usual technical and publicity concerns.

Some nights we were wined and dined. Once our hosts took us to the Forbidden City to eat where the empress herself had been served. A young girl played a lute-like instrument. A traditional Peking duck dinner was prepared, consisting of what seemed like dozens of courses of every part of the duck cooked every possible way—except my favorite part, the foie gras. We ate the duck feet and the web between the toes. There was also some pungent type of fish, curious meats, and parts of animal bodies that I chose not to examine too closely. It is said that the Chinese will eat anything on four legs, except a table, and anything that flies, except an airplane. Much of what we ate, however, was spectacular.

At my table were Chinese government officials and some foreign ambassadors. In the center was a big Lazy Susan. I've traveled a lot and eaten everything from crickets to worms; I don't much like either, but they didn't kill me. But some of the dishes that night were difficult to handle, so whenever anything suspicious revolved past, I just pretended I didn't see it. The head of the Chinese National Art and Culture Corporation was to my left, and every time I let something go he would grab it and put it on my plate, saying, "You *must* taste this, it's a Chinese delicacy."

I'd put a little in my mouth and go, "Hmm. This is nice." Danny sat to my right, and I heard him laughing because he knew I was faking it. I turned to my Chinese friend and said, "You know, this is *so good*. I think Mr. O'Donovan would like some, too!" Our host put some pieces on Danny's plate and he didn't laugh at me after that.

After dinner we had a drink—their grappa—that tastes like socks fermented in gasoline. (Sorry, China.) Drink one shot of that and you can eat *anything*. I remember getting pretty bombed that night and thinking perhaps I should have drunk some *before* the meal.

Two things happened in the Forbidden City that jeopardized our concerts. Thankfully both only involved the weather. One night it was so cold that I didn't think that the women—the violinists and cellists—could stand the air in their strapless dresses. Also, somehow the Chinese had neglected to tell us that in May it rains all the time. It poured for a week before the concerts because of a hurricane off the coast. I'd never been rained out before, but the concert dates and times were fixed, and if they didn't happen, that would be that. I didn't have insurance in case everything fell through.

Well, actually I did: My mother, brother and sister had come to the Forbidden City. Both nights it had rained on my way to the show. But my mother was in the car with Linda and me, and she would take Linda's hand and slip away into some private place—and the rain would stop. Both nights it rained all around the Forbidden City, but it never rained on us.

The first night was also quite windy, perhaps fifty-mile-an-hour gusts. There's no way you can do a concert with that wind. Three hours before our first show at eight o'clock, the wind was howling. I went to the sound board and asked Anthony, "How strong are the light towers? What kind of gusts can they take?"

"Oh, seventy-five, maybe."

I said, "Where's the wind now?"

"Fifty-five. Sixty."

I closed my eyes and saw the wind calm down. And it did.

I was told that Chinese audiences would be a bit on the subdued side, that they wouldn't jump up and down, that they certainly wouldn't roar. Instead, they went crazy. When people first started standing up, the police—who were always present—got them to sit down, but there were no incidents. The audience was awesome. Whenever I played a familiar song from the Acropolis album, they cheered. It was soccer match intensity and as far away as could be from anything I had been told about the Chinese culture.

The shows went off with only one minor drama. We had a camera platform forty-five feet high, for a 360-degree panorama shot George wanted to get from Tiananmen Square into the Forbidden City. We recorded a bunch of those spin-around shots. Sure enough, later that night, Chinese troops came marching in and went up on the tower. George later told me he'd heard the commotion in his headset. The soldiers told the cameraman to stop—at gunpoint—and demanded our tapes. In a way I understood: It was four days before the Tiananmen Square anniversary. We were 300 yards away with some twenty cameras—and they didn't want anyone snooping around. Even journalists had been banned from the area. Who knows what we might have picked up.

We turned over the tapes, but I'm not sure *which* tapes. Knowing George, I'm not sure they were the ones the Chinese actually wanted. Besides, they weren't shot in a format easily playable there. Our liaison, Chen, was a trouper. She went ballistic at the intrusion. I don't know what she said, but it certainly seemed to involve name-calling. She was unbelievably ballsy. Eventually, everyone backed off.

Otherwise, there were no problems, though there could have been, because of what I said between songs about everyone being equal, and the message of tolerance, acceptance, and love. Instead, I was applauded, not censored, and that was all the more impressive when you consider that whatever I said in English was simultaneously translated into Chinese, and that the concert was broadcast on CCTV to hundreds of millions of Chinese homes as well as to other Asian countries. The Chinese had risked exposure to how we looked and spoke and what we said, which might have made it much more difficult for the government to convince the people that the West is bad and dangerous, and that our way of thinking is wrong.

My only regret is not having met the then–Chinese leader, Jiang Zemin. I received word he would have liked to be at my concert, but that for political reasons—namely, the impending Tiananmen Square anniversary—he could not. However, his entire family was there to enjoy the performance. A few days before, at the Beijing Capital Gymnasium show, I had met Jiang's right-hand man; during the break I was notified that someone I had to see—and see now, as in drop everything—had arrived. We had a polite conversation while his people and mine stood at attention around us.

On the flight home to begin months of work on the album and video of the Taj Mahal and Forbidden City concerts, visit my parents, and get ready for another world tour, I met a man who said he worked for AT&T. "We've been in India for six years, trying to make a deal," he said. "How the hell did you guys get the Taj Mahal?"

I laughed. We had a flight ahead of us just long enough for me to tell him, but I was exhausted. I went to sleep instead.

12

WARRIOR WITHOUT A WAR

Tribute and the accompanying concert video, including the documentary *No Borders, No Boundaries*, narrated by Christopher Plummer, were released in late 1997. The album entered high on the *Billboard* charts and kept moving up. Even before airing nationwide on PBS, the video generated $200,000 in pledges on station WLRN in Miami, Florida, where our old friend Gustavo Sagastume now worked.

My shows at the Taj Mahal and Forbidden City also convinced the press to treat me differently. The *Wall Street Journal* put me on the front page. I appeared on *Larry King.* The *Los Angeles Times* wrote about how I'd won over the people of China. Suddenly—not so suddenly to me; years of work usually precede any "overnight" recognition—I'd evolved into the world musician I'd hoped to become. American critics still didn't rave about my music, or try much to understand it, but I felt genuine respect from most quarters about what I had tried to accomplish.

Work on the album and video took all summer, and I

delayed my usual vacation in Greece until September, after which
I went to Europe to do press. I spent October rehearsing for an
impending world tour and kicked it off in early November with
five consecutive sold-out concerts at the Auditorio Nacionale in
Mexico City.

I never looked back. I played Puerto Rico, then most of
Florida before taking a Christmas and New Year's break in the
Caribbean. Then it was on to New York for a record ten sold-out
shows at Radio City Music Hall. Before I was through I'd play
every major arena in the United States—and some twice—as
well as in Canada, with dates in South America and Asia to
come. One hundred twenty-five shows in all.

For a guy who doesn't like to know ahead of time what he's
having for dinner that night, I found that knowing what I'd be
doing for the next year was pure hell. I should have known better. The *Tribute* project, no matter how ultimately gratifying,
had been like a military expedition. I did it because I didn't
know it couldn't be done, and somewhere along the way I ex-
ceeded the limits of my stamina.

With a world tour looming, I realized I'd allowed myself to
get into something I didn't know how to get out of. As I went
from hotel to hotel, and arena to arena, in city after city, I grew in-
creasingly unsettled and unbalanced. I was both restless and tired,
driven yet low on passion. Exhaustion hit me, not all at once, but
relentlessly, day by day. Sometimes I'd wake up in the middle of
the night and not remember what city I was in, or the way to the
bathroom. I'd order breakfast in the morning and when asked for
my room number, not know it. "Is that a trick question?" Sometimes I'd forget the hotel name or the floor I was on.

I'd been on the go nonstop for almost six years—and by
nonstop I mean *nonstop*. I accepted that as part of my commitment to both have a career and never play safe with it. But

more often, now that I was sought after, I kept asking myself why I had so rarely taken the time to stop and enjoy my success. Sure, there were moments when I sat by the fireplace, drink in hand, proud—gloating?—over reports that my albums were selling through the roof, and that millions of people had seen my videos, but then I would go right back to work. I may have said, "Let's take off, go on holiday, charter a boat, go see Mom, hang out . . . ," but I never seriously considered it. A plan for a month-long vacation—other than in August—would turn into ten days, then a week, then disappear entirely. I felt guilty not working.

It's very scary to wake up every morning in a bad mood. Nothing interested me. I'd wonder, What would I like to do today? Do I go to the best restaurant in the world because now I can afford it, and bring lots of friends? Once that had seemed exciting; now it just bored me. Go to a movie? Mundane. See friends? Yawn.

Someone who hasn't lived my life might say, "Man, what's wrong with you? Come on. Don't you remember the old days? You used to make $150 a week, and eating at McDonald's was your highlight. What's the matter with you? Snap out of it. Be grateful."

I was. But after years of being the center of attention, of night after night performing in front of thousands of cheering fans who adored me, who wanted to touch me, were inspired by me, took pictures with me, who would have been thrilled to have a single hair from my head, I'd lost focus. I adored my fans and the music, but I'd misplaced the real reasons why. I can't put my finger on when I began to lose the feeling and cross the line, but I had the sense that there was no more Yanni. Perhaps *this* was the new lesson that life had in store for me, the answer to my question: What could possibly compare to the stress of the Acropolis experience? But typical of someone who had neglected himself for years—and who believed with all his heart in the nobility of taking the pain—I ignored how I felt.

At times during the tour I came close to breaking down. But I don't break down.

Part of the problem was being without Linda. We'd broken up.

It's hard to know when the relationship actually began to unravel. We were on vacation in Kalamata, then flew to Spain and France. The French didn't really know me yet, so my record company wanted to use Linda to advertise me. I was really mad about that.

> LINDA: *It was hard for Yanni to need me for anything like that; he didn't like it when he got on some television show only because I went with him. I didn't want him to be upset at me because he needed me. In fact, his vulnerability is part of what's so beautiful about him—when he showed it. Those moments were dear to me; Yanni couldn't be sweeter than when he needed me to be there for him.*

Other than my parents, I've allowed myself to be dependent only on Linda and Tom Paske. Linda knew I didn't like that feeling. Whenever Linda felt me detach from her because I wanted to do something by myself, or I was getting ready to go on the road, she'd say, "You're getting into your protective mode now. Survival mode." She'd tease me and say, *mono mu,* "by myself."

> LINDA: *The real issue for me was that after India and China Yanni remained driven and I didn't think he had to be. Once the album was done and the video edited, and he'd publicized them, he could have let go and relaxed. I had*

asked Yanni, for the first time in our relationship, if we could put some focus on me instead of just him. But he responded in exactly the opposite way and got more difficult. It was like he couldn't do what I needed even if he wanted to. So in Paris I just said, "Bye. Go do it," and left.

I don't think he believed I would ever do that, but I didn't know what else to do. Yanni was under tremendous stress because his dreams were so big. He was flying high and difficult to be around. I knew that once he had an intention for something, he got it. Part of why I left is that I saw his intention for me wasn't there. I felt like he'd finally got caught in the game—years before I'd told him he might—and I didn't want to spend my whole life on his career, his career, his career, forever. Nine years was enough. I was ready to just have some fun, just play and be. He wasn't. I didn't even know if Yanni loved me anymore.

I did neglect Linda. A normal human would need about fifty times as much as I gave, and she had asked for so little. But when one person gives and gives and the other gets used to taking and taking, sometimes you take too much without thinking. If you're a carpet, even your best friend will step on you someday—because you are a carpet! I'd like to think that I didn't step on Linda, but I know that she had needs I could not meet. Instead she had to put up with me trading my personal life for time in the studio and on the road. She totally understood and did everything to encourage me, which was part of the early attraction. Yet the day-to-day reality—especially during India and China—is that I must not have been a fun guy to hang out with. There was so much stress; so much going there and coming back. Malaria pills. Jet lag. Flying to England on the Concorde for one night to do a TV show; doing a show in New York on the return. It's difficult for anyone who doesn't live like that to understand what really goes on, and Linda *had* lived that way once. She knew. Paris was the first visible crack in our relationship.

I'm not going to go back and forth about who did what to whom. Honestly, I can't. In the big picture we didn't do anything to each other but change focus and drift apart. No cheating. No fighting. We never played head games; as soon as you start the first one, it's over. We were real. There was no manipulation. No cold shoulders.

Linda is and always will be a great woman. Even as the fire went out, Linda was my best friend. I wondered if what I felt was the truth or if I was just fried and hating everything because of the stress. But either way I was killing her and I didn't want to cause any more hurt. I felt terrible. I knew I wasn't going to find another woman like Linda. There aren't a lot of Lindas walking around. In fact, there's only one.

It's not that I didn't love Linda; there's nothing *not* to love about her. At the time I thought I wasn't *in* love anymore. Maybe I took refuge in my responsibilities and ambitions as a way out, as a way to avoid the inevitable confrontation. But I also believe we need to be whole—by ourselves—if we are to ever have a successful relationship with another human being. By the time the end came I could tell I was no longer whole.

Linda and I didn't break up immediately, but stayed in a kind of limbo. In fact, I asked her to join me on St. Martin in the Caribbean for the holidays. I thought perhaps we could work it out. Reconnect. We stayed in a very nice hotel. Great beach. Dinner every night. Romantic. Loving. But I knew before the two weeks were over that I couldn't enjoy it. I felt numb. I couldn't stop thinking about the year of touring that lay ahead.

Danny O'Donovan came to St. Martin to help us celebrate the New Year, then he and I went to Puerto Rico and New York. Linda and I left matters unresolved, or at least unspoken, and went our separate ways. But whatever I was feeling must have shown. Don Bath, my head of security—now my personal assistant, and the man who keeps my life in order—picked me up from the airport in New York, took one look at me, and said, "Buddy, if you continue like this, I don't think you're going to make it through the tour. You look like shit."

I appreciated the honesty. I always do.

A few minutes after I got to my room I called Linda. I started talking and the words just came tumbling out. "I don't think we should go on." I had imagined the moment, I knew the day would come, but I hadn't planned it. It was just instinctive. I couldn't resist.

My mother had come to visit from Greece; she was waiting in the hotel room next door to see me. When Don knocked I said, "Don't bring her in yet." I was still on the phone with Linda, and crying. Linda wasn't. She made it easy. She said, "You'll be fine on your own. You don't need me."

My mom walked in just as I hung up. My eyes were red and she got worried. I said, "Sit down, I have something to tell you."

"Things like that happen," she said afterward. "Maybe you'll get back together."

Besides the obvious personal cost of breaking up with Linda, I had an additional problem: how to handle interviews on tour. We were in the public eye big time, and I was afraid the separation would be the only topic. Plus, I didn't want to announce anything in case we changed our minds. A couple of days later, I was on *The View* and I managed to avoid telling the ladies anything.

Eventually we had to say something, so we told the truth: The decision was mutual. Our needs had changed. It was no one's fault. Articles were written about the breakup, but since there had been no other woman and no other man, the attention went away quietly.

Often during concerts I would ask the audience if they had any questions for me. Usually I'd hear, "How old are you?" "Is Yanni your real name?" "What kind of underwear do you wear?" Now I expected, "Where's Linda?" but that happened only once, and I heard half the audience go, "Shhh!" They didn't torture me, and I was very grateful for that.

LINDA: *The Yanni I left was not the guy I first met who was content to just be every moment wherever he was, whatever he did. The Yanni I met had no responsibility to anybody but his music and himself, and being true to that. The Yanni that I knew only loved the creative process and giving birth to that music. When he got in the game it became about more than the music. Before, he wrote because it was in his soul to do it; then he got an audience, and along with it opinions about him, his career, his music.*

Yanni doesn't want to fail, and that's the place he—most of us—got lost. He has tremendous responsibilities. I know he supports people around the world. He has relatives; some work for him and many of them need money. He sent an Albanian girl who cleaned his parents' house to college in America. He loves doing that, but if he nose-dives and blows it all, he's not going to be able to help everybody forever.

I wish he could go to the top of a mountain and look over everything—the magic that he's created, the beauty that he's made, how it's happened, how it's unfolded—and then think about what he wants to do now. After India and China, I think he was stunned that his dream cost him so much emotionally and physically; it took him to the end of his ability to be strong.

He is still scared. With all my money and all my fame, and the world loving me, I still had all this stuff in me that I dragged along with me. That's why I wanted to get out, because it's such a game. Thank God for Aaron Spelling and money, so I could just leave, be sixty years old, and not worry about going to work. I don't think Yanni's quite able to admit his fear. He has a lot of responsibility, but I think in his heart he would give anything to be free.

I couldn't just *be.* I was forty-three, and for years I'd looked to the future, seen the rainbow, and raced headlong in its direction. Now, for the first time, I felt the rainbow was gone. Everywhere I looked was a black thunderstorm. I didn't know how to deal with that. I'd lost interest in my career. Linda was gone. I didn't want to talk to Tom Paske. I wasn't going to call my dad and dump my problems on him. Usually, I was the guy everyone talked to when *they* had problems.

And *they*—meaning my musicians—had problems, too. I wasn't the only one under stress. Everybody was stressed-out and breaking down. For instance, when the tour began I heard there was infighting and tension between the band members. I got on the bus with them and said, "Okay guys, let me explain something to you. I just broke up with my girlfriend. I'm about ready to go into a mental institution. If any one of you guys quits or has a problem, I can't replace you. I don't have the energy to go into rehearsals anymore. If anyone leaves, the tour is off. So think twice and very seriously about what you'll have to say to the crew if they have to go home to their families, out of a job. I'm not going to baby-sit anybody anymore. Get it together on your own."

It worked. Peace returned. Usually I wouldn't have given it another thought; thanks to my upbringing I always assumed that the future would take care of any problems. But suddenly I wasn't so sure.

Instead, I felt completely isolated and had only one concern: How do I keep going? My tour schedule put me in five different cities a week, waking up at 5 A.M. for television shows and interviews, wearing makeup and posing for pictures. I knew I was crumbling, and although they might not even notice, I didn't want to play for audiences that way. I'd rather have gotten a root canal.

Don Bath tried to pull me through with activity unrelated to touring. We worked out every day. Don is an incredibly strong yet gentle giant. Intelligent, from solid midwestern stock out of Wisconsin, I trust him with my life. Wherever there was a pool, we'd go swimming. Exercise helped, at least for a couple of hours, until I had to battle the depression again. During a short break in the spring I went to Bali with Danny, returned to do another leg of the tour, then went back to Bali for another brief hiatus. I was grateful for any diversion.

I even looked for a new home. Los Angeles was too busy and the air was too polluted; my eyes burned and I had headaches all the time. After the Acropolis I'd bought a house on Puget Sound with a great view over the water. I started renovating but got so heavily into my career that I didn't have time to buy furniture, deal with the color of carpeting, choose bathroom fixtures and door handles—or pay attention at all. When the house was done I never moved in. I stayed with Linda instead. I suspect that part of me knew I couldn't settle in the Northwest; the weather, while not as harsh as Minnesota's, was too often overcast, and a Greek likes the sun. But another part of me knew I'd never really given myself the chance to find out.

However, I did love Florida. I asked my sister to find me a house by the ocean. I kept saying, "I've got to get into a place with a nice climate where the sun shines and I can be right next to the water." Just looking out at the infinite openness helps me focus and create life again. I can see my future. I've got to see the horizon.

Anda looked at buildings from Key West to Jupiter Island and beyond, and sent me videotapes while I was on the road. Nothing appealed to me. On one day off I took the tour jet and flew to Florida to look at houses north of Miami. I found nothing. After my second trip to Bali I came through Florida again and checked into a hotel, waiting for a real estate agent to show me properties. On the coffee table were a couple of magazines. I started thumbing through and saw a photo of a house on the beach, with the wind blowing through the palms, white sand, blue water. I thought, That looks good, I wonder why they're not showing me this house? I wonder where this town is?

When the agent came in I asked where the town was. She said, "You're in it. This is it!" And we were less than a mile away from the house.

I said, "Why didn't you show it to me before?"

"The house is a teardown," she explained. "Not exactly what you're looking for."

"Never mind. It looks *exactly* like what I'm looking for."

We drove over. I walked in, took a right turn, looked out the picture window at the ocean, and went, "Uh-oh." I wanted it. I knew the place was very expensive, but the property had enough room to build a studio and a beautiful pool. And to have my own private beach . . . I made an offer to buy the house and then went back on the road.

The third leg of the tour—which eventually went into the record books as the highest-grossing tour of that first half of

1998, and the second highest for the year—ended near Toronto, Ontario, on July fifth. I'd already canceled all the remaining dates, including swings through South America and Asia. I needed time off, but I didn't know if that meant three months or three years. I only knew this: There was trouble in paradise. I had accomplished my dream, I'd reached my goals, I'd gotten everything beyond any stretch of imagination—and I was still unhappy. I had no sense of direction. Everything seemed flat, dark, without meaning. I realized I was in real deep trouble. That terrified me, because what can you do to fix your life if having everything you've ever wanted doesn't do it for you? I wished I could go back twenty years and reclaim what I'd lost: my infinite ocean of optimism.

The next morning I awoke feeling very alone, as if I were in one of those science fiction stories where suddenly you are the only person left on Earth. The sun shone through a break in the window curtains, and the room—the world—was eerily quiet. After speeding at 160 miles per hour, nonstop, for years, life as I'd known it screeched to a halt overnight. It wasn't so much like slamming into a wall as it was like disintegrating into thin air in slow motion. I had nowhere to go and nothing to do. I'd have gone back to sleep, but I had a life hangover and a headache. I was wired and tired and frustrated and angry and beaten. I was a warrior without a war, a man who had forgotten who he was when the battle began. I lay in bed and stared at my hands until I realized without a shred of emotion that I didn't care if I ever touched a piano again.

Like every brave, smart guy, I ran away. I was still negotiating on the Florida house and didn't have a home, so I went to Greece and hung out with my family for a month. This was different from my regular visits. I didn't go to the nightclubs. I didn't go out with all my friends. My parents knew I was in trouble, but they trusted me to work it out. They must have wondered, though, because I never touched the piano. Whenever the craving to play or write music appeared I pushed it away, as if I were withdrawing from drugs. I treated my career as if it were an addiction.

I didn't try to forget my problems, though, nor did I want anyone to tell me that everything would be okay. I wanted to take the bull by the horns, go into my anguish, wallow in it, think it through. Where I found fear, I went into the fear. Where I found pain, I let it hurt me for a while. I knew from experience that this was the road to freedom.

Some days I'd wake up with an overpowering instinct: This is going to be a bad day. I'd let myself go into it and feel miserable, because I knew that eventually I'd get bored with the pain and pull out and feel better. I just didn't know how long that relief would last.

This is what worked for me. I'm not saying anyone else should do it. I never feel that I can tell people how life is, because I really don't know anything except how life is for me. That's the key. When people ask me for advice, I will always say, "I don't know if I have the right to tell you."

Every morning I'd walk in the mountains with my father, then do it again in the evening. We'd talk about whatever: the birds, the view, the meaning of life. Sometimes I stayed up late with my mother, and we'd sit outside under the stars, on the same balcony where I thought about playing the Acropolis. Yet I still didn't talk about my pain.

A month of this routine began to heal me. Finally, I talked to my dad and said, "I'm not really sure if I want to go back into the music business." I had forced myself to remain open to that possibility, if only to remove the pressure and eventually make a clear decision.

I said, "It may be three years before I come back. Maybe ten years. Maybe never. I could move to some little Pacific island and stay for twenty years."

I meant it. Once, people thought I would never quit swimming, that I would become a great champion. They couldn't believe I'd just walk away. Same thing when I studied psychology. But I did very well both times, so why should music be the end of the line? It would be very difficult to quit again, but it could be done.

"You will decide," my father said, "but you don't have to decide that right now. You can leave, though. It's okay. It's up to you. You've done enough. You've written so much music; any composer would be proud to have done that much in a lifetime. You don't ever need to write another piece of music again. You are in the history books. Now it's a matter of how you want to live your life. Ask yourself: What will keep me interested?"

He said everything I felt inside. Of course, I'm not completely satisfied with everything I've written, but I feel very proud about most of my work. Still, my father reaffirmed my instincts and reminded me of something my grandma Anna always said. When I'd call home, my parents would put her on the phone. Our conversations were always fairly short. She'd say, "I hear about all your successes and it's really great. Congratulations. But don't forget to take care of Yanni."

I'd brush her aside gently. "Yeah, Grandma. I'm fine."

She wasn't easy to brush. "Good. But don't forget: Take care of Yanni." In fact, she never said anything else. "You're playing in China? That's very nice. Don't forget to take care of Yanni." She never was impressed with my career. She just wanted me to have a good life.

My father had been more direct—"Get a life"—and my friends had echoed him. They were right, only I didn't know how to do nothing. I could risk $20 million on a tour, fight in the Supreme Court of India to play at the Taj Mahal, and charm Chinese dignitaries. I could lock myself in a studio for days, not eat and hardly sleep, but I didn't know how to have fun.

That evening my father and I walked again in the mountains until sunset, and although we did not talk I heard his wisdom in my head. "Look at the sunset. If it pleases you, you're a happy man."

After Greece I more or less followed the sun. I went to Indonesia, Malaysia, Singapore, and Thailand. I left the trip open-ended because I didn't want to place a deadline on my rehabilitation. I did not engage in conversations about my career, or touring; I didn't do interviews. I didn't want the star treatment; I didn't want to be fussed over. I took Don Bath. Anthony Stabile visited for a couple of weeks, but otherwise I hung out with friends I'd made on tour, like Brian Marcar, in Thailand. I swam, ate good food. I began to heal a little more. Soon I began to wake up without pain.

Often I simply sat on white, sparkling beaches watching the world and trying to answer my father's question: Is there a future I'd be interested in? I also read—not books, but fan letters. My sister, Anda, sent care packages of letters every couple of weeks. I think she did it to help me reconnect. I didn't want to open them at first, but I finally did out of curiosity and I discovered that in my darkest hours I'd forgotten that I meant something to people.

The letters came from teachers, therapists, lawyers, housewives, soldiers, truckers, merchants, recovering addicts, the inspired, rabbis, reverends, and more. They reminded me of who I was, and I cried. I wanted to let go and get as far away from Yanni and the music as possible, but it was the music that had meant so much to the fans. The letters made it clear that no matter how depressed I felt at the moment, no matter how much I wanted to abandon music, my life had not been wasted.

Most began with, "I've never written a fan letter before, but I thought you should know that . . ." and told me a story that moved me deeply. I was struck by how everyone believed they had connected with me personally through my songs with no words. They wrote of inspiration and uplift.

I also read about how the music had helped a woman through her mother's death, and how it had comforted that same mother during her illness. Others wrote of how the music motivated kids in school and even helped rehabilitate the incarcerated. I got one letter from a teenager that described how listening to my music at his darkest hour had stopped him from committing suicide. (Later, he and his family came backstage after a concert to thank me. It was so poignant, everyone standing there, crying. It was a great, great moment. So amazing.) Another time, during the *Tribute* tour, I met a young boy who had gone through chemotherapy. He told me he would listen to my music and visualize the tumor getting smaller and smaller. And it did. The hospital gave him a medal for surviving. We met at a concert when he stood up during the question-and-answer period, approached the stage, and gave the medal to me. I still have it in my office.

Every letter forced me to accept that something I'd created not only connected emotionally but had a clarity that, for many people, had cut past the bull.

One mother wrote to tell me that her very young daughter had been struck with a mysterious disease, could no longer talk or even feed herself, and would eat only when my music played. Another told of a baby with serious birth defects—and her mother's helplessness—and the moments of peace they enjoyed together, dancing slowly to something I'd written. When she passed away at only a month old, the parents played "Until the Last Moment" at the funeral.

Anda sent one letter that I had already read, but its impact was even greater the second time. It was written by a twenty-four-year-old military doctor in Colombia, in broken English, and it had originally arrived when I was in the midst of my headaches over India and China, feeling sorry for myself, thinking maybe this was too big of a project for anyone to handle. The young doctor told of being in combat, of coming under fire while hauling the wounded back to his helicopter. He said he'd carried a soldier out of the jungle who'd been shot near the heart and was beyond help.

"I put pressure on the wound but I was losing him. I tried to find the bleeding point but there was nothing to do; the hurt was so big and the heart was hit. I put my finger into the hole in the right ventricle, but it wasn't enough. This young man was going away. The situation was desperate and I did the only other thing I could do: be with him like brothers. I hugged him in my arms, waiting, waiting."

Just before the soldier died he opened his eyes and looked at the doctor and said, "Lieutenant, do you hear the music? This must be heaven. I have no fear. I feel at peace. Don't feel bad for me. I'm not in pain. This is beautiful. This silence and this music. This is the way to heaven, isn't it, Lieutenant? Don't you hear it? The music? It's got to be heaven—I hear this music."

And then he died, with "a soft smile on his face. And, yes, a celestial melody filled the air and I did not know what it was. Then I realized that the 'music' he'd heard was coming from the headphones around my neck."

To calm his own nerves on the helicopter ride to the battlefield, before evacuating the wounded, the doctor had been listening to the *Live at the Acropolis* CD. That's what the dying soldier had heard.

"The song was yours, Yanni. 'One Man's Dream.' And then I remembered your words, 'We are all the same.'

"I am here now, making a promise to this friend that I never knew, the promise to tell everybody that, like Yanni says, *'We are all the same.'*"

When I read the story I burst into tears. How could I respond any other way?

The letters reminded me that music is the ultimate language, the one that made all my life choices worthwhile. I had often asked myself: Would I wake up when I was sixty or seventy and look back and say, "What the hell was that all about?" Would not having a wife and family have been worth it? Was there meaning to creating the music? Or was I just a kid with a toy? Was it merely an overblown hobby?

Those letters helped me find an answer.

Even in my pain there was pleasure. For me. I mean that I can always find something positive in the experience. I don't waste my pain. It makes me stronger. It makes me more intelligent. I become more alert because I'm in extreme danger. It's taught me how to stay calm and not lose my cool and not give up. I know this because every time I've emerged on the other side, I've never wanted to change the experience. Once I'm through it, I'm better off.

My hiatus taught me to work as hard at pleasure as at anything else. I understood the concept but had never really pursued it; I'd just said, "Yeah, yeah. Okay." But it's true: Just be nice to yourself. You don't have to be able to afford to spend months on a remote island; there are many ways to treat yourself with care. Anyone can do it in half an hour. When I finally did tend to myself, my guilt at not working diminished and I felt better than I had in years.

In the end it came down to this simple, not original, rule. It isn't over until you say it is. Failures are battles, not the war. And the war is not over until you say it's over.

I came back to America, to Florida. In Los Angeles I'd lived in a small house and slept on a bad mattress. I didn't mind because my career was exploding and I was often on the road. Yet even though I eventually became a millionaire I'd never moved out, because I had my studio in my house and a studio is a difficult thing to build. I was even willing to enter the bathroom sideways for the convenience.

When I finally moved into my new home in Florida, it was the first time in my life I allowed myself to have creature comforts. I could say I wanted a bed like *this,* a bathroom like *that.* I could build the studio of my dreams. I could improve on the mattress quality.

My new home nourishes my spirit, creativity, and well-being because it's right on the ocean, like the place where I grew up. I created a little Kalamata, and it's just what I needed. There's openness. Looking at the ocean allows my eyes to focus on the distance. The ocean is alive and I'm not in control of it and I never will be. The ocean changes every day and I never know what I will wake up to. That's what I love.

In the summer of 1999 I got heavily into building my studio. It became my healing project. Though the work was quite difficult and demanding, it was risk-free. The stress was nothing compared to the last twenty years. Instead, it was a joy to sit in my new home, walk on the beach, and build my studio the way I wanted it: state-of-the-art, with all the equipment I'd ever dreamed of—and then some. No compromises. Great acoustic design. Every day I'd talk with the workers, pitch in with physical labor.

But I still hadn't touched a piano.

When the studio was done and the moment finally came, I confess I had to have a few vodkas first. I looked at the piano and was terrified. An old saying I knew from Greece rang in my ears: "You leave it once, it's going to leave you ten times," meaning that if you don't play the instrument just once, it will distance itself from you tenfold. I was afraid that the muscles in my fingers had become weak. But I knew my mind was still very musical. I'd been hearing songs in my head again, as I had since I was a kid. I had been trying to push them away, but they tugged at me more and more intensely, saying, "Come on, let's go!" I was scared. I wondered how long it would take for me to get back in shape. Six days? Six months? I thought; maybe I should just write music and not ever tour again—do what pleases me without the pressure.

My habit in the studio had always been to turn on a tape recorder and then sit at the piano, focus on surrendering to the black, and wait for something to come out of me. I don't play things I've already written, I just play whatever comes forth. It's all improvisation. It always has been.

That first night I walked into the studio—which is the bottom floor of a two-story building—and closed the soundproofed doors behind me. Again, I asked myself, What will my hands do? Will my fingers respond? Do I need months of training?

I rolled the DAT machine, sat on the piano bench, closed my eyes, and let the music play in my head. I don't know how long I sat there; perhaps an hour or two. Then suddenly I was

playing the piano as if I had never stopped. My fingers flew almost flawlessly. I got goose bumps and a rush. My body began to
vibrate. The creative moment for me is hot, and I felt the heat. I
knew the music was good.

I played for maybe five hours, stopping once in a while to
pace myself, to avoid cramps and overheating. I didn't want to
push too hard. I didn't know if my battery was fully charged or
had just a little juice. Maybe I'd write a song or two and it would
be all over. Instead, I found an unending supply of music, which
showed me once again what I've always believed: Creativity is
boundless. All I had to do was to mentally arrive at the place
where I could let go. It's not a matter of logic or control. I could
be depressed or happy. I could be empty or full.

I had no problem surrendering to the black. I soared again,
the way I always had.

When I was done I had worked on three different pieces, all
of which ended up on my next album, *If I Could Tell You*. They
just came out. I was ready.

The next day I listened to the tape and was dumbfounded at
my dexterity. But when I tried to repeat the music I'd recorded the
night before, my fingers kept hitting the wrong notes. It wasn't
just that my hands were sore; I wasn't in the same mental place.
Then I had played with my soul. Now, using memory and logic
just didn't work for me. I stumbled, flat-fingered, if you will. My
hands acted the way I'd *expected* them to act the night before.

That stunned me. And it reminded me again of what I
knew but sometimes forgot: Creativity cannot be controlled.
Only in surrender does it come.

I returned to the studio with a vengeance and in 2000 released a
new album, *If I Could Tell You*, but did not tour. Instead, I

focused on a balanced life and found it with friends and family. I remained close to Linda and we often talked about life. I still call her for advice; I value and trust her like a member of my family. I traveled and composed. I lived the way Linda had wanted, and my father and I had always spoken of, but I had just imagined: as a human being who could just *be*. Thank goodness my father has never lost his innocence. I watched him in the mountains a couple of years ago, jumping from cliff to cliff. The wind was howling. I said, "Don't go so close to the edge, Dad."

In his face I saw the eight-year-old Sotiri. Our roles had reversed.

Here's the best I've figured it out for me so far. Life is change, and it always will be. It's never stationary. I expect twenty years from now I'll have a different perspective on all this and I may even change my mind about what I've just written. But for now, this is what I've learned and this is how much I understand.

When I read that Socrates had said, "I only know one thing: I know nothing," I thought he was being pseudo–modest. Now I know he was right. As I get older, I understand more how little I really know.

The lessons I've learned have allowed me the opportunity to think deeply about life: where I came from, where I've been, where I'm going next—and the miracle of creativity that has made it all possible. I am grateful and excited to have tasted and felt so many things, and to have been welcomed all around the world. I am humbled to have achieved and surpassed my wildest dreams. Given that space to reflect, I decided the moment had come to talk about everything I'd been through, in this book. I also created another album, *Ethnicity*, and decided to tour again. I haven't played in front of an audience for a long, long time, but I'm looking forward to it because once again I'm doing it for myself and for the music.

. . .

If today I could talk to the little boy from Kalamata who wanted to live on his own terms and never gave up the dream that he could do what so many said he couldn't, the boy in my heart as I performed in the light of the Parthenon, I would say, "Keep on going. You're doing the right thing."

I wouldn't change my life. I have no regrets. I'm not proud of all my choices, and I've made mistakes, but most of what I've done has been for the good, and all of it makes me who I am today. I can't change even a small part and remain who I am.

I can only write the music because of what I've experienced.

And if the little boy from Kalamata could talk to me, what might he say? I believe he'd look up at me and go, "Whew! Wow! Man! What the heck did you do? We said make it big, but this is ridiculous. Can we just cool it for a while? Can we slow it down a bit?

"Can we remember to take care of Yanni?"

13

CREATIVITY

Throughout this book about a life of challenges, lessons, dreams, and obstacles overcome, I've used one word again and again: creativity. Without it there would be no book. The act of creation gives me an alert mind, a physical rush, and an overall sense of well-being. Creation leads to satisfaction. The music I write is so in tune with who I am that when I play it back, it heals me.

Next to my loved ones, my ability to write music is the most important part of my life, and for years I've explored what that requires with a single-minded passion. In these pages I've called the creative process "going into the music," and "facing the black." I've talked about loving the unknown instead of fearing it. I've said that creativity is about surrender, not control. But what do I mean by creativity? Is it a thing? A place? A quality? An action?

For me, creativity is best described as surrender and clarity. Picture it taking place in a zone, or in a private music universe in my head. There, I am one with what I create. I don't *think* about the music; I just wait in the light at the edge of the black, or un-known, and bathe in the silence until the music comes to me, all at once. It is abundant and it flows freely. I don't observe the process—if I do, the process stops—I *am* the process. I don't ana-lyze or manipulate what comes, and most of all I do not judge. Creativity and judgment are opposites; both are valid, but they can't exist in the same place at the same time. The instant I judge my creation—good, bad, indifferent—I find myself on the out-side looking in, and the creative moment vanishes.

People ask: Is this kind of creativity accessible and available to everyone? Must you have a "gift" or natural talent? (No.) Does it require lots of money, a secluded aerie, and leisure time to spare? (No.) How about a dank garret, personal demons, and a drinking problem? (I think not.) Can a middle-class housewife who wants to write a novel be creative even though she has three kids, a grumpy husband, and a full schedule? (Yes.) Can students be creative? (Naturally.) The elderly? (Absolutely.) Everybody, from the company CEO to the janitor who cleans the office building, from the chef to the teacher, salesperson, and two-year-old, is in some way creative *every day*.

Creativity is extremely easy. Effortless.

So why does it seem so tough to achieve?

When people want to express themselves artistically, in any genre, at the beginning they tend to confuse the journey to cre-ativity with the destination. The road to creativity is full of men-tal potholes. The mind plays games, has doubts, lacks clarity. We're so diffused and unfocused in society. We're juggling so many different things all at once. You wake up in the morning and have to take the kids to school, make the insurance payment, take the car to get fixed, go to work; you get home at seven and you're fried. Then you prepare dinner, watch the news, deal with the kids . . . your brain is anything but sharp. How could you create anything under these conditions?

Life gets in the way.

There is a learning curve, no question. Creativity requires commitment. That adage about genius being 5 percent inspiration and 95 percent perspiration—it's true. The challenge is in setting up and getting to the place where you can be creative. To do that requires only this: passion, hard work, discipline, patience, focused will, and an open mind. Like I said, there's a learning curve.

In the beginning, I played the piano in a college dormitory lounge, improvising without thinking, having no clue about the elements that made creativity possible. It just happened, but not necessarily when I willed it to. Later, when I confined myself to my basement studio and promised not to emerge until I had written something, I came face-to-face with my limitations, and realized I had to learn how to manipulate myself into a place conducive to creativity, a place where the music in the black is revealed. I don't know what's going to come, but I know it will be exciting. "The black" is the source of everything. The idea of the unknown usually scares people, but to me it's a great friend. I love standing at the very edge of the lit area—my knowledge—trying to see what's beyond. My second album is called *Out of Silence* for a reason: That's where the music is. In silence.

Tom Paske used to say (with a smile), "You go into the studio and don't talk to anybody for two weeks, and that's weird. You're weird."

I have learned over the years that certain preconditions aid the creative process. Before I could focus my will, I had to learn to detach. I'm a natural worrier about all that I have to do. Anxiety about the minutiae of daily life keeps us from being creative. Most people can't avoid these tasks, but concern about them can be handled by making a list. I write down what I need to accomplish outside the creative space, when I'll do it, and how. For instance, "Tomorrow at ten call the book editor to go over changes." Then I let go because I've already decided on a course of action. In the same way, you can temporarily put aside worries about the insurance payment, your girlfriend's birthday, or about who said what to whom at the party last night. Make the list; let it go. The more you do it, the easier it becomes. It's over. Done. Empty your plate.

It helps to have a personal, protected space. I have my studio. You could close the den or bedroom door, or whatever. Just find peace, quiet, solitude. I dim the lights because seeing distracts me while I'm playing. The darker it gets, the more my ears take over. The less external input my brain has, the better off I am. If you're a writer or painter, you can't turn out the lights, but you can limit noise and other diversions. Then allow your mind to fly.

It's not easy to do, especially because you've got to forget who you are. To enter creativity you must leave your baggage outside. Preconceived notions and fears and insecurities can't, by definition, come through the door. Inside you're naked.

Your creative space should also be clear of distractions. In the old days, I'd be in the studio, zoning out, clearing my mind, focusing on only one thought—and the phone would ring. Like an idiot, I would answer it. On the other end somebody would want to talk about everything *except* what I was doing. I'd get upset. "Why are you calling me? What are you saying? I can't think about this right now." Then I'd hang up and feel bad because I'd been rude. When I'd try to go back to work I couldn't, because I was upset. I'd have to call back and say, "Listen, I'm sorry. I'm writing this song and . . ."

I learned to tell everyone, "Unless there is a nuclear explosion, don't knock on my door. On second thought, even if there is a nuclear explosion I'll find out soon enough." Eventually I learned just not to answer the phone. My father says it can be the most inconsiderate visitor.

Creativity is my job. My life is devoted to writing, recording, touring and, if I've learned the lessons of this book, living. When I'm in the studio, I have the luxury of being able to leave my creative sessions open-ended. I can say, "I'm going to work for two hours or twenty." But as a rule I don't give myself a deadline. I just say, "I'm going to do this *now*." Whatever happens, happens. I don't force it. When will it end? It doesn't matter.

Most people can't devote the time I do, but for however long you work, when you're there, don't push or feel you have to come up with anything. Take what comes. Even if nothing happens, the time is well spent. Learning how to focus is good practice.

When I'm finally comfortable, sitting in my studio, I don't just begin playing the piano. I roll my DAT tape, relax, focus, and wait for the music to come. The emotion appears first. Sometimes it has been with me for a day or two. I've felt it, pushed it away, noticed it pushing back, as if it were telling me I must write a piece of music with that feeling. I don't know what the notes are yet, I just sense the emotional quality. Once, the emotion might have taken a week to reappear. Now it takes fifteen minutes, half an hour, an hour at the most. After many years I've trained myself to become open and receptive fairly quickly. Once I get to the edge of the black there's nothing left to do but surrender.

After I know the emotion, it's easy for the appropriate rhythm, melody, instruments, and so on to come to me. For example, will the song begin with a cello, a drumbeat, or a big orchestra hit?

What I do *not* do is say, "Here's the drumbeat, now let's put a bass line underneath it." I don't play piano waiting to accidentally stumble on a riff. The song appears to me all at once. At first, it's in liquid form. The structure isn't absolute. It's more of a general sensibility, like a splash of paint on a canvas. I know that in one corner I'll have a tree, so I put a bit of green there, and brown. I don't have to do every leaf. I'll do that later. Then I see where the ocean goes, and a little boat, and maybe some people walking on the beach.

These choices are easy because the emotion fills me and my whole body vibrates on that frequency. Even more important, when I latch on to the feeling, *I don't let go.* I don't spend an hour and then pick up the phone and call my friends. I'm in the process until I've finished recording most of the song. I stay with it. That's why everyone knows to leave me alone and not call or come by. You may not have the same luxury of time that I do, but in whatever time you've got, stick with the emotion and don't let go.

The emotion is the key. I know that if a piece of music touches my soul, it will touch the souls of others. It's no different for any creative person: What's true inside of you connects to the truth inside everyone.

When I first began composing in earnest, nothing happened right away. In fact, despite my list-making and other techniques, life kept popping up in my head.

I eventually figured out not to fight it. Unlike some meditators who seek to empty their minds, I just go with whatever thoughts arise. The trick is to pick one thought and focus on that intently. For me, it can be about a difficult adagio or my dry cleaning; there is no such thing as a wrong thought. I simply immerse myself in whatever comes up in the same way I do at night, sitting at the foot of the bed, reviewing the day or my emotions.

Follow the thought all the way to the end. You can have mundane thoughts; that's okay. "Did I leave the iron on?" or "Was I a little harsh on the phone today?" Even, "Why aren't I creating?" Don't resist. More serious thoughts will emerge. You're training yourself to concentrate on one idea or emotion, to stay with it, to go deeply into it, to become it. At first, your mind will be a mishmash of turbulence. But as you learn to focus and become one with that thought, you transform. Like a diamond, you cut through glass. A single focused thought is very powerful. Eventually your art will show itself. And when it comes, it's unconditional. The creative moment is made of truth. Your creations are your truth. It's the pure you.

I don't have to be in the studio or creating music to focus so intensely. I might be able to create a butterfly landing on my finger, or stop the wind before a concert. Why? *Because creativity is not only about creating music; it is about creating your life.* While I'm in this space I will often close my eyes and surrender and ask life to give me what is good for me. I see life as I want it to be.

Focused intent is the instrument of power. The source of power is in faith. How clear can you be and how much faith can you have? How little doubt can you have in what you're creating? The more doubt you have, the less likely it is that the creation will come to life. Creating music teaches me how to create life. I cannot prove it and I don't want to. What matters to me is that I had faith, and when the butterfly settled on my index finger and I stood up with her still there, it blew me away.

The process is extremely personal, and sometimes, because I've been embarrassed to close my eyes and do it in public, I've even done it in a bathroom. But focusing is focusing. It doesn't matter where you do it. You don't have to be by the beach or on a dramatic cliff with the wind howling.

In the studio, when I'm in the music and the moment of clarity happens, when I'm flying and the music is coming, and I'm feeling the rush and having a great time, it's very easy to turn the spotlight on my life and say, "Here's what I want." I try to do it well. I approach it humbly and allow the wisdom of life to make the decision. In my experience, when I feel that strongly, when I am that passionate what I see usually happens. Remember, passion is the fuel.

This is magic. It's also matter-of-fact. I don't like to use big words or concepts to describe it because I don't think of the process as a big deal. In fact, it might all be just a giant coincidence, and maybe the universe is playing a joke on me. But I don't care. Whatever's happening works for me. I've learned to trust that it works. It's not mystical, it's not difficult (now), and it's not mysterious. Either it's true and it works for everything, or it won't work for anything. There's no middle ground.

Everyone can learn how to tap into creativity. Trust, belief, and focused will form the pool of creativity; all that's left is to dive in and let the magic begin.

The more time you spend in that space, the more creative you'll become, and the more effective you'll become. But just as with everything else in life, you have to work at it.

Part of the difficulty in getting there is that in our culture we're really not taught to trust the instinctive moment. We're told to rely on facts and figures, probability and analysis, history and reason. All are fine—in their place. We also have voices in our heads—parents, teachers, the media, ourselves— that interfere by judging. "That's not good enough." "Who do you think you are, Mozart?" "No one will care about what I'm doing."

When I was younger I got in my own way by asking myself questions like, How long does a piece need to be? What kind of music should I write? The answer is to write what you like. The piece is going to be as long as it keeps you interested. If it bores you, cut it.

Society does everything it can to fill you with a distrust of yourself and others. We grow up in an environment where we're laughed at or criticized for thinking that what we create could profoundly affect people and maybe make a difference in their lives—or be worth doing for nobody but ourselves.

Even when you're not trying to be creative, you should work on getting rid of those voices. To take some time each day to sit quietly in a room without any distractions, or to walk, or even just to turn off the TV is probably one of the most valuable things you can do. Left alone with your own thoughts, you will exercise focusing your mind. Like a muscle, the ability to focus will keep getting stronger.

If I could keep someone in a room for a few hours with no outside distractions, she'd be amazed at what she could create. She may spend only five minutes or five seconds in the zone, without judgment, and come up with only one line. But what if the line is, "To be or not to be, that is the question"?

With time the process gets easier, and there are rewards along the way. Just don't expect to be Shakespeare overnight.

When a creative moment happens, no matter how briefly it lasts, you will recognize it forevermore. Physically, I get hot. Sometimes I get goose bumps. I feel the rush. I can try to describe it until I turn blue in the face, but words fall short.

You'll know it, I promise.

Then you'll try to get it back as often as possible. The levels I go to when I write are pretty high. I float. I feel happy, peaceful, empowered. It's an incredible experience. To me, it's heaven, if you will. There is enormous pleasure associated with creativity.

Creativity is addictive.

Everyone, and I mean everyone, falls into the trap of judging material as it emerges. That kills the creativity. I have screwed up the process in every which way possible. I always felt intelligent and experienced enough to think I could mold the music instead of just letting it happen. That's using logic and knowledge and experience, and sometimes I messed up so badly I had to throw away entire songs. They weren't among my better ones, and you've never heard them.

It took me years to accept this truth: Let it be.

Once I've let go of everything and I'm calmly facing the unknown, the music comes. Give up control and something comes. I guarantee it.

However, be prepared. What comes out may not be what you're expecting or hoping for. Remember, creativity is not linear. Like I said before: You may know *A* and *B* and end up finding *Q* without knowing quite how. It's a quantum leap. You're just there.

Was Shakespeare thinking, "I've got to come up with a line that contains the essential dilemma of existence?" He didn't think the words "To be or not to be" *before* he thought them—impossible, right?—they just came. He wrote. Did he cause them, or did they cause him to write?

Once, in an hour and a half, I worked on six different pieces of music, and all six of them made it onto the *Tribute* album. It's all on a DAT tape, number thirty, in my safe. Every ten minutes a different piece of music came out. On the tape you can hear me play "Tribute"—the entire piece—for the first time. A couple of minutes later "Renegade" came out.

When I get into the zone I find an unlimited amount of music. My most difficult decision is which piece to do. What do I bring down into the world? It can be a rock 'n' roll piece, a jazz piece, a classical piece. When I decide, I bring it down by surrendering to it, not grasping at it. It has to come to me the way a butterfly lands on your fingertip. I can't say it often enough: Trust there is light at the end of the tunnel. Trust the outcome and don't destroy your creation. If you don't trust, you ain't got jack.

Trust is also important because when I play, I don't know whether the music tells me where it wants to go or I tell it where to go. Any writer will tell you this: At first he tells his characters what to do, then they tell him.

Writing a piece of music is like being on a roller coaster. You go up and down, there are twists to the left, twists to the right. And there are no rules. Take a song like "Nostalgia" with a run coming down and a series of runs climbing up. It's maybe twenty years old, and I've played it in every concert. It taught me about ups and downs. I remember playing it for the first time; at the very moment I felt like changing directions—as in diving—the music had already begun diving. The moment I felt it should turn, it had already turned. I didn't know if I was telling it to turn or if it was turning and I was just following. Now, I describe the process as *allowing*. I allow the piece of music to tell me what it wants to be. Logically I must be causing it, but in my experience I can't really tell. All I know is that at the outset I don't know what's going to happen, but in retrospect I realize the song couldn't have turned out any other way.

At first the feeling of creativity lasted only seconds, but I've learned how to make it endure. I spent years investigating this. Could I make ten seconds become eleven seconds? And how do I get it started in the first place? What do I have to do to get there? Eventually, rules emerged and made sense—and I've tried to share some of them here.

Creativity has always been practical and down-to-earth to me. It just comes slowly, like learning how to play the piano. I didn't practice for three hours and know everything. In fact, after playing for a month I thought, I'm never going to learn how to do this. Often the process is more disappointing than encouraging, but there is *always* a little bit of encouragement every time, and you must trust the outcome. I trust instincts. I've always wanted to find out for myself. *I trust that life will guide me into this power*. It's like learning to shoot skeet. You fire and, at first, have no sense of how to hit anything—and you don't. But after you actually hit the clay pigeon, your improvement is tenfold because now your mind and body have a sense of what it took to hit it. It's the same with creativity. Once you have the first positive outcome, the next few positives are quicker and easier because you have a sense of what your body and psyche feel like when it happens. Once you know how it feels, you know what to look for.

CREATIVITY

If you have a passion for anything—painting, writing, music, whatever—these suggestions might help, because creativity is the same for everybody. We all go to the same place.

You can talk about anything you want, but you can only *truly* know what you actually experience. That is yours. If you use your art to express only what you know, then your art will be original. Just tell the truth about what life feels like to you.

I show what life feels like to me.

The reward has always been discovering that I am far from alone.

So dive in, and let the magic begin.

ACKNOWLEDGMENTS

YANNI

Words have never been my medium. I never thought I'd ever write a book. But life is full of surprises, and this story of my life—so far—has been one of the most satisfying. The philosophies and experiences are mine, but it took more than just me to bring this book to life.

First, I'd like to thank David Rensin for going with me into the black and putting the magic into words. That's the highest praise. This book could not have been written without him.

I'm grateful to Tom Paske, Linda Evans, Danny O'Donovan, and George Veras for their gracious contributions, impeccable memories, inexhaustible passion, and unwavering support. I'm amazed that Tom still remembers our phone conversations. I'm even more amazed that he could write them down. Thank you, Stanley.

Special thanks to Don Bath for his caring and unconditional support. He's the only reason I made it through the last tour and still know what I'm supposed to do every day.

Thanks as well to Robert Barnett, who opened the doors, and to Jonathan Burnham, Peter Guzzardi, and the entire Miramax Books team, whose enthusiasm and honesty made the project a reality.

I'm also indebted to Anda Allenson, Richard Allenson, Yorgo Chryssomallis and family, Toula Mavrea, Bill MacDonald, George Rapp, Shirley McNeill, Dugan McNeill, Tommy Sterling, Wes Hayne, Anthony Stabile, Charlie Adams, Mark Macpherson, Terry Randolph, Richard Ginsburg, Kip Kilpatrick, Beth Lewis, Roger Moore, Tom White, Bruce Lipton, Sig Gesk, Peter Baumann, Sam Schwartz, Jeff Klein, Ron Goldstein, Guilio Proietto, Stuart Rubin, Lee Phillips, Jody Graham-Dunitz, Larry Winokur, Andreas Potamianos, Theodoros Kassimis, Dora Bakoyanni, Andy Christos, Fotis Tritsis, Roula Koromila, Pedro Eustache, Karen Briggs, Ricc Fierabracci, Ming Freeman, Erin Hanson, Dione Dirito, Diane Kramer, Catherine Yatrakis, Peter Dorsey, Brian Brown, Mori-san, Ken Berry, Phil Quartararo, Ray Cooper, Ken Pedersen, Romesh Bhandari, Venkat Vardhan, Ram Kholi, Biptee Ram, Chen Jixen, Lu Changhe, Wang Cheng, Xiang Xiaowei, Maria Rogina Kooistra, and everyone else along the way whose participation in my life made this story worth telling.

Some people should have been in the book but were not. My apologies. In trying to tell the whole story I simply could not tell every story. Nonetheless, your presence and influence is felt. And if I've forgotten to mention anyone here, again it's only because there are so many to mention. You know who you are. Thank you.

DAVID RENSIN

Cynthia Price, Bill Zehme, Brian DeFiore, Bernie and Carrie Brillstein, Lisa Kusel, Larry Winokur, and Team Yanni, most of all, encouraged me to follow my instincts and supported me along the way. All more than deserve my humble thanks—and especially my wife, Suzie Peterson, and son, Emmett Rensin. Their love, wisdom, patience, grace, and joy in life make all things possible, and they mean everything to me.

My deepest thanks and enduring respect are for Yanni, whose love of family, pursuit of clarity, fearless embrace of the unknown, and determination to be true to himself always is an example for us all. I am grateful to have earned his trust. He is an original.

Shari'a